# Quantum Computing in Practice with Qiskit® and IBM Quantum Experience®

Practical recipes for quantum computer coding at the gate and algorithm level with Python

**Hassi Norlén**

BIRMINGHAM—MUMBAI

# Quantum Computing in Practice with Qiskit® and IBM Quantum Experience®

**Commissioning Editor**: Kunal Chaudhari

**Acquisition Editor**: Alok Dhuri

**Senior Editor**: Nitee Shetty

**Content Development Editor**: Ruvika Rao

**Technical Editor**: Gaurav Gala

**Copy Editor**: Safis Editing

**Project Coordinator**: Deeksha Thakkar

**Proofreader**: Safis Editing

**Indexer**: Manju Arasan

**Production Designer**: Prashant Ghare

First published: November 2020

Production reference: 1201120

Published by Packt Publishing Ltd.

Livery Place

35 Livery Street

Birmingham

B3 2PB, UK.

ISBN 978-1-83882-844-8

www.packt.com

*To my family: Tova, Ella, and Noah. Without your infinite patience and support, this adventure would never have taken place! And to my parents, Rolf and Ingegerd, who have always supported me in following my dreams and ideas, no matter where they might lead.*

Packt.com

Subscribe to our online digital library for full access to over 7,000 books and videos, as well as industry leading tools to help you plan your personal development and advance your career. For more information, please visit our website.

## Why subscribe?

- Spend less time learning and more time coding with practical eBooks and Videos from over 4,000 industry professionals

- Improve your learning with Skill Plans built especially for you

- Get a free eBook or video every month

- Fully searchable for easy access to vital information

- Copy and paste, print, and bookmark content

Did you know that Packt offers eBook versions of every book published, with PDF and ePub files available? You can upgrade to the eBook version at packt.com and as a print book customer, you are entitled to a discount on the eBook copy. Get in touch with us at customercare@packtpub.com for more details.

At www.packt.com, you can also read a collection of free technical articles, sign up for a range of free newsletters, and receive exclusive discounts and offers on Packt books and eBooks.

# Contributors

## About the author

**Hassi Norlén** is an educator, physicist, and software developer, long fascinated with computer programming, both small and large, new and old. He stumbled into the quantum-computing universe a few short years ago and has since then been lucky enough to engage in this fascinating field both professionally and as a hobby.

In his day job with IBM, he designs content in the AI Applications division. In his spare time, he spreads the word on the Qiskit® open source SDK and quantum computing as an IBM Quantum Ambassador and Qiskit Advocate: lecturing, coding, and hosting quantum-computing workshops.

He traces his roots back to Sweden, with the United States being his recently adopted homeland, and is currently enjoying the Bavarian Alps in southern Germany on an IBM Global assignment.

*Thank you to:*

*Denise Ruffner for taking a chance, and Andi Couilliard, for unwavering support!*

*James Weaver, Robert Loredo, Charles Robinson, Steven Margolis, and Gabriel Chang, for ideas, sparring and support.*

*Jerry Chow (for my first glimpse of an IBM quantum computer Jay Gambetta, Bob Sutor, and the entire IBM Quantum® team, for making quantum computing real!*

## About the reviewer

**James Weaver** is a developer, author, and speaker with a passion for quantum computing. He is a Java Champion, and a JavaOne Rockstar. James has written books including *Inside Java*, *Beginning J2EE*, the *Pro JavaFX* series, and *Java with Raspberry Pi*. As an IBM Quantum Developer Advocate, James speaks internationally about quantum computing with Qiskit® at quantum and classical computing conferences.

## Packt is searching for authors like you

If you're interested in becoming an author for Packt, please visit `authors.packtpub.com` and apply today. We have worked with thousands of developers and tech professionals, just like you, to help them share their insight with the global tech community. You can make a general application, apply for a specific hot topic that we are recruiting an author for, or submit your own idea.

# Table of Contents

# 5

# Touring the IBM Quantum® Hardware with Qiskit®

# 6

## Understanding the Qiskit® Gate Library

# 7

## Simulating Quantum Computers with Aer

# 8
# Cleaning Up Your Quantum Act with Ignis

# 9
# Grover's Search Algorithm

# 10
# Getting to Know Algorithms with Aqua

# Other Books You May Enjoy

# Index

# **Preface**

**IBM Quantum Experience®** with **Qiskit®** together form a popular and easy-to-use quantum computing platform. They let you access and program actual IBM quantum computer hardware in the cloud, but you can also run your code on local and cloud-based simulators.

This book is designed to teach you how to implement quantum programming in a Python® environment, first at an elementary level, and later moving to more advanced examples. The locally installable **Quantum Information Science Toolkit (Qiskit)** software is built on Python and represents the most accessible tool available today for learning quantum computing.

Throughout the recipes of this book, we will introduce the Qiskit classes and methods step by step, starting with the very basic concepts such as installing and upgrading Qiskit, checking which version you are running, and so on. We then move on to understanding the building blocks that are required to create and run quantum programs and how to integrate these Qiskit components in your own hybrid quantum/classical programs to leverage Python's powerful programming features.

We'll explore, compare and contrast **Noisy Intermediate-Scale Quantum (NISQ)** computers and universal fault-tolerant quantum computers using simulators and actual hardware, looking closely at simulating noisy backends and how to mitigate for noise and errors on actual hardware, implementing the Shor code method for quantum error correction of a single qubit.

Finally, we'll take a look at quantum algorithms to see how they differ from classical algorithms. We will take a closer look at coding Grover's algorithm, and then use Qiskit Aqua to run versions of Grover's and Shor's algorithms to show how you can reuse already constructed algorithms directly in your Qiskit code. We do all of this as a sweeping tour of Qiskit, IBM's quantum information science toolkit, and its constituent layers: Terra, Aer, Ignis, and Aqua.

We will also use the online IBM Quantum Experience® user interface for drag-and-drop quantum computing. Everything we do in this book, and way more, can be coded in the cloud on IBM Quantum Experience®.

Each chapter contains code samples to explain the principles taught in each recipe.

# Who this book is for

This book is for developers, data scientists, researchers, and quantum computing enthusiasts who want to understand how to use Qiskit® and IBM Quantum Experience® to implement quantum solutions. Basic knowledge of quantum computing and the Python programming language is beneficial.

# What this book covers

This cookbook is a problem-solution- and exploration-based approach to understanding the nuances of programming quantum computers with the help of IBM Quantum Experience®, Qiskit®, and Python.

*Chapter 1, Preparing Your Environment,* walks you through how to install Qiskit® as a Python 3.5 extension on your local workstation. You'll also register with IBM Quantum Experience®, get your API key, and grab the sample code.

*Chapter 2, Quantum Computing and Qubits with Python,* shows how to use Python to code simple scripts to walk you through the concept of bits and qubits and how quantum gates work without Qiskit® or IBM Quantum Experience®.

*Chapter 3, IBM Quantum Experience® – Quantum Drag and Drop,* looks at IBM Quantum Experience®, IBM Quantum's online, cloud-based drag-and-drop tool for programming quantum computers. Here you will code a simple program and learn how to move between Qiskit® and IBM Quantum Experience®.

*Chapter 4, Starting at the Ground Level with Terra,* explores a set of basic quantum programs, or circuits, to examine fundamental concepts such as probabilistic computing, superposition, entanglement, and more. We will also run our first programs on an actual physical IBM quantum computer.

*Chapter 5, Touring the IBM Quantum® Hardware with Qiskit®,* looks at the IBM Quantum® backends, exploring various physical aspects that impact the results of your quantum programs.

*Chapter 6, Understanding the Qiskit® Gate Library,* gives an overview of the quantum gates that are offered out of the box with Qiskit® to see what they do to your qubits. We take a look at the universal quantum gates from which all other quantum gates are built, and also expand from one-qubit gates, to the two-, three-, and more qubit gates needed for more advanced quantum circuits.

*Chapter 7, Simulating Quantum Computers with Aer,* helps you run your circuits on a collection of simulators that you can use locally or in the cloud. You can even set your simulators up to mimic the behavior of an IBM Quantum® backend, to test your circuits under realistic conditions on your local machine.

*Chapter 8, Cleaning Up Your Quantum Act with Ignis,* explains how to clean up your measurement results by understanding how our qubits behave, and looks at how we can correct for noise by using noise mitigation circuits such as the Shor code.

*Chapter 9, Grover's Search Algorithm,* builds Grover's search algorithm, a quadratic speedup of classical search algorithms. We will use a unique quantum tool, quantum phase kickback. We build several different versions of the algorithm to run on both simulators and IBM Quantum® backends.

*Chapter 10, Getting to Know Algorithms with Aqua,* uses premade Qiskit Aqua versions of two of the most well-known quantum algorithms: Grover's search algorithm and Shor's factoring algorithm. We also take a quick tour of the Qiskit Aqua algorithm library.

# To get the most out of this book

It helps if you have acquainted yourself a little bit with basic quantum computing concepts; we will not spend too much time with proofs or the deeper details. Python programming skills are also helpful, especially when we start building slightly more complex hybrid quantum/classical programs. A basic understanding of linear algebra with vector and matrix multiplication will definitely help you understand how quantum gates work, but we let Python and NumPy do the hard work.

Qiskit® supports Python 3.6 or later. The code examples in this book were tested on Anaconda 1.9.12 (Python 3.7.0) using its bundled Spyder editor with Qiskit® 0.21.0, and on the online IBM Quantum Experience® Code lab environment. We recommend our readers to use the same.

| Software/hardware covered in the book | OS requirements |
|---|---|
| Python 3.7 | Windows, macOS, and Linux (any) |
| Qiskit 0.21.0 | Python 3.5+ |
| Anaconda Navigator 1.9 | Windows, macOS, and Linux (any) |

**If you are using the digital version of this book, we advise you to type the code yourself or access the code via the GitHub repository (link available in the next section). Doing so will help you avoid any potential errors related to the copying and pasting of code.**

# Download the example code files

You can download the example code files for this book from GitHub at https://github.com/PacktPublishing/Quantum-Computing-in-Practice-with-Qiskit-and-IBM-Quantum-Experience. In case there's an update to the code, it will be updated on the existing GitHub repository.

We also have other code bundles from our rich catalog of books and videos available at https://github.com/PacktPublishing/. Check them out!

# Download the color images

We also provide a PDF file that has color images of the screenshots/diagrams used in this book. You can download it here: https://static.packt-cdn.com/downloads/9781838828448_ColorImages.pdf.

# Conventions used

There are a number of text conventions used throughout this book.

Code in text: Indicates code words in text, database table names, folder names, filenames, file extensions, pathnames, dummy URLs, user input, and Twitter handles. Here is an example: "The log_length(oracle_input,oracle_method) function takes as input the oracle input (log or bin) and the oracle method (logical expression or bit string) and returns the ideal number of iterations the Grover circuit needs to include."

A block of code is set as follows:

```
def log_length(oracle_input,oracle_method):
    from math import sqrt, pow, pi, log
    if oracle_method=="log":
        filtered = [c.lower() for c in oracle_input if
            c.isalpha()]
        result = len(filtered)
```

Any command-line input or output is written as follows:

```
$ conda create -n environment_name python=3
```

**Bold**: Indicates a new term, an important word, or words that you see onscreen. For example, words in menus or dialog boxes appear in the text like this. Here is an example: "Clicking the job results box opens the **Result** page, and displays the final result of the job you just ran."

> **Tips or important notes**
> Appear like this.

# Sections

In this book, you will find several headings that appear frequently (*Getting ready, How to do it..., How it works..., There's more...,* and *See also*).

To give clear instructions on how to complete a recipe, use these sections as follows:

## Getting ready

This section tells you what to expect in the recipe and describes how to set up any software or any preliminary settings required for the recipe.

## How to do it...

This section contains the steps required to follow the recipe.

## How it works...

This section usually consists of a detailed explanation of what happened in the previous section.

## There's more...

This section consists of additional information about the recipe in order to make you more knowledgeable about the recipe.

## See also

This section provides helpful links to other useful information for the recipe.

# Get in touch

Feedback from our readers is always welcome.

**General feedback**: If you have questions about any aspect of this book, mention the book title in the subject of your message and email us at customercare@packtpub.com.

**Errata**: Although we have taken every care to ensure the accuracy of our content, mistakes do happen. If you have found a mistake in this book, we would be grateful if you would report this to us. Please visit www.packtpub.com/support/errata, selecting your book, clicking on the Errata Submission Form link, and entering the details.

**Piracy**: If you come across any illegal copies of our works in any form on the Internet, we would be grateful if you would provide us with the location address or website name. Please contact us at copyright@packt.com with a link to the material.

**If you are interested in becoming an author**: If there is a topic that you have expertise in and you are interested in either writing or contributing to a book, please visit authors.packtpub.com.

# Reviews

Please leave a review. Once you have read and used this book, why not leave a review on the site that you purchased it from? Potential readers can then see and use your unbiased opinion to make purchase decisions, we at Packt can understand what you think about our products, and our authors can see your feedback on their book. Thank you!

For more information about Packt, please visit packt.com.

# 1
# Preparing Your Environment

Before you can start working on your quantum programs, you must have a Python environment to execute your code. The examples in this book can be run both on your local machine by using the Qiskit® developer environment provided by IBM Quantum® and in an online environment on IBM Quantum Experience®.

In this chapter, we will take a look at both environments, get you a login account on IBM Quantum Experience®, and install a local version of **Qiskit**®. We will also discuss the fast-moving environment that is open source Qiskit®, and how to keep your local environment up to date.

We will cover the following recipes:

- Creating your IBM Quantum Experience® account
- Installing Qiskit®
- Downloading the code samples
- Installing your API key and accessing your provider
- Keeping your Qiskit® environment up to date

So, let's get started. This chapter, and its contents, is pretty important as it provides you with the foundation on which you can start building your Qiskit® future. Do spend a moment or two setting this up, and then get going with the recipes in this book to get started with quantum programming on Qiskit®. To get you started quickly, you can also grab and run the sample recipe code that is provided with this book.

# Technical requirements

The recipes that we will discuss in this chapter can be found here: `https://github.com/PacktPublishing/Quantum-Computing-in-Practice-with-Qiskit-and-IBM-Quantum-Experience/tree/master/Chapter01`.

You can run the recipes in this book in your local Qiskit® environment that you set up as a part of this chapter. You can also run most of them in the **Quantum Lab** environment of the online IBM Quantum Experience®. This is also true for the `c1_r1_version.py` recipe in this chapter, which lists the installed version of Qiskit® in the environment in which you run the recipe.

For information about how to download the recipes, see *Downloading the code samples*.

The local environment in which you choose to install Qiskit® must have **Python 3.5 or higher** installed (as of this book's writing). For detailed information about the most current requirements for Qiskit® installation, see the Qiskit® requirements page at `https://qiskit.org/documentation/install.html`.

IBM Quantum® recommends using the Anaconda distribution of Python (`https://www.anaconda.com/distribution/`), and to use virtual environments to keep your Qiskit® installation isolated from your usual Python environment.

---

**New to virtual environments?**

Virtual environments provide isolated Python environments that you can modify separately from each other. For example, you can create an isolated environment for your Qiskit® installation. You will then install Qiskit® only in that environment, and not touch the Python framework in the base environment which will then contain an untarnished version of Python.

As Qiskit® releases new versions of their packages, there is technically nothing stopping you from creating a new isolated environment for each updated version of Qiskit® to retain your old and stable version for your Qiskit® quantum programming, and a new environment where you can test updated versions of Qiskit®. You will find more on this in the *Keeping your Qiskit® environment up to date* recipe.

---

# Creating your IBM Quantum Experience® account

Your key to exploring quantum computer programming with IBM is your *IBM Quantum Experience® account*. This free account gives you access to the online IBM Quantum Experience® interface, and the programming tools that are available there. An IBM Quantum Experience® account is not technically required to test out IBM Quantum Experience® or to install Qiskit® but is required to run your programs on the freely available IBM quantum computers, which are, after all, probably why you are reading this book in the first place.

## Getting ready

To set up your IBM Quantum Experience® account, you can log in with an IBMid, or with one of the following:

- A Google account
- A GitHub account
- A LinkedIn account
- A Twitter account
- An email address

## How to do it...

1. In your browser (Google Chrome seems to work best), go to this link: `https://quantum-computing.ibm.com/login`.

2. Enter your IBMid credentials or select another login method.

   You can also skip the sign-in, which will give you access to IBM Quantum Experience® but with a limit of 3 qubits for your quantum circuits, and with simulator backends only.

3.  Once you have logged in, you now have an activated IBM Quantum Experience®
    account, and will find yourself at the main dashboard:

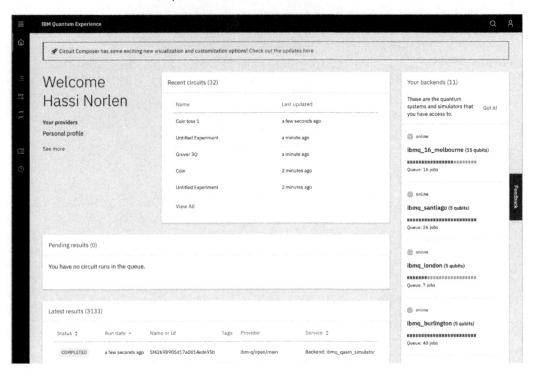

Figure 1.1 – The IBM Quantum Experience® home page

4.  From here, you have a couple of paths:

Go to a composer to start building your quantum programs in a graphical user
interface. Click the **Circuit composer** left-menu icon ( ) and then go to *Chapter
3, IBM Quantum Experience® – Quantum Drag and Drop*.

If you want to start writing your quantum programs in Python without first
installing a local Qiskit® instance, you can go to the Qiskit® notebooks to start
working on your quantum programs in a Jupyter Notebook Python environment.
Click on the **Quantum Lab** left-menu icon ( ), click **New Notebook**, and then go
to *Chapter 4, Starting at the Ground Level with Terra*.

If you want to continue down the Qiskit® path for which this book was written,
you can now log out of IBM Quantum Experience®, and continue with installing
Qiskit® on your local machine.

## See also

- *IBM Quantum Experience is quantum on the cloud*: `https://www.ibm.com/ quantum-computing/technology/experience/`.

- *Quantum computing: It's time to build a quantum community*: `https://www. ibm.com/blogs/research/2016/05/quantum-computing-time- build-quantum-community/`.

# Installing Qiskit®

With your Python environment prepared and ready to go, and your IBM Quantum Experience® account set up, you can now use `pip` to install the Qiskit® Python extension. The process should take about 10 minutes or so, after which you can use your Python command line, or your favorite Anaconda Python interpreter to start writing your quantum programs.

## Getting ready

This recipe provides information about the generic way to install Qiskit® and does not go into any detail regarding operating system differences or general installation troubleshooting.

For detailed information about the most current requirements for Qiskit® installation, see the Qiskit® requirements page at `https://qiskit.org/documentation/ install.html`.

## How to do it...

1. Create your Anaconda virtual environment:

```
$ conda create -n environment_name python=3
```

This will install a set of environment-specific packages.

2. Activate your virtual environment:

```
$ conda activate environment_name
```

3. Verify that you are in your virtual environment.

Your Command Prompt should now include the name of your environment; I used something like this for my own environment with the name `packt_qiskit`:

```
(packt_qiskit) Hassis-Mac:~ hassi$
```

> **Nomenclature**
>
> In this chapter, I will print out the full prompt like this `(environment_name) … $` to remind you that you must execute the commands in the correct environment. In the rest of the book, I will assume that you are indeed in your Qiskit-enabled environment and just show the generic prompt: $.

4.  If needed, do a `pip` update.

    To install Qiskit®, you must use `pip` as Qiskit® is not distributed as `conda` packages. The latest Qiskit® requires pip 19 or newer.

    If you have an older version of `pip`, you must upgrade using the following command:

    ```
    (environment_name) … $  pip  install  -U  pip
    ```

5.  Install Qiskit®.

    So, with everything set up and prepared, we can now get on to the main course, installing the Qiskit® code in your environment. Here we go!

    ```
    (environment_name) … $  pip install qiskit
    ```

> **Failed wheel build**
>
> As part of the installation, you might see errors that the *wheel* failed to build. This error can be ignored.

6.  Use Python to Verify that Qiskit® installed successfully.

    Open Python:

    ```
    (environment_name) … $  python3
    ```

    Import Qiskit®:

    ```
    >>> import qiskit
    ```

    This is a little bit exciting; we are going to use Qiskit® code for the first time. Granted, not exactly for programming a quantum computer, but at least to make sure that we are now ready to start programming your quantum programs.

    List the version details:

    ```
    >>> qiskit.__qiskit_version__
    ```

This should display the versions of the installed Qiskit® components:

```
{'qiskit-terra': '0.15.2', 'qiskit-aer': '0.6.1',
 'qiskit-ignis': '0.4.0', 'qiskit-ibmq-provider': '0.9.0',
 'qiskit-aqua': '0.7.5', 'qiskit': '0.21.0'}
```

Congratulations, your Qiskit® installation is complete; you are ready to go!

By using `pip install` from your virtual environment, you can install Qiskit® in just that environment, which will then stay isolated from the rest of your Python environment.

## There's more...

Qiskit® also comes with some optional visualization dependencies to use visualizations across the Qiskit® components. You can install these with the following command:

```
(environment_name) … $ pip install qiskit[visualization]
```

> **Note**
> If you are using the zsh shell you must enclose the component in quotes:
> pip install `'qiskit[visualization]'`

## See also

For a quick introduction to Anaconda environments, see *Managing environments* in the Anaconda docs: `https://docs.conda.io/projects/conda/en/latest/user-guide/tasks/manage-environments.html`.

This book does not, in any way, act as a Qiskit® installation troubleshooting guide, and you might conceivably run into issues when installing it, depending on your local OS, versions, and more.

But fear not, help is on the way. Here are a couple of good and friendly channels on which to reach out for help:

- **Slack**: `https://qiskit.slack.com/`
- **Stack Exchange**: `https://quantumcomputing.stackexchange.com/questions/tagged/qiskit`

# Downloading the code samples

The recipes in this book include short, and some not so short, sample programs that will lead you through your first steps in programming quantum computers. You can type in these programs directly from the instructions in the book if you want, but for convenience, you can also grab the sample code directly from the Packt Cookbook GitHub organization.

The Python samples are written for Python 3.5+ and the Qiskit® extension that you installed in your Python environment. The Python samples all have the extension: `.py`.

## Getting ready

While you can type the recipes directly into your Python environment, or into Jupyter Notebooks on IBM Quantum Experience® or on your local Anaconda environment, it is somewhat more efficient to download or use **Git** to clone the sample code to your local environment. The advantage of cloning is that you can later refresh your local files from the remote repository if any updates are made.

If you do not plan to use Git, but instead to download the recipes as a compressed file, continue on with *How to do it*.

To use Git to clone the sample code, you must first do the following:

1. Get a GitHub account. These are free and you can sign up for one at `https://github.com`.

2. Install Git in your local environment. For more information, see `https://git-scm.com/book/en/v2/Getting-Started-Installing-Git`.

3. If you are a user interface person, you might also want to install GitHub Desktop, available here: `https://desktop.github.com/`.

## How to do it...

You have several different options to download the sample recipes to your local machine.

For each, start by opening your web browser and then go to the *Quantum-Computing-in-Practice-with-Qiskit-and-IBM-Quantum-Experience* GitHub repository at `https://github.com/PacktPublishing/Quantum-Computing-in-Practice-with-Qiskit-and-IBM-Quantum-Experience`.

## Downloading the repository as a compressed file

The easiest way to get the recipes is to just grab the sample files as a compressed directory and decompress it on your local machine:

1. At the preceding URL, click the **Clone or download** button and select **Download zip**.

2. Download the compressed file and select a location.

3. Decompress the file.

## Cloning the repository using git

1. Click the **Clone or download** button and copy the URL.

2. Open your command line and navigate to the location where you want to clone the directory.

3. Enter the following command:

```
$ git clone https://github.com/PacktPublishing/Quantum-
Computing-in-Practice-with-Qiskit-and-IBM-Quantum-
Experience.git
```

The command should result in something like the following:

```
Cloning into 'Quantum-Computing-in-Practice-with-Qiskit-
and-IBM-Quantum-Experience'...
remote: Enumerating objects: 250, done.
remote: Counting objects: 100% (250/250), done.
remote: Compressing objects: 100% (195/195), done.
remote: Total 365 (delta 106), reused 183 (delta 54),
pack-reused 115
Receiving objects: 100% (365/365), 52.70 MiB | 5.42
MiB/s, done.
Resolving deltas: 100% (153/153), done.
```

## Cloning the repository using GitHub Desktop

1. Click the **Clone or download** button and select **Open in desktop**.

2. In the GitHub Desktop dialog, select a directory to clone the repository to and click **OK**.

You can now browse the recipes in this cookbook. Each chapter includes one or more recipes. If you want, you can copy and paste the recipes directly into your Python environment, or into Jupyter Notebooks on IBM Quantum Experience® or on your local Anaconda environment.

## Opening a recipe file

So far, you have done everything with the command line. So how about you grab the following Python program and run it from your favorite Python interpreters, such as **Anaconda Spyder** or **Jupyter Notebooks**?

If you have downloaded the sample files, the recipe file is available in the following local directory:

```
<The folder where you downloaded the files>/https://github.
com/PacktPublishing/Quantum-Computing-in-Practice-with-
Qiskit-and-IBM-Quantum-Experience/blob/master/Chapter01/
ch1_r1_version.py
```

The ch1_r1_version.py code sample lists the version numbers of the Qiskit® components that we just installed:

```
# Import Qiskit
import qiskit

# Set versions variable to the current Qiskit versions
versions=qiskit.__qiskit_version__

# Print the version number for the Qiskit components

print("Qiskit components and versions:")
print("===============================")

for i in versions:
    print (i, versions[i])
```

When run, the preceding code should give an output similar to the following:

```
Qiskit components and versions:
===============================
qiskit-terra 0.15.2
qiskit-aer 0.6.1
qiskit-ignis 0.4.0
qiskit-ibmq-provider 0.9.0
qiskit-aqua 0.7.5
qiskit 0.21.0
```

Figure 1.2 – A list of the Qiskit® components and versions

The following sections cover how to run the script in the environments that we have available.

## Python scripts in Spyder

In your local environment, you can now open the Python scripts in the Python interpreter of your choice; for example, Spyder, which is included with Anaconda:

> **Important**
>
> Be sure that you run your interpreter in the virtual environment in which you installed Qiskit®. Otherwise, it will not be able to find Qiskit®, and the program will not run correctly.

1.  Open your Anaconda user interface.

2.  Select your virtual environment.

3.  Click the **Spyder** tile. If Spyder is not yet installed for your virtual environment, it will now install. This might take a while. Be patient!

4.  In Spyder, open the Python script that is included with this chapter:

```
<The folder where you downloaded the files>/https://
github.com/PacktPublishing/Quantum-Computing-in-
Practice-with-Qiskit-and-IBM-Quantum-Experience/blob/
master/Chapter01/ch1_r1_version.py
```

5.  Click **Run**. The script will now pull out the version numbers of the installed Qiskit® components. You can also open the Python scripts in a Jupyter notebook, for example, in the online IBM Quantum Experience® environment, but this takes a little extra work.

## Jupyter Notebooks in Anaconda

1.  Open your Anaconda user interface.

2.  Select your virtual environment.

3.  Click the **Jupyter Notebooks** tile. If Jupyter Notebooks is not yet installed for your virtual environment, it will now install.

4.  Your default web browser opens at your root directory. Browse to and open the following:

```
<The folder where you downloaded the files>/https://
github.com/PacktPublishing/Quantum-Computing-in-
Practice-with-Qiskit-and-IBM-Quantum-Experience/blob/
master/Chapter01/ch1_r1_version.py
```

5.  The sample script opens in a Jupyter text editor. You can now see the code but not run it.

6.  Go back to the Jupyter browser and click **New | Notebook**.

7.  Copy and paste the Python script code into the new notebook. You can now click **Run** and see the code execute.

## Jupyter Notebooks in IBM Quantum Experience®

1.  To run the Python scripts in the online IBM Quantum Experience® notebooks, log in to IBM Quantum Experience® at `https://quantum-computing.ibm.com/login`.

2.  On the main dashboard, click on the **Quantum Lab** left-menu icon ( ), then click **New Notebook** and follow the process we discussed *in the Jupyter Notebooks in Anaconda* section.:

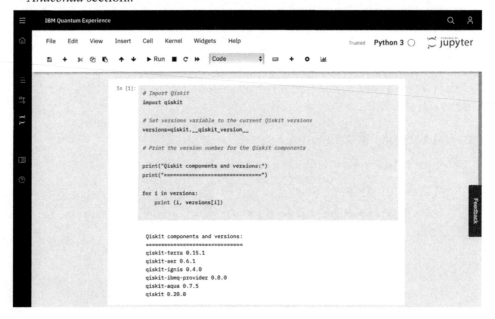

Figure 1.3 – Running your Qiskit® code on IBM Quantum Experience®

## How it works...

The Qiskit®-based Python code that we will be going through in the chapters that follow can be run in any Python environment that meets the Qiskit® requirements, so you have free reins to pick the environment that suits you. And with that environment, you can also freely pick your favorite tools to run the programs.

For this book, I have tested running the code in both the **Spyder** editor that comes as standard with **Anaconda** and with the **Jupyter Notebook** environments on both IBM Quantum Experience® and Anaconda.

# Installing your API key and accessing your provider

Now that you have installed Qiskit®, you can immediately start creating your quantum programs and run these on local simulators. If, however, at some point, you want to run your quantum code on actual IBM Quantum® hardware, you must install your own unique API key locally.

> **API keys on IBM Quantum Experience®**
>
> If you are running your Qiskit® programs in the IBM Quantum Experience® notebook environment, your API key is automatically registered.

## Getting ready

Before you can install your API key, you must first have an IBM Quantum Experience® account. If you have not yet created one, go back and do it (see the *Creating your IBM Quantum Experience® account* section).

## How to do it...

Let's take a look at how to install the API key locally:

1. Log in to IBM Quantum Experience® at `https://quantum-computing.ibm.com/login`.

2. On the IBM Quantum Experience® dashboard, find your user icon in the upper-right corner, click it, and select **My account**.

3. On the account page, find the **Qiskit in local environment** section, and click **Copy token**.

4.  You can now paste your token in a temporary location or keep it in the clipboard.

5.  On your local machine, access your Qiskit® environment. We have done this one, but here's a repeat of the process if you are using Anaconda.

6.  Activate your virtual environment:

```
$ conda activate environment_name
```

7.  Open Python:

```
$(environment_name) … $  python3
```

Verify that the Python header displays and that you are running the correct version of Python:

```
Python 3.7.6 (default, Jan  8 2020, 13:42:34)
[Clang 4.0.1 (tags/RELEASE_401/final)] :: Anaconda, Inc.
on darwin
Type "help", "copyright", "credits" or "license" for more
information.
>>>
```

8.  Get the required IBMQ class:

```
>>> from qiskit import IBMQ
```

9.  Install your API token locally:

```
>>> IBMQ.save_account('MY_API_TOKEN')
```

Here, instead of MY_API_TOKEN, paste in the API token that you just copied from IBM Quantum Experience®: Keep the single quotes as they are required for the command.

10. Load your account.

Now that the token is in place, let's verify that all is in order and that your account has the correct privileges:

```
>>> IBMQ.load_account()
```

This should display the following output:

```
<AccountProvider for IBMQ(hub='ibm-q', group='open',
project='main')>
```

This is the provider information for your account, with hub, group, and project.

## How it works...

The main class that you import for this exercise is IBMQ, which is a toolbox for working with the quantum hardware and software that is provided by IBM in the cloud.

In this chapter, we used save.account() to store your account locally. As we go forward, in the recipes where we will access the IBM Quantum® machines, we will use the IBMQ.load_account() and IBMQ.get_provider() classes in your quantum programs to make sure that you have the correct access.

> **Updating your API key**
>
> If for some reason, you need to create a new API token on IBM Quantum Experience® and update your locally saved token, you can use the following command:
>
> ```
> >>> IBMQ.save_account('NEW_API_TOKEN',
> overwrite=True)
> ```

## There's more...

In the code that follows in the recipes in this cookbook, we will set a provider variable to hold the provider information for your account by using the following command:

```
>>> provider = IBMQ.get_provider()
```

We can then use the provider information when selecting the IBM Quantum® computer, or backend, to run your quantum programs on. In the following example, we select a quantum computer that is called **IBM Q 5 Yorktown** (ibmqx2) as our backend. The internal reference for this machine is ibmqx2:

```
>>> backend = provider.get_backend('ibmqx2')
```

# Keeping your Qiskit® environment up to date

Qiskit® is an open source programming environment that is in *continuous flux*. Over the course of writing this book, I have passed through many minor and major version updates of the software.

It is generally a good idea to stay updated with the latest version, but with some updates, components of the code might change behavior. It is always a good idea to have a good look at the release notes for each new version. Sometimes changes are introduced that will change the way your code behaves. In those cases, you might want to hold off on upgrading until you have verified that your code still works as expected.

If you are using Anaconda environments, then you can maintain more than one environment at different Qiskit® levels, to have a fallback environment in case an upgraded Qiskit® version breaks your code.

> **Qiskit® moves fast**
>
> The IBM Quantum Experience® Notebook environment always runs the latest version of Qiskit®, and it might be a good idea to test drive your code in that environment before you upgrade your local environment.

You can also subscribe to notification updates, to find out when a new release has been offered:

1.  Log in to IBM Quantum Experience® at `https://quantum-computing.ibm.com/login`.

2.  On the IBM Quantum Experience® dashboard, find your user icon in the upper-right corner, click it, and select **My account**.

3.  On the account page, under **Notification** settings, set **Updates and new feature announcements** to **On**.

## Getting ready

Before you begin, verify which version of Qiskit® you are running for each of your environments (if you have more than one).

For each environment, launch Python, either from the command line, from an IDE such as Spyder, or as a Jupyter notebook, then execute the following code:

```
>>> import qiskit
>>> qiskit.__qiskit_version__
```

If you have an old version of Qiskit® installed, the preceding code might result in the following output:

```
{'qiskit-terra': '0.9.0', 'qiskit-aer': '0.3.0', 'qiskit-ibmq-provider': '0.3.0', 'qiskit-aqua': '0.6.0', 'qiskit': '0.12.0'}
```

You can then go to the Qiskit® release notes to find out if there is a more up-to-date version available: `https://qiskit.org/documentation/release_notes.html`

This is a lot of steps just to make sure. The whole process is automated in Python. To go down that path, go to the next section.

# How to do it...

1. Activate your virtual environment:

```
$ conda activate environment_name
```

2. Run the following command to check for outdated `pip` packages for your virtual environment:

```
(environment_name) … $  pip list --outdated
```

3. This will return a list of all your `pip` packages that are currently outdated and list the available versions:

```
Example:
Package                    Version   Latest    Type
------------------------   -------   -------   -----
…
qiskit                     0.19.6    0.21.0    sdist
qiskit-aer                 0.5.2     0.6.1     wheel
qiskit-aqua                0.7.3     0.7.5     wheel
qiskit-ibmq-provider       0.7.2     0.9.0     wheel
qiskit-ignis               0.3.3     0.4.0     wheel
qiskit-terra               0.14.2    0.15.1    wheel
…
```

4. It is then a breeze to update Qiskit® using `pip`:

```
(environment_name) … $  pip install qiskit --upgrade
```

5. From the command line, verify that Qiskit® is installed:

```
(environment_name)… $ pip show qiskit
```

This will result in an output similar to the following:

```
Name: qiskit
Version: 0.21.0
Summary: Software for developing quantum computing
programs
Home-page: https://github.com/Qiskit/qiskit
Author: Qiskit Development Team
Author-email: qiskit@us.ibm.com
License: Apache 2.0
Location: /Users/hassi/opt/anaconda3/envs/packt_qiskit/
lib/python3.7/site-packages
Requires: qiskit-aer, qiskit-terra, qiskit-aqua, qiskit-
```

```
ignis, qiskit-ibmq-provider
Required-by:
...
```

6. Verify that Qiskit® is integrated with Python in your isolated environment.

Open Python:

```
(environment_name)... $ python3
```

Import Qiskit®:

```
>>> import qiskit
```

List the version details:

```
>>> qiskit.__qiskit_version__
```

This should display the versions of the installed Qiskit® components:

```
{'qiskit-terra': '0.15.2', 'qiskit-aer': '0.6.1',
'qiskit-ignis': '0.4.0', 'qiskit-ibmq-provider': '0.9.0',
'qiskit-aqua': '0.7.5', 'qiskit': '0.21.0'}
```

Congratulations, your Qiskit® upgrade worked; you are now running the latest code!

## How it works...

Depending on how you consume this book, you might be looking over this process as part of your first read-through, and no upgrades were available. If so, go ahead and bookmark this recipe, and come back to it at a later time when there has been a Qiskit® upgrade.

The pip tool will manage your upgrade for you for each virtual environment. As I mentioned before, it might be a good idea to do a staged upgrade of your environments if you have more than one.

For example, you can upgrade one environment and test run your quantum programs in that environment to make sure that the new version did not break anything in your code.

OK, with this you should be reasonably set with one or more Qiskit® environments on which to run your quantum programs. If you feel ready for it, you can now take the plunge and go directly to *Chapter 4, Starting at the Ground Level with Terra*, to start writing quantum programs in Python using Qiskit®. If you are up for some prep work to get a feel for what programming a quantum computer is all about, start with *Chapter 2, Quantum Computing and Qubits with Python*, to get an introduction to qubits and gates, or *Chapter 3, IBM Quantum Experience® – Quantum Drag and Drop*, to get a visual feel for quantum programs by using the IBM Quantum Experience® drag-and-drop programming interface.

No matter which path you take, don't worry, we'll let Python do the hard work. Again, have fun!

# 2
# Quantum Computing and Qubits with Python

Quantum computing is a fairly new and fairly old field at the same time. The ideas and concepts used to achieve quantum computing (such as quantum mechanical superposition and entanglement) have been around for almost a century and the field of quantum information science was founded almost 40 years ago. Early explorers, such as Peter Shor and Lov Grover, produced quantum computing algorithms (Shor's algorithm and Grover's algorithm) that are now starting to become as well known as foundational physics concepts such as $E=mc^2$. For details, see the references at the end of the chapter.

At the same time, real quantum computers that utilize these effects are a relatively recent invention. The requirements for building one were outlined by DiVincenzo in the 1990, and IBM opened up its IBM Quantum Experience® and Qiskit® in 2016, effectively the first time anyone outside of a research lab could start exploring this nascent field for real.

So, what is the difference between classical computing and quantum computing? One way to start exploring is by taking a look at the basic computational elements used by each—the classical bits and the quantum qubits.

In this chapter, we will contrast bits and qubits, play with some generic linear algebra to explore them in more detail, and contrast deterministic (classical) computation and probabilistic (quantum) computation. We will even take a quick look at some basic Qiskit® presentation methods to visualize a qubit.

In this chapter, we will cover the following recipes:

- Comparing a bit and a qubit
- Visualizing a qubit in Python
- A quick introduction to quantum gates

# Technical requirements

The recipes that we discuss in this chapter can be found here: `https://github.com/PacktPublishing/Quantum-Computing-in-Practice-with-Qiskit-and-IBM-Quantum-Experience/tree/master/Chapter02`.

For more information about how to get the recipe sample code, refer to the *Downloading the code samples* section in *Chapter 1, Preparing Your Environment*.

# Comparing a bit and a qubit

So, let's start with the obvious—or perhaps, not so obvious—notion that most people who read this book know what a bit is.

An intuitive feeling that we have says that a bit is something that is either **zero** (**0**) or **one** (**1**). By putting many bits together, you can create bytes as well as arbitrary large binary numbers, and with those, build the most amazing computer programs, encode digital images, encrypt your love letters and bank transactions, and more.

In a classical computer, a bit is realized by using low or high voltages over the transistors that make up the logic board, typically something such as 0 V and 5 V. In a hard drive, the bit might be a region magnetized in a certain way to represent 0 and the other way for 1, and so on.

In books about quantum computing, the important point to drive home is that a classical bit can only be a 0 or a 1; it can never be anything else. In the computer example, you can imagine a box with an input and an output, where the box represents the program that you are running. With a classical computer (and I use the term classical here to indicate a binary computer that is not a quantum computer), the input is a string of bits, the output is another string of bits, and the box is a bunch of bits being manipulated, massaged, and organized to generate that output with some kind of algorithm. An important thing, again, to emphasize is that while in the box, the bits are still bits, always 0s or 1s, and nothing else.

A qubit, as we will discover in this chapter, is something quite different. Let's go explore.

## Getting ready

As recipes go, this one isn't really that much to brag about. It is just a quick Python and NumPy implementation that defines a bit as a 2x1 matrix, or a vector representing 0 or 1. We also introduce the Dirac notation of $|0\rangle$, $|1\rangle$, and $a|0\rangle + b|1\rangle$ to represent our qubits. We then calculate the probability of getting various results when measuring the bits and qubits.

The Python file for the following recipe can be downloaded from here: https://github.com/PacktPublishing/Quantum-Computing-in-Practice-with-Qiskit-and-IBM-Quantum-Experience/blob/master/Chapter02/ch2_r1_bits_qubits.py.

## How to do it...

1. Let's start by importing numpy and math, which we will need to do the calculations:

```
import numpy as np
from math import sqrt, pow
```

2. Create and print the bit and qubit vectors for 0, 1, $|0\rangle$, $|1\rangle$, and $a|0\rangle + b|1\rangle$ as [1,0], [0,1], [1,0], [0,1], and [a,b], respectively:

```
# Define the qubit parameters for superposition
a = sqrt(1/2)
b = sqrt(1/2)
if round(pow(a,2)+pow(b,2),0)!=1:
    print("Your qubit parameters are not normalized.
        \nResetting to basic superposition")
    a = sqrt(1/2)
```

```
      b = sqrt(1/2)
 bits = {"bit = 0":np.array([1,0]),
     "bit = 1":np.array([0,1]),
     "|0\u27E9":np.array([1,0]),
     "|1\u27E9":np.array([0,1]),
     "a|0\u27E9+b|1\u27E9":np.array([a,b])}
# Print the vectors
for b in bits:
   print(b, ": ", bits[b].round(3))
print ("\n")
```

Notice the Unicode entries here: \u27E9. We use this instead of just > to create the nice-looking Dirac qubit rendering |0⟩ in the output.

---

**You must provide the correct a and b parameters**

Note that the parameter verification code checks whether the values for a and b are *normalized*. If not, then a and b are reset to a simple 50/50 superposition by setting a = $\frac{1}{\sqrt{2}}$ and b = $\frac{1}{\sqrt{2}}$.

---

3.  Measure the qubits by creating a measurement dictionary, and then calculate the probability of getting 0 and 1 from the bit vectors we created:

```
print("'Measuring' our bits and qubits")
print("--------------------------------")
prob={}
for b in bits:
    print(b)
    print("Probability of getting:")
    for dig in range(len(bits[b])):
        prob[b]=pow(bits[b][dig],2)
        print(dig, " = ", '%.2f'%(prob[b]*100), percent")
    print ("\n")
```

The preceding code should give the following output:

```
Ch 2: Bits and qubits
------------------------
bit = 0 :  [1 0]
bit = 1 :  [0 1]
|0) :  [1 0]
|1) :  [0 1]
a|0)+b|1) :  [0.707 0.707]


'Measuring' our bits and qubits
-------------------------------
bit = 0
Probability of getting:
0  =  100.00 percent
1  =  0.00 percent


bit = 1
Probability of getting:
0  =  0.00 percent
1  =  100.00 percent


|0)
Probability of getting:
0  =  100.00 percent
1  =  0.00 percent


|1)
Probability of getting:
0  =  0.00 percent
1  =  100.00 percent
|

a|0)+b|1)
Probability of getting:
0  =  50.00 percent
1  =  50.00 percent
```

Figure 2.1 – Simulating bits and qubits with NumPy

Now we know what the probabilities of getting the values of 0 or 1 are when measuring the bits and qubits. For some of these (0, 1, |0⟩, and |1⟩) the outcome is what we expected, 0 or 100%; the bit or qubit is either 0 or 1 and nothing else. For one (a|0⟩ + b|1⟩), which is a qubit that is in a superposition of 0 and 1, the probability of getting either is 50%. This is an outcome that can never happen for a classical bit, only for a qubit. We will explain why in the next section.

## How it works...

What we have seen in this recipe is that the probability of reading a classical bit will always be *100%*, either 0 or 1; there are no other options. But for a qubit that can be expressed as a|0⟩ + b|1⟩, the probability of a 0 or 1 is proportional to $|a|^2 + |b|^2 = 1$. For pure |0⟩ and |1⟩ states, $a$ or $b$ is always 1, and the probability of measuring each is 100%. But for the qubit that we labeled a|0⟩ + b|1⟩, a and b are both $\frac{1}{\sqrt{2}}$, giving a probability of 50% for 0 or 1

$(|\frac{1}{\sqrt{2}}|^2 + |\frac{1}{\sqrt{2}}|^2 = 0.5 + 0.5 = 1)$.

---

**Measuring a bit and a qubit**

The word **measure** means two slightly different things in classical computing and quantum computing. In classical computing, you can measure your bits at any time without seriously disturbing the calculations that you are doing. For a quantum computer, measuring is a more definite act that results in your qubit reverting from a bit that behaves quantum-mechanically to a bit that behaves classically. After you measure a qubit, you are done. You can do no further quantum actions on that qubit.

---

Due to the quantum mechanical nature of a qubit, we can describe it as a vector similar to the vector we use for a bit. To clarify that, when we are talking about qubits, we do not just use 0 and 1 as labels, but rather the Dirac *ket* notation, $|0\rangle$ and $|1\rangle$, indicating that these are state vectors in a vector space.

We can write out the state vector, $|\psi\rangle$ (psi), of a qubit like this:

- $|\psi\rangle = |0\rangle$ for a qubit in the *ground state*, representing 0

- $|\psi\rangle = |1\rangle$ for a qubit in the *excited state*, representing 1

Here, we have used **ground state** and **excited state** as one way of categorizing qubits. This is appropriate as the Josephson junctions that the IBM Quantum® qubits use are quantum systems with two energy levels. Depending on the underlying physical system, qubits can also be based on other two-level quantum systems, such as electron spin (up or down) or photon polarization (horizontal or vertical).

So far, nothing is intuitively much different from classical bits, as each represents just the value 0 or 1. But now we add a complexity: a qubit can also be a superposition of the two states, $|0\rangle$ and $|1\rangle$.

$|\psi\rangle = a|0\rangle + b|1\rangle$, where $a$ and $b$ are complex numbers. These numbers are normalized so that $|a|^2 + |b|^2 = 1$, which geometrically means that the resulting vector, $|\psi\rangle$, has a length of 1. This is important!

Going back to the simplest cases, these can be described as follows:

- $|\psi\rangle = |0\rangle = a|0\rangle + b|1\rangle = 1|0\rangle + 0|1\rangle$ for a qubit in the ground state. In this case, a=1 and b=0.

- $|\psi\rangle = |1\rangle = a|0\rangle + b|1\rangle = 0|0\rangle + 1|1\rangle$ for a qubit in the excited state. In this case, a=0 and b=1.

So far, so good, but now we add the quantum twist: superposition. The following qubit state vector is also supported:

$$|\psi\rangle = \frac{1}{\sqrt{2}}|0\rangle + \frac{1}{\sqrt{2}}|1\rangle$$

Just to check that we are still normalized, in this case,

$$|a|^2 + |b|^2 = |\frac{1}{\sqrt{2}}|^2 + |\frac{1}{\sqrt{2}}|^2 = \frac{1}{2} + \frac{1}{2} = 1.$$

But what does this state vector mean?

The qubit is set up in a state where it is exactly halfway between $|0\rangle$ and $|1\rangle$; it exists in a superposition of the two basic states. It is behaving quantumly.

---

**Important Note**

The quantum superposition state of a qubit can only be sustained while we are doing calculations on the quantum computer. The same is true for an actual particle in nature, such as a photon that behaves quantum-mechanically. For example, the polarization of the photon can be described as a superposition of horizontal and vertical orientations while the photon is in flight, but when you add a polarizer in its path, you will measure it as either horizontal or vertical, and nothing else.

---

Going back to the computer-as-a-box example, for a quantum computer we have a similar image, a string of bits as input and another string of bits as output. The difference comes inside the box where the qubits can exist in superposition while we are doing our calculations.

As soon as we measure the qubits to get that string of output bits however, the qubits must decide, quantum-mechanically, if they are a $|0\rangle$ or a $|1\rangle$, and here is where those $a$ and $b$ parameters come in.

The $|a|^2 + |b|^2 = 1$ formula not only states that the vector is normalized to the length 1, but it also describes the probability of getting the $|0\rangle$ and $|1\rangle$ outputs. The probability of getting $|0\rangle$ is $|a|^2$, and $|1\rangle$ is $|b|^2$. This is the core of the difference between a quantum computer and a classical computer. The quantum computer is probabilistic—you cannot know in advance what the end result will be, only the probability of getting a certain result—whereas the classical computer is deterministic—you can always, at least in theory, predict what the answer will be.

> **About probabilistic computing**
>
> People often get a little confused about quantum computers and probabilistic outcomes and visualize the whole quantum programming concept as qubits spinning randomly and uncontrollably in all different states at the same time. This is not a true picture; each qubit is initialized in a specific known state, $|\psi\rangle$, and then acted upon by quantum gate manipulations. Each manipulation is strictly deterministic; there is nothing random. At each stage in a quantum state evolution, we know exactly what our qubit is doing, expressed as an $a|0\rangle + b|1\rangle$ superposition. It is only at the end, when we measure and force the qubit to be either 0 or 1, that the probabilistic nature shows with the probability of measuring 0 or 1 set by the $a$ and $b$ parameters ($|a|^2 + |b|^2 = 1$).

## See also

For more information about qubits and how to interpret them, refer to the following excellent books:

- *Dancing with Qubits, How quantum computing works and how it can change the world*, Robert S. Sutor, Packt Publishing Ltd., 2019, *Chapter 7, One Qubit*

- *Quantum Computation and Quantum Information*, Isaac L. Chuang; Michael A. Nielsen, Cambridge University Press, 2010, *Chapter 1.2, Quantum bits*

- *Quantum Mechanics: The theoretical minimum*, Leonard Susskind & Art Friedman, Basic Books, 2015, *Lecture 1: Systems and experiments*

- *Shor, I'll do it*, Scott Aaronson's blog, `https://www.scottaaronson.com/blog/?p=208`

- *What's a Quantum Phone Book?*, Lov Grover, Lucent Technologies, `https://web.archive.org/web/20140201230754/http://www.bell-labs.com/user/feature/archives/lkgrover/`

- *The Physical Implementation of Quantum Computation*, David P. DiVincenzo, IBM, `https://arxiv.org/abs/quant-ph/0002077`

# Visualizing a qubit in Python

In this recipe, we will use generic Python with NumPy to create a vector and visual representation of a bit and show how it can be in only two states, 0 and 1. We will also introduce our first, smallish foray into the Qiskit® world by showing how a qubit can not only be in the unique 0 and 1 states but also in a superposition of these states. The way to do this is to take the vector form of the qubit and project it on the so-called **Bloch sphere**, for which there is a Qiskit® method. Let's get to work!

In the preceding recipe, we defined our qubits with the help of two complex parameters—*a* and *b*. This meant that our qubits could take values other than the 0 and 1 of a classical bit. But it is hard to visualize a qubit halfway between 0 and 1, even if you know *a* and *b*.

However, with a little mathematical trickery, it turns out that you can also describe a qubit using two angles—**theta** ($\theta$) and **phi** ($\varphi$)—and visualize the qubit on a Bloch sphere. You can think of the $\theta$ and $\varphi$ angles much as the latitude and longitude of the earth. On the Bloch sphere, we can project any possible value that the qubit can take.

The equation for the transformation is as follows:

$$|\psi\rangle = \cos\left(\frac{\theta}{2}\right)|0\rangle + e^{i\varphi}\sin\left(\frac{\theta}{2}\right)|1\rangle$$

Here, we use the formula we saw before:

$$|\psi\rangle = a|0\rangle + b|1\rangle$$

*a* and *b* are, respectively, as follows:

$$a = \cos\left(\frac{\theta}{2}\right)$$

$$b = e^{i\varphi}\sin\left(\frac{\theta}{2}\right)$$

I'll leave the deeper details and math to you for further exploration:

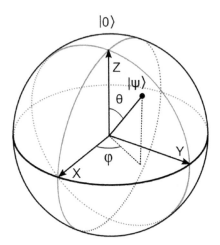

Figure 2.2 – The Bloch sphere.

The poor classical bits cannot do much on a Bloch sphere as they can exist at the North and South poles only, representing the binary values 0 and 1. We will include them just for comparison.

The reason 0 points up and 1 points down has peculiar and historical reasons. The qubit vector representation of $|0\rangle$ is $\begin{bmatrix}1\\0\end{bmatrix}$, or up, and $|1\rangle$ is $\begin{bmatrix}0\\1\end{bmatrix}$, or down, which is intuitively not what you expect. You would think that 1, or a more exciting qubit, would be a vector pointing upward, but this is not the case; it points down. So, I will do the same with the poor classical bits as well: 0 means up and 1 means down.

The latitude, the distance to the poles from a cut straight through the Bloch sphere, corresponds to the numerical values of $a$ and $b$, with $\theta = 0$ pointing straight up for $|0\rangle$ (a=1, b=0), $\theta = \pi$ pointing straight down for $|1\rangle$ (a = 0, b = 1), and $\theta = \frac{\pi}{2}$ points to the equator for the basic superposition where $a = b = \frac{1}{\sqrt{2}}$.

So, what we are adding to the equation here is the *phase* of the qubit. The $\varphi$ angle cannot be directly measured and has no impact on the outcome of our initial quantum circuits. Later on in the book, in *Chapter 9, Grover's Search Algorithm*, we will see that you can use the phase angle to great advantage in certain algorithms. But we are getting ahead of ourselves.

## Getting ready

The Python file for the following recipe can be downloaded from here: `https://github.com/PacktPublishing/Quantum-Computing-in-Practice-with-Qiskit-and-IBM-Quantum-Experience/blob/master/Chapter02/ch2_r2_visualize_bits_qubits.py`.

## How to do it...

For this exercise, we will use the $\theta$ and $\varphi$ angles as latitude and longitude coordinates on the Bloch sphere. We will code the 0, 1, $|0\rangle$, $|1\rangle$, and $\frac{(|0\rangle + |1\rangle)}{\sqrt{2}}$ states with the corresponding angles. As we can set these angles to any latitude and longitude value we want, we can put the qubit state vector wherever we want on the Bloch sphere:

1.  Import the classes and methods that we need, including numpy and `plot_bloch_vector` from Qiskit®. We also need to use `cmath` to do some calculations on imaginary numbers:

```
import numpy as np
import cmath
from math import pi, sin, cos
from qiskit.visualization import plot_bloch_vector
```

2.  Create the qubits:

```
# Superposition with zero phase
angles={"theta": pi/2, "phi":0}
# Self defined qubit
#angles["theta"]=float(input("Theta:\n"))
#angles["phi"]=float(input("Phi:\n"))
# Set up the bit and qubit vectors
bits = {"bit = 0":{"theta": 0, "phi":0},
    "bit = 1":{"theta": pi, "phi":0},
    "|0\u27E9":{"theta": 0, "phi":0},
    "|1\u27E9":{"theta": pi, "phi":0},
    "a|0\u27E9+b|1\u27E9":angles}
```

From the code sample, you can see that we are using the theta angle only for now, with theta = 0 meaning that we point straight up and theta = $\pi$ meaning straight down for our basic bits and qubits: 0, 1, |0⟩, and |1⟩. Theta $\frac{\pi}{2}$ takes us halfway, to the equator, and we use that for the superposition qubit, a|0⟩ + b|1⟩.

3.  Print the bits and qubits on the Bloch sphere.

The Bloch sphere method takes a three-dimensional vector as input, but we have to build the vector first. We can use the following formula to calculate the $X$, $Y$, and $Z$ parameters to use with `plot_bloch_vector` and display the bits and qubits as Bloch sphere representations:

$$\text{bloch} = (\cos \varphi \sin \theta, \sin \varphi \sin \theta, \cos \theta)$$

This is how it would look in our vector notation:

$$\text{bloch} = \begin{bmatrix} \cos \varphi \sin \theta \\ \sin \varphi \sin \theta \\ \cos \theta \end{bmatrix}$$

And this is how we set this up in Python:

```
bloch=[cos(bits[bit]["phi"])*sin(bits[bit]
    ["theta"]),sin(bits[bit]["phi"])*sin(bits[bit]
    ["theta"]),cos(bits[bit]["theta"])]
```

We now cycle through the bits dictionary to display the Bloch sphere view of the bits and qubits, as well as the state vectors that correspond to them:

$$|\psi\rangle = a|0\rangle + b|1\rangle = \begin{bmatrix} a \\ b \end{bmatrix}$$

The state vector is calculated using the equation we saw previously:

$$|\psi\rangle = \cos\left(\frac{\theta}{2}\right)|0\rangle + e^{i\varphi}\sin\left(\frac{\theta}{2}\right)|1\rangle$$

What we see now is that $a$ and $b$ can actually turn into complex values, just as defined.

Here's the code:

```
for bit in bits:
    bloch=[cos(bits[bit]["phi"])*sin(bits[bit]
        ["theta"]),sin(bits[bit]["phi"])*sin(bits[bit]
        ["theta"]),cos(bits[bit]["theta"])]
    display(plot_bloch_vector(bloch, title=bit))
    # Build the state vector
    a = cos(bits[bit]["theta"]/2)
    b = cmath.exp(bits[bit]["phi"]*1j)*sin(bits[bit]
        ["theta"]/2)
    state_vector = [a * complex(1, 0), b * complex(1, 0)]
    print("State vector:", np.around(state_vector,
        decimals = 3))
```

4.  The sample code should give an output similar to the following examples.

First, we show the classical bits, 0 and 1:

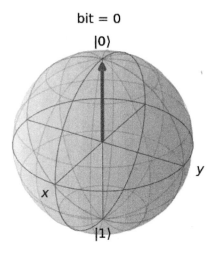

State vector: [1.+0.j 0.+0.j]

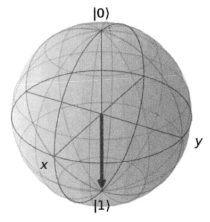

Figure 2.3 – Bloch sphere visualization of classical bits

5.    Then, we show the quantum bits, or qubits, $|0\rangle$ and $|1\rangle$:

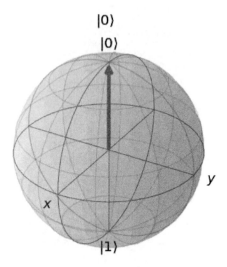

State vector: [1.+0.j 0.+0.j]

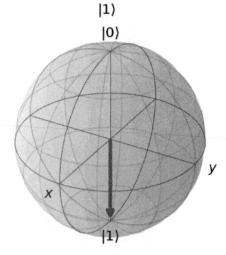

State vector: [0.+0.j 1.+0.j]

Figure 2.4 – Bloch sphere visualization of qubits

6.    Finally, we show a qubit in superposition, a mix of $|0\rangle$ and $|1\rangle$:

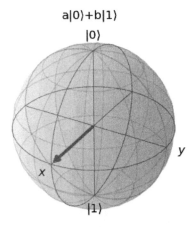

State vector: [0.707+0.j 0.707+0.j]

Figure 2.5 – Bloch sphere visualization of a qubit in superposition

So, there is very little that is earth-shattering with the simple 0, 1, $|0\rangle$, and $|1\rangle$ displays. They simply point up and down to the north and south pole of the Bloch sphere as appropriate. If we check what the value of the bit or qubit is by measuring it, we will get 0 or 1 with 100% certainty.

The qubit in superposition, calculated as $\dfrac{|0\rangle + |1\rangle}{\sqrt{2}}$, on the other hand, points to the equator. From the equator, it is an equally long distance to either pole, thus a 50/50 chance of getting a 0 or a 1.

In the code, we include the following few lines, which define the `angles` variable that sets $\theta$ and $\varphi$ for the $a|0\rangle + b|1\rangle$ qubit:

```
# Superposition with zero phase
angles={"theta": pi/2, "phi":0}
```

# There's more...

We mentioned earlier that we weren't going to touch on the phase ($\varphi$) angle, at least not initially. But we can visualize what it does for our qubits. Remember that we can directly describe $a$ and $b$ using the angles $\theta$ and $\varphi$.

To test this out, you can uncomment the lines that define the angles in the sample code:

```
# Self-defined qubit
angles["theta"]=float(input("Theta:\n"))
angles["phi"]=float(input("Phi:\n"))
```

You can now define what your third qubit looks like by manipulating the $\theta$ and $\varphi$ values. Let's test what we can do by running the script again and plugging in some angles.

For example, we can try the following:

$$\theta = \frac{\pi}{2} \approx 1.570$$

$$\varphi = \frac{\pi}{8} \approx 0.392$$

You should see the final Bloch sphere look something like the following:

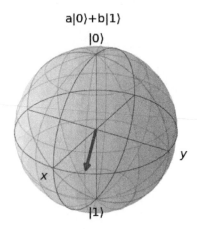

Figure 2.6 – The qubit state vector rotated by $\frac{\pi}{8}$

Note how the state vector is still on the equator with $\theta = \frac{\pi}{2}$ but now at a $\frac{\pi}{8}$ angle to the $x$ axis. You can also take a look at the state vector: [0.707+0.j   0.653+0.271j].

We have now stepped away from the Bloch sphere prime meridian and out into the complex plane, and added a phase angle, which is represented by an imaginary state vector component along the $y$ axis: $|\psi\rangle = 0.707|0\rangle + (0.653 + 0.271i)|1\rangle$

---

**Let's go on a trip**

Go ahead and experiment with different $\theta$ and $\varphi$ angles to get other $a$ and $b$ entries and see where you end up. No need to include 10+ decimals for these rough estimates, two or three decimals will do just fine. Try plotting your hometown on the Bloch sphere. Remember that the script wants the input in radians and that theta starts at the North Pole, not at the equator. For example, the coordinates for Greenwich Observatory in England are 51.4779° N, 0.0015° W, which translates into: $\theta = 0.6723$, $\varphi = 0.0003$.

---

Here's Qiskit® and a globe displaying the same coordinates:

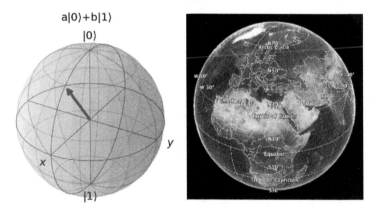

Figure 2.7 – Greenwich quantumly and on a globe

# See also

*Quantum Computation and Quantum Information*, Isaac L. Chuang; Michael A. Nielsen, Cambridge University Press, 2010, *Chapter 1.2, Quantum bits,* and *Chapter 4.2, Single qubit operations.*

# A quick introduction to quantum gates

Now that we have sorted out the difference between bits and qubits, and have also understood how to visualize the qubit as a Bloch sphere, we know all that there is to know about qubits, correct? Well, not quite. A qubit, or for that matter, hundreds or thousands of qubits, is not the only thing you need to make a quantum computer! You need to perform logical operations on and with the qubits. For this, just like a classical computer, we need logical gates.

I will not go into any great detail on how logical gates work, but suffice to say that a quantum gate, operates on the input of one or more qubits and outputs a result.

In this recipe, we will work our way through the mathematical interpretation of few quantum gates by using matrix multiplication of single- and multi-qubit gates. Don't worry, we will not dig deep, just a little to scratch the surface. You will find a deeper look quantum gates in *Chapter 6, Understanding the Qiskit Gate Library*.

Again, we will not be building any actual Qiskit quantum circuits just yet. We are still using more or less plain Python with some NumPy matrix manipulations to prove our points.

## Getting ready

The Python file for the following recipe can be downloaded from here: `https://github.com/PacktPublishing/Quantum-Computing-in-Practice-with-Qiskit-and-IBM-Quantum-Experience/blob/master/Chapter02/ch2_r3_qubit_gates.py`.

## How to do it...

This recipe will create vector and matrix representations of qubits and gates, and use simple algebra to illustrate the behavior of the qubits as gates are applied to them:

1.  In your Python environment, run `ch2_r3_qubit_gates.py` and respond to the **Press return to continue** prompts to move along the program.

2.  First, we see the vector representations of three qubit states: $|0\rangle$, $|1\rangle$, and $\frac{|0\rangle + |1\rangle}{\sqrt{2}}$:

```
Ch 2: Quantum gates
-------------------
Vector representations of our qubits:
------------------------------------
|0)
 [1 0]
|1)
 [0 1]
(|0)+|1))/√2
 [0.707 0.707]

Press return to continue...
```

Figure 2.8 – Qubits as vectors

3. Next, we display the matrix representation of a couple of gates.

   We will use the Id (does nothing), X (flips the qubit), and H (creates a superposition) gates:

```
Matrix representations of our quantum gates:
--------------------------------------------
id
 [[1 0]
  [0 1]]
x
 [[0 1]
  [1 0]]
h
 [[ 0.707  0.707]
  [ 0.707 -0.707]]
```

Figure 2.9 – Single-qubit gates as matrices

4.  The final step for our single-qubit setup is to see how each gate manipulates the qubits.

This is done using matrix multiplication of the qubit vector and the gate matrix:

```
Gate manipulations of our qubits:
------------------------------------
Gate: id
|0)
  [1 0] -> [1 0]
|1)
  [0 1] -> [0 1]
(|0)+|1))/√2
  [0.707 0.707] -> [0.707 0.707]


Gate: x
|0)
  [1 0] -> [0 1]
|1)
  [0 1] -> [1 0]
(|0)+|1))/√2
  [0.707 0.707] -> [0.707 0.707]


Gate: h
|0)
  [1 0] -> [0.707 0.707]
|1)
  [0 1] -> [ 0.707 -0.707]
(|0)+|1))/√2
  [0.707 0.707] -> [1. 0.]
```

Figure 2.10 – Gates acting on qubits

5.  With the single qubits done, we now move on to working with combinations of two qubit states: $|00\rangle, |01\rangle, |10\rangle$, and $|11\rangle$:

```
Vector representations of our two qubits:
------------------------------------------
|00)
  [1 0 0 0]
|01)
  [0 1 0 0]
|10)
  [0 0 1 0]
|11)
  [0 0 0 1]
|PH)
  [ 0.5 -0.5  0.5 -0.5]
```

Figure 2.11 – Two qubits as vectors

6.  Like for the single qubits, we now show the matrix representations of the two-qubit quantum gates.

    Here, we use CX (controlled NOT, flips one qubit if the other is 1) and swap (swaps the values of the two qubits):

```
Matrix representations of our quantum gates:
--------------------------------------------
cx
  [[1 0 0 0]
   [0 1 0 0]
   [0 0 0 1]
   [0 0 1 0]]
swap
  [[1 0 0 0]
   [0 0 1 0]
   [0 1 0 0]
   [0 0 0 1]]
```

Figure 2.12 – Two-qubit gates as matrices

7.  Finally, let's see gate manipulations of our multi-qubit states.

    Again, we have a matrix multiplication of the qubits vector and the gate matrix:

```
Gate manipulations of our qubits:
---------------------------------
Gate: cx
|00)
 [1 0 0 0] -> [1 0 0 0]
|01)
 [0 1 0 0] -> [0 1 0 0]
|10)
 [0 0 1 0] -> [0 0 0 1]
|11)
 [0 0 0 1] -> [0 0 1 0]
|PH)
 [ 0.5 -0.5  0.5 -0.5] -> [ 0.5 -0.5 -0.5  0.5]


Gate: swap
|00)
 [1 0 0 0] -> [1 0 0 0]
|01)
 [0 1 0 0] -> [0 0 1 0]
|10)
 [0 0 1 0] -> [0 1 0 0]
|11)
 [0 0 0 1] -> [0 0 0 1]
|PH)
 [ 0.5 -0.5  0.5 -0.5] -> [ 0.5  0.5 -0.5 -0.5]
```

Figure 2.13 – Multi-qubit gates acting on two qubits

That's it... we have now witnessed Python-generated linear algebra that describes how our qubits are defined and how they behave when gates are applied to them.

## How it is works...

The previous section contained a lot of printed information with very little explanation of how we got those results. Let's dig into the sample code to see how the output is generated:

> **Tip**
>
> The numbered steps that follow correspond to the same numbered steps in the preceding *How to do it...* section. Refer back to those steps to see the result of the code samples that follow.

1.  Let's start by importing the math tools we need:

```python
import numpy as np
from math import sqrt
```

2.  Set up the basic vectors for our qubits.

    A qubit set to the value 0 is labeled $|0\rangle$ in the Dirac ket notation and is mathematically represented by the $\begin{bmatrix} 1 \\ 0 \end{bmatrix}$ vector, if it is set to 1 as $|1\rangle$, or the $\begin{bmatrix} 0 \\ 1 \end{bmatrix}$ vector. So far, so good, still only 0 and 1. As we have seen, the real magic comes when you have a qubit set to a superposition value represented by a vector pointing to the equator of the Bloch sphere, or anywhere except the poles—for example, $\frac{|0\rangle + |1\rangle}{\sqrt{2}}$, which would be represented by the following vector:

$$\begin{bmatrix} \dfrac{1}{\sqrt{2}} \\ \dfrac{1}{\sqrt{2}} \end{bmatrix}$$

> **The generic way of writing a qubit**
>
> Remember, the generic way of writing a qubit in superposition is $|\psi\rangle = a|0\rangle + b|1\rangle$, with $a$ and $b$ as complex numbers and $|a|^2 + |b|^2 = 1$.

This is how we create the $|0\rangle$ qubit vector using NumPy:

```python
np.array([1,0])
```

Here's how we create a dictionary of our qubits in the sample:

```
qubits = {"|0\u27E9":np.array([1,0]),
    "|1\u27E9":np.array([0,1]),
    "(|0\u27E9+|1\u27E9)/\u221a2":1/sqrt(2)*np.
    array([1,1])}
for q in qubits:
    print(q, "\n", qubits[q].round(3))
```

3. Set up the basic matrices for our quantum gates.

For qubits, any single-qubit gate can be represented by a 2x2 matrix like this:
$\begin{bmatrix} a & b \\ c & d \end{bmatrix}$.

For single qubits, the math that we have implemented is a matrix operation that corresponds to the truth table for the two operations, *ID* and *NOT* (or *X*, as the quantum gate is called):

$$\text{ID: } \begin{bmatrix} 1 & 0 \\ 0 & 1 \end{bmatrix}$$

$$\text{X: } \begin{bmatrix} 0 & 1 \\ 1 & 0 \end{bmatrix}$$

But here, we also add another example, the *H* (or Hadamard) gate that does something completely new:

$$\text{H: } \frac{1}{\sqrt{2}} \begin{bmatrix} 1 & 1 \\ 1 & -1 \end{bmatrix}$$

When we run $|0\rangle$ through an H gate, you get the superposition result:

$$0.707|0\rangle + 0.707|1\rangle$$

The same is true when you run $|1\rangle$ through the gate, but with the sign flipped for the $|1\rangle$ component:

$$0.707|0\rangle - 0.707|1\rangle$$

Finally, when you run a qubit in the generic 50/50 superposition ($|\psi\rangle = 0.707|0\rangle + 0.707|1\rangle$) through the H gate, you get one of the base qubits back:

$$|0\rangle \text{ or } |1\rangle$$

This is our first tangible demonstration of another aspect of quantum gates that we'll touch on in the *There's more...* section. They are reversible. This means that no information is lost as you apply a gate to your qubit. You can always run the gate backward and end up where you started by applying its inverse.

Here's how you create the X gate as a NumPy matrix:

```
np.array([[0, 1], [1, 0]])
```

Here's how we create a dictionary of our gates in the sample:

```
gates ={"id":np.array([[1, 0], [0, 1]]),
    "x":np.array([[0, 1], [1, 0]]),
    "h":1/sqrt(2)*np.array([[1, 1], [1, -1]])}
for g in gates:
  print(g, "\n", gates[g].round(3))
```

4.  Now, let's use NumPy to apply the defined gates on our qubits.

    The application of a gate on a qubit can be expressed as a vector multiplication of the qubit and the gate. Here's the NumPy matrix dot multiplication for an X gate on the $|0\rangle$ qubit:

```
np.dot(np.array([[0, 1], [1, 0]]), np.array([1,0]))
```

In our sample, we step our way through the two dictionaries that we created, applying the matrix multiplication to each gate/qubit combination:

```
for g in gates:
    print("Gate:",g)
    for q in qubits:
        print(q,"\n",qubits[q].round(3),"->",
              np.dot(gates[g],qubits[q]).round(3))
```

Here, we see the expected behavior of the gates on our qubits: the ID gate does nothing, the X gate flips the qubit, and the H gate creates or uncreates a superposition.

If you want to experiment a little, you can take a look at the vector representations of the various quantum gates that we show in *Chapter 6, Understanding the Qiskit® Gate Library*, and see whether you can add these gates to the **gates** dictionary.

In this first example, we took a look at how to build our single qubits and gates as vectors and matrices, and how to run our qubits through the gates by using vector multiplication. Now let's do the same with two qubits…

5.  Set up our multi-qubit vectors.

    First, we expand our Dirac-noted qubit combinations: $|00\rangle$, $|01\rangle$, $|10\rangle$, and $|11\rangle$.

These represent, respectively, both qubits 0, first qubit 1 and second 0, first qubit 0 and second 1, and both qubits 1. Here, we are using the **backward Qiskit® notation** for our qubits, starting with the first qubit ($q_0$) as the **Least Significant Bit (LSB)** in the vector notation, like this: $|q_1\ q_0\rangle$.

The vector representation of these are, respectively, as follows:

$$\begin{bmatrix}1\\0\\0\\0\end{bmatrix}, \begin{bmatrix}0\\1\\0\\0\end{bmatrix}, \begin{bmatrix}0\\0\\1\\0\end{bmatrix}, \text{and} \begin{bmatrix}0\\0\\0\\1\end{bmatrix}$$

We already know how to build our qubits as 2x1 NumPy arrays, so let's extend that to 4x1 vectors. With NumPy, this is how we create, for example, the $|00\rangle$ qubit vector:

```
np.array([1,0,0,0])
```

In the sample code, we set up a dictionary with the multi-qubit arrays:

```
twoqubits = {"|00\u27E9":np.array([1,0,0,0]),
    "|01\u27E9":np.array([0,1,0,0]),
    "|10\u27E9":np.array([0,0,1,0]),
    "|11\u27E9":np.array([0,0,0,1]),
    "|PH\u27E9":np.array([0.5,-0.5,0.5,-0.5])}
for b in twoqubits:
  print(b, "\n", twoqubits[b])
```

6.  Set up our multi-qubit gate matrices.

    The two-qubit quantum gates are represented by 4x4 matrices, such as the **controlled-NOT (CX)** gate, which flips the first qubit ($q_0$) if the controlling second qubit ($q_1$) is set to 1:

    $$CX: \begin{bmatrix}1&0&0&0\\0&1&0&0\\0&0&0&1\\0&0&1&0\end{bmatrix}$$

    Gate matrices like these, where one qubit acts as the control and the other as controlled, differ somewhat depending on which qubit you select as the control. If the CX gate points the other way, with the first qubit ($q_0$) as the controlling qubit, the matrix will look like this instead:

    $$CX = \begin{bmatrix}1&0&0&0\\0&0&0&1\\0&0&1&0\\0&1&0&0\end{bmatrix}$$

Here's how we build the gates:

```
twogates ={"cx":np.array([[1, 0, 0, 0], [0, 1, 0, 0],
    [0, 0, 0, 1], [0, 0, 1, 0]]),
    "swap":np.array([[1, 0, 0, 0], [0, 0, 1, 0],
    [0, 1, 0, 0], [0, 0, 0, 1]])}
```

Here's a NumPy matrix dot multiplication example for a CX gate on the $|11\rangle$ qubit:

```
np.dot(np.array([[1, 0, 0, 0], [0, 1, 0, 0],
    [0, 0, 0, 1], [0, 0, 1, 0]]), np.array([0,0,0,1]))
```

Here's the sample code:

```
twogates ={"cx":np.array([[1, 0, 0, 0], [0, 1, 0, 0],
    [0, 0, 0, 1], [0, 0, 1, 0]]),
    "swap":np.array([[1, 0, 0, 0], [0, 0, 1, 0],
    [0, 1, 0, 0], [0, 0, 0, 1]])}
for g in twogates:
  print(g, "\n", twogates[g].round())
print ("\n")
```

7.  Then, we'll apply the gates to our bits and see the results:

```
for g in twogates:
    print("Gate:",g)
    for b in twoqubits:
        print(b,"\n",twoqubits[b],"->",
            np.dot(twogates[g],twoqubits[b]))
    print("\n")
```

The main takeaway with the multi-qubit matrix manipulations is that the output is a vector of the same dimensions as the input vector; no information is lost.

## There's more...

One other aspect of quantum gates that is generally not true of classical gates is that they are reversible. If you run the gate backward, you end up with the input states of your qubits, and no information is lost. The final recipe in this chapter illustrates this.

## The sample code

The sample file for the following recipe can be downloaded from here: `https://github.com/PacktPublishing/Quantum-Computing-in-Practice-with-Qiskit-and-IBM-Quantum-Experience/blob/master/Chapter02/ch2_r4_reversible_gates.py`:

1. Let's start by importing all we need:

```
import numpy as np
from math import sqrt
```

2. Set up the basic qubit vectors and gate matrices. When printing out the gates, we compare the gate matrix with its complex conjugate. If these are the same, the gate and its inverse are identical:

```
qubits = {"|0\u232A":np.array([1,0]),
    "|1\u232A":np.array([0,1]),
    "(|0\u232A+|1\u232A)/\u221a2":1/sqrt(2)*np.
    array([1,1])}
for q in qubits:
  print(q, "\n", qubits[q])
print ("\n")
gates ={"id":np.array([[1, 0], [0, 1]]),
    "x":np.array([[0, 1], [1, 0]]),
    "y":np.array([[0, -1.j], [1.j, 0]]),
    "z":np.array([[1, 0], [0, -1]]),
    "h":1/sqrt(2)*np.array([[1, 1], [1, -1]]),
    "s":np.array([[1, 0], [0, 1j]])}
diff=""
for g in gates:
  print(g, "\n", gates[g].round(3))
  if gates[g].all==np.matrix.conjugate(gates[g]).all:
      diff="(Same as original)"
  else:
      diff="(Complex numbers conjugated)"
  print("Inverted",g, diff, "\n",
    np.matrix.conjugate(gates[g]).round(3))
print ("\n")
```

3. Demonstrate that the basic quantum gates are reversible by applying the gate then its complex conjugate, and then comparing the outcome with the input. For the quantum gates, which are reversible, this will bring the qubit back to the starting state:

```python
for g in gates:
    input("Press enter...")
    print("Gate:",g)
    print("-------")
    for q in qubits:
        print ("\nOriginal qubit: ",q,"\n",
            qubits[q].round(3))
        print ("Qubit after",g,"gate: \n",
            np.dot(gates[g],qubits[q]).round(3))
        print ("Qubit after inverted",g,"gate.","\n",
            np.dot(np.dot(gates[g],qubits[q]),
            np.matrix.conjugate(gates[g])).round(3))
    print("\n")
```

## Running the sample

When you run this `ch2_r4_reversible_gates.py` script, it will do the following:

1. Like before, create and print out vector and matrix representations of our qubits and quantum gates.

   This time, we add three new gates:

   $$Y: \begin{bmatrix} 0 & -i \\ i & 0 \end{bmatrix}$$

   $$Z: \begin{bmatrix} 1 & 0 \\ 0 & -1 \end{bmatrix}$$

   $$S: \begin{bmatrix} 1 & 0 \\ 0 & i \end{bmatrix}$$

   Here, $Y$ and $Z$ perform $\pi$ rotation around the corresponding axes, in essence acting as NOT gates along the $y$ and $z$ axes on the Bloch sphere. The S gate adds a new functionality to the gates, $\pi/2$ rotation around the $z$ axis. We will return to these gates in more detail in *Chapter 6, Understanding the Qiskit® Gate Library*:

```
Ch 2: Reversible quantum gates
--------------------------------------
|0⟩
  [1 0]
|1⟩
  [0 1]
(|0⟩+|1⟩)/√2
  [0.707 0.707]


Matrix representations of our gates:
--------------------------------------
 id
 [[1 0]
  [0 1]]
Reversed id = id (Same as original)
 [[1 0]
  [0 1]]

 x
 [[0 1]
  [1 0]]
Reversed x = x (Same as original)
 [[0 1]
  [1 0]]

 y
 [[ 0.+0.j -0.-1.j]
  [ 0.+1.j  0.+0.j]]
Reversed y = y† (Complex numbers conjugated)
 [[ 0.-0.j -0.+1.j]
  [ 0.-1.j  0.-0.j]]

 z
 [[ 1  0]
  [ 0 -1]]
Reversed z = z (Same as original)
 [[ 1  0]
  [ 0 -1]]

 h
 [[ 0.707  0.707]
  [ 0.707 -0.707]]
Reversed h = h (Same as original)
 [[ 0.707  0.707]
  [ 0.707 -0.707]]

 s
 [[1.+0.j 0.+0.j]
  [0.+0.j 0.+1.j]]
Reversed s = s† (Complex numbers conjugated)
 [[1.-0.j 0.-0.j]
  [0.-0.j 0.-1.j]]
```

Figure 2.14 – Quantum gates and their inverses

The complex conjugate of a complex number is obtained by changing the sign of its imaginary part, so for gates with only real numbers in their matrices, the complex conjugate does nothing, and the gate is its own reverse.

2. Then, for each of our qubits, we apply each gate and then its reverse gate and show that we end up with the same qubit state as we started with.

The examples that follow are for the X and S gates:

```
Gate: x
———————

Original qubit:   |0⟩
   [1 0]
Qubit after x gate:
   [0 1]
Qubit after reversed x gate.
   [1 0]

Original qubit:   |1⟩
   [0 1]
Qubit after x gate:
   [1 0]
Qubit after reversed x gate.
   [0 1]

Original qubit:   (|0⟩+|1⟩)/√2
   [0.707 0.707]
Qubit after x gate:
   [0.707 0.707]
Qubit after reversed x gate.
   [0.707 0.707]
```

Figure 2.15 – The effects of the X gate and reversed X gate on three qubit states

The reversed X gate is simply itself, and applying it twice to a qubit brings back the original qubit state:

```
Gate: s
———————

Original qubit:   |0⟩
   [1 0]
Qubit after s gate:
   [1.+0.j 0.+0.j]
Qubit after reversed s gate.
   [1.+0.j 0.+0.j]

Original qubit:   |1⟩
   [0 1]
Qubit after s gate:
   [0.+0.j 0.+1.j]
Qubit after reversed s gate.
   [0.+0.j 1.+0.j]

Original qubit:   (|0⟩+|1⟩)/√2
   [0.707 0.707]
Qubit after s gate:
   [0.707+0.j    0.    +0.707j]
Qubit after reversed s gate.
   [0.707+0.j 0.707+0.j]
```

Figure 2.16 – The effects of the S and reversed S gate (S†) on three qubit states

The reverse of the S gate is called the S† gate, where S† is the complex conjugation of S. Applying S followed by S† brings back the original qubit state.

# See also

- *Quantum Computation and Quantum Information*, Isaac L. Chuang; Michael A. Nielsen, Cambridge University Press, 2010, *Chapter 4.2, Single qubit operations*, and *Chapter 4.3, Controlled operations*.

- *The Feynman Lectures on Physics*, Feynman, Richard P.; Leighton, Robert B.; Sands, Matthew, 1965, Addison-Wesley. Take a look at the online version, and the chapter on amplitudes and vectors, for more about Dirac notation: `https://www.feynmanlectures.caltech.edu/III_08.html#Ch8-S1`.

- For a quick interactive look at a single qubit Bloch sphere representation, take a look at the **grok bloch** application by Qiskit Advocate James Weaver: `https://github.com/JavaFXpert/grok-bloch`.

- You can install and run it from your own Python environment, or run it online here: `https://javafxpert.github.io/grok-bloch/`.

- The application supports the simple X and H gates that we have tested so far, as well as additional gates that we will be touching on in the following chapters, such as Y, Z, Rx, Ry, Rz, and more. For a deeper dive into the quantum gates that are available with Qiskit®, refer to *Chapter 6, Understanding the Qiskit® Gate Library*.

# 3
# IBM Quantum Experience® – Quantum Drag and Drop

Something pretty amazing happened in the cloud in early 2016; a new type of computer opened its arms to the world—a programmable quantum computer.

In this chapter, we will talk briefly about the early history of IBM Quantum Experience®, how to get there, and how to open a user account. We will take a look at the drag-and-drop user interface for programming the IBM quantum computers (Circuit Composer).

Also, we will take a quick peek at how you can move back and forth between IBM Quantum Experience® and Qiskit® by using the underlying OpenQASM coding.

In this chapter, we will cover the following recipes:

- Introducing IBM Quantum Experience®
- Building quantum scores with Circuit Composer

- Tossing a quantum coin
- Moving between worlds

We will not stay long here; just long enough to scratch the surface, present a quantum circuit we will play with later in *Chapter 4, Starting at the Ground Level with Terra*, and get a feel for the plethora of gates that are available to use.

# Technical requirements

The quantum programs that we will discuss in this chapter can be found here: `https://github.com/PacktPublishing/Quantum-Computing-in-Practice-with-Qiskit-and-IBM-Quantum-Experience/tree/master/Chapter03`.

If you haven't already, get yourself an IBM Quantum Experience® account. For information, see *Creating your IBM Quantum Experience® account* in *Chapter 1, Preparing Your Environment.*

# Introducing IBM Quantum Experience®

**IBM Quantum Experience®** is an open platform available for someone to start their quantum computing journey. In it, you have free access to a number of IBM quantum computers, ranging in size from a single qubit to 15 qubits (at the time of writing), as well as a 32-qubit simulator that runs on IBM POWER9™ hardware. That's a lot of power at your fingertips.

IBM Quantum Experience® opened its doors in May 2016, in a world-first announcement that the public would now have access to actual quantum computing hardware in the cloud. Since then, several other companies have announced similar initiatives and opened up for cloud quantum computing, initially on *simulators*. Notable among this crowd are Google, Microsoft, Rigetti, Qutech, and more. As of this book's writing, IBM gives free access to both hardware and software quantum computing through its IBM Quantum Experience®, we will focus on that platform.

From your web browser, go to the following URL, and log in with your IBM Quantum Experience® account: `https://quantum-computing.ibm.com/`.

You are now on the main IBM Quantum Experience® landing page from which you can access all the quantum experience tools.

From here, you will see the following:

- In the right pane, we have backends that are available to you. Clicking on each brings up a data page with the access status, provider access, chip structure and error rate data, the number of qubits, a list of basis gates, and more.

- In the center area, you find your workbench. There's a list of recent circuits, currently running experiments, and your previous experiment results; when you first drop in here, it will be quite empty. From this area, you can also manage your user profile, configure notifications, get your API key, and more.

- To the left, we have the main tools and help resources. These are described in more detail in the next section's *How to do it....*

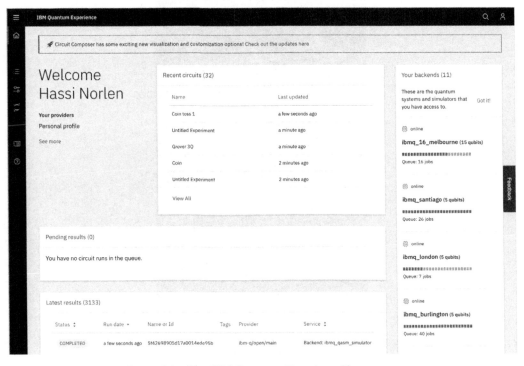

Figure 3.1 – The IBM Quantum Experience® home page

Now that we have successfully logged in and looked around, let's take a look at the quantum computing programming tools at our disposal. From the main menu on the right, you can access the following pages:

- **Results**
- **Circuit Composer**
- **Quantum Lab**

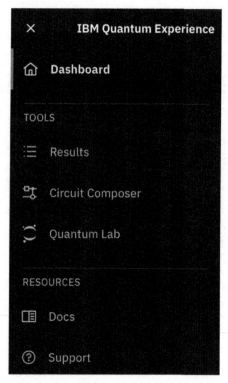

Figure 3.2 – The IBM Quantum Experience® programming tools

Let's look at each of those pages now.

# Results

The **Results** section of IBM Quantum Experience® is just a long list of your pending jobs and your previously run quantum computing programs. You can search, sort, and filter by variables such as execution time, services (backends), and more:

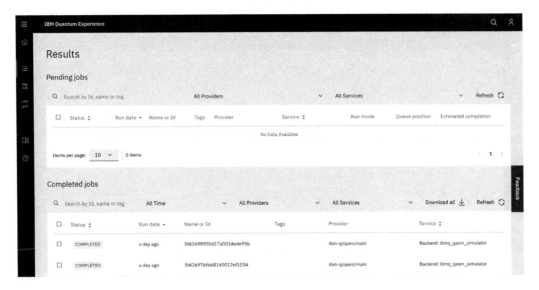

Figure 3.3 – The Results page

The **Results** pane in IBM Quantum Experience® includes not only the jobs that are run from the **Circuit Composer** but also all jobs that you run on IBM Quantum® backends from your local Qiskit® with the same ID.

Each job includes not only the results of your job but also other data such as how long the job stayed in each stage of processing, how long it took to run, the status of the job, the **transpiled** circuit diagram, and the OpenQASM code for the circuit.

# Circuit Composer

The Circuit Composer is the main tool for working with your quantum scores (which is what IBM Quantum Experience® calls quantum programs built using the Circuit Composer tool). We will go through it in detail in the recipes in this chapter, but I will provide you with a quick overview of its components here:

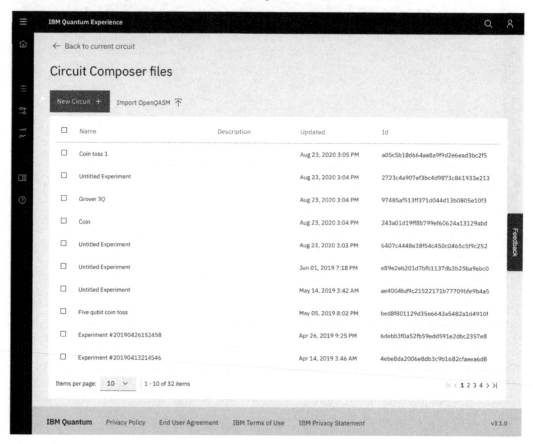

Figure 3.4 – The Circuit Composer files page

Just like the **Results** pane has a list of jobs, the **Circuit Composer files** pane has a list of your *circuits*. From here, you can open and run all circuits that you have created using the Circuit Composer.

You can also click **New Circuit** to start from scratch, which opens Circuit Composer on an untitled circuit:

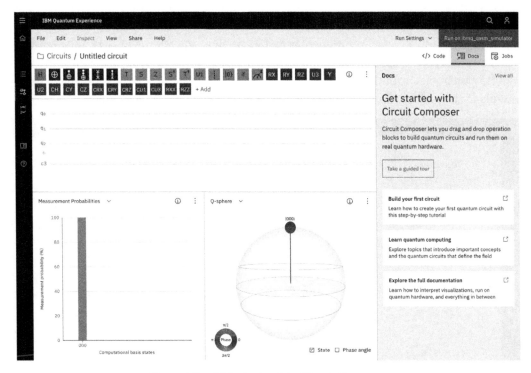

Figure 3.5 – A blank circuit in Circuit Composer

**No Qiskit® overlap**

The Circuit Composer window does not (in contrast to the **Results** pane) contain any of the circuits that you have run from a local Qiskit® environment. Only the quantum scores that you have created in IBM Quantum Experience® are available here. If you want to see your Qiskit® circuits here, you must import them as OpenQASM code. See the *Moving between worlds* recipe at the end of this chapter.

Once you have opened or created a circuit, a set of new tools open up to help you build your quantum score. These are covered in the next recipe, *Building quantum scores with Circuit Composer*.

# Quantum Lab

The third toolkit is a collection of Jupyter Notebook tutorials put together by the Qiskit® team. You can access them all from the **Qiskit tutorials** tile. You can also create your Jupyter Notebooks from this pane, and these will show up in this window much like the circuits in the previous one:

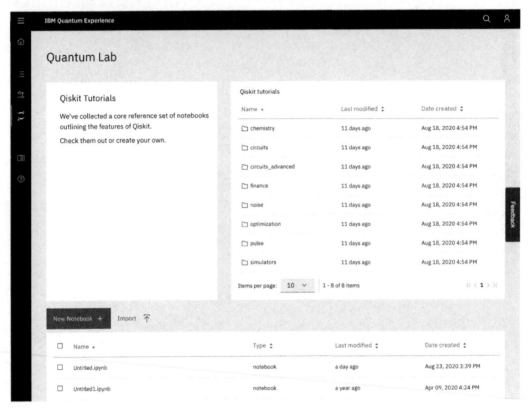

Figure 3.6 – Quantum Lab

---

**Running Python programs in notebooks**

You can also use the Jupyter Notebook environment to run the quantum computing Python sample scripts that we include in this book. Take a look at the *Downloading the code samples* recipe in *Chapter 1, Preparing Your Environment*, for a quick reminder.

---

In addition to the tools that you will use to code your quantum programs, IBM Quantum Experience® also includes some extended help in the form of two additional pages:

- **Docs**: This page includes a collection of getting started tutorials, a more extensive set of instructions for Circuit Composer, algorithms, and more. This is a good starting point to explore IBM Quantum Experience® when you are done working your way through this book.

- **Support**: As IBM Quantum Experience® is built on Qiskit®, the support resources are tailored directly for this type of experience via a Slack workspace and Stack Exchange tags for IBM Quantum Experience® (ibm-q-experience) and Qiskit® (qiskit). These social environments are vibrant and responsive, and you can bounce around questions, ideas, and more in a give-and-take manner. Questions are not long left unanswered by knowledgeable members and moderators!

# Building quantum scores with Circuit Composer

This recipe will walk you through the basic steps of creating a quantum score in IBM Quantum Experience®, to get a feel for how the composer works, how to build and modify a score, and finally how to analyze the score step by step using the **Inspect** feature.

> Drag-and-drop programming
>
> The recipes in this chapter will be run in the IBM Quantum Experience® web environment, using the drag-and-drop interface, which nicely visualizes what you are doing in an intuitive way.

## How to do it...

Let's build ourselves a little quantum score:

1.  From your web browser (Chrome seems to work best), go to the following URL, and then log in with your IBM Quantum Experience® account: https://quantum-computing.ibm.com/.

2.  In the left pane, select **Circuit Composer**.

    This opens the composer to a blank **Untitled circuit**.

3.  Optional: Set the number of qubits to play with.

    In the default setting, you will see three lines, much like a music score (hence the term quantum score). Each line represents one of your qubits, and the basic score is designed for a 5-qubit machine. As you will see in the *Comparing backends* recipe in *Chapter 5, Touring the IBM Quantum® Hardware with Qiskit®*, this is currently the most common setup for the free IBM quantum machines.

    For this example, we want to use only 1 qubit for clarity. If we use all five, the results that will be displayed will also include the results of the four we won't be using, which can be confusing.

    So, in the **Untitled circuit** tab that you just opened, hover over a qubit label ($q_0$). The label shifts to a trash can icon. Use this icon to remove qubits until you have one left. Your quantum score now has only one line.

    Prepending that line is the label, $q_0$, which is the name of your qubit:

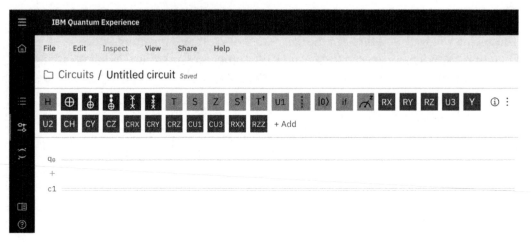

Figure 3.7 – A blank 1-qubit quantum score

4.  Add a ⊕ gate to the score.

5.  Now select and drag the ⊕ gate to the $q_0$ line of your score.

> **Tip**
>
> As you will see further in *Chapter 4*, *Starting at the Ground Level with Terra*, in Qiskit®, the NOT gate is represented by an **X**.

You have now added an X, or NOT gate, which will flip the qubit from its initial set value 0 to 1:

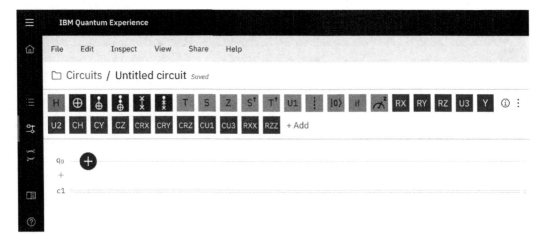

Figure 3.8 – NOT gate added

> **A glossary of operations**
>
> To get more information about the available instructions, click the (**i**) icon in the upper-right corner of Circuit Composer and select **Operations glossary** to open up an exhaustive guide to all instructions (gates, measurements, and more) that are available to you.

6.  Now, add a measurement instruction to finish off your circuit.

The measurement instruction is required if you want to run your score and get a result. It measures the state of the $q_0$ qubit and writes the result (0 or 1) to the classical register (**c1**) so that you can see the outcome of your experiment.

In multi-qubit circuits, there is no need to display all the classical registers as lines. Instead, they are represented by one line labeled with the number of classical registers that it represents; for example, **c5** for five classical registers:

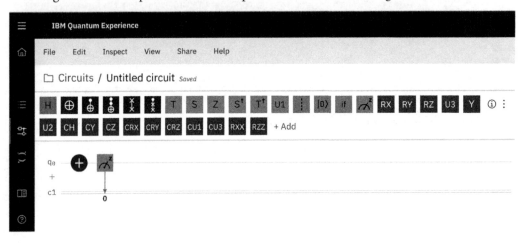

Figure 3.9 – Measurement instruction added

7.  You can now run your circuit.

    Optionally, save the circuit by first selecting **Untitled circuit** and giving the experiment a good name.

    Click the **Run on ibmq_qasm_simulator** button.

8.  Take a look at the results.

    To see the results of your job, click the **Jobs** icon right beneath the **Run** button. The results of your job are displayed:

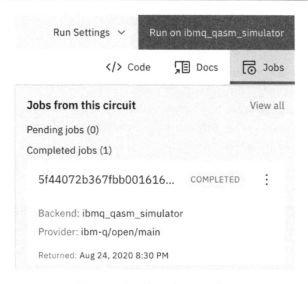

Figure 3.10 – The job results box

Clicking the job results box opens the **Result** page, and displays the final result of the job you just ran. In this case, we got a result of **1**, with **100%** certainty:

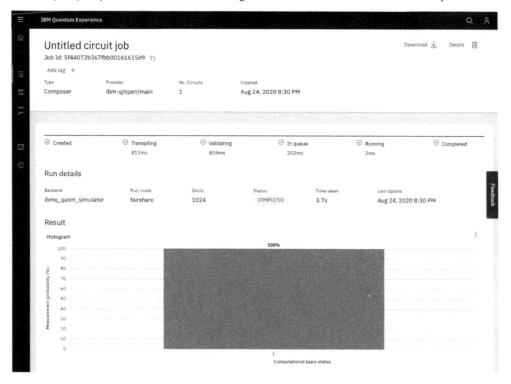

Figure 3.11 – Job result: 1 with 100% certainty

9.  Now, go ahead and play a little.

    Drag some more quantum instructions into your score willy-nilly, and adjust the
    number of qubits up and down. You are now building complex quantum circuits,
    but not necessarily working quantum programs or algorithms. This would be like
    soldering on random gates to your classical computer or cooking by randomly
    adding ingredients to your pot. You would get some kind of result, but probably
    nothing useful or edible. But it is fun!

    Here's an example – see if you can recreate it and then inspect it to see what it does
    (if anything):

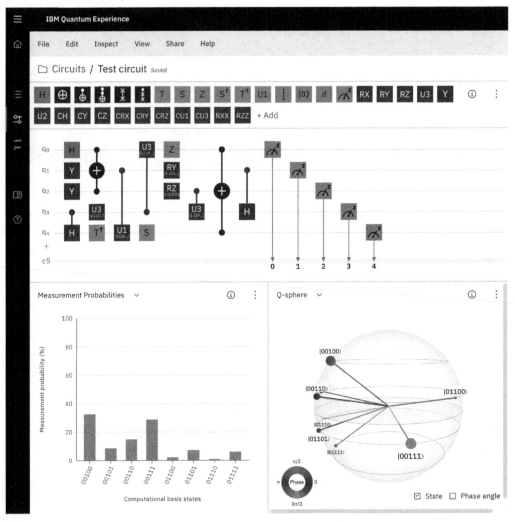

Figure 3.12 – Randomly dragged and dropped circuit

Just look at the complex results of that circuit. I wonder what it does? And also, note the two graphical boxes at the bottom of the page: **Measurement Probabilities** and **Q-sphere**. I have ignored them until now, but let's take a look and see what they are.

## There's more

The score is read, much like a music score, from left to right, in time. This means that the gates on the left side of the score execute before the ones more to the right. You can inspect how your circuit should behave by using the **Inspect** feature of the composer:

1.  In IBM Quantum Experience®, open the circuit that you just created, with a single qubit, a single NOT gate, and a measurement instruction.

2.  From the top menu, select **Inspect**.

    In the **Inspector** window that opens, you can now step your way through your score to see how the statevector that represents your qubit changes as you apply the gates by clicking >. You will also see the so-called Q-sphere, which is a graphical representation of the possible outcomes of your circuit. We first encountered the state vector in *Chapter 2, Quantum Computing and Qubits with Python*. More about the Q-sphere can be found in *Chapter 6, Understanding the Qiskit® Gate Library*.

    In our case, with just a single X gate, as we set up our qubit to start as 0, we expect the statevector to start at $1|0\rangle + 0|1\rangle$ and then become $0|0\rangle + 1|1\rangle$ as we apply the first X gate:

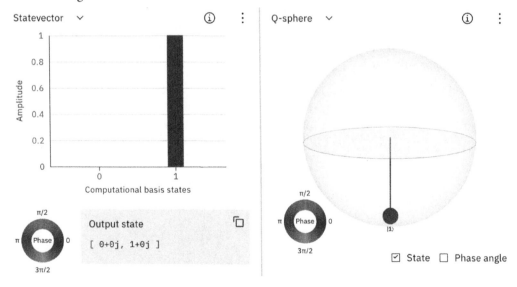

Figure 3.13 – Visualizing the X gate action on our qubit as a statevector and as a Q-sphere

The Q-sphere indicates that we will get only one outcome and that this outcome will be |1⟩. If you switch the **Statevector** display to the **Measurement Probabilities** option instead, you can verify my statement that the circuit should, indeed, produce the result 100% of the time:

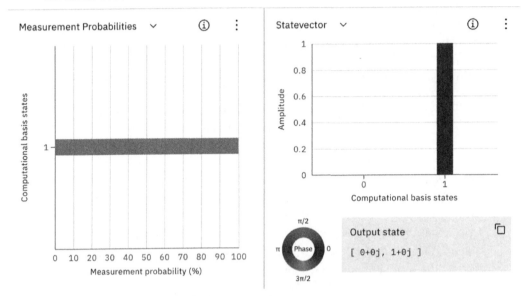

Figure 3.14 – The result 1 with 100% certainty

The **Inspect** tool lets you test your circuit at any gate. This is not possible when running on an actual quantum computer, as testing a qubit would be the same as measuring it, and then the qubit loses its quantumness and behaves like a classical bit. What is done here is a quick run of the circuit up to that point using a statevector simulator.

If you want to include the initial |0⟩ state in the inspection, then add a barrier instruction before the first gate of your circuit. The barrier doesn't manipulate the qubit but will let the **Inspect** tool register the initial state of the qubit:

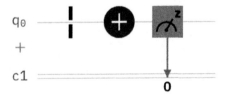

Figure 3.15 – Adding a barrier gate before the first gate

In the chapters that follow, we will create a variation of this **Inspect** feature to look through our circuits before we run them. For more information, see the *Visualizing circuits and results* recipe in *Chapter 4, Starting at the Ground Level with Terra*.

# Tossing a quantum coin

One of the examples I use is what is arguably the simplest useful quantum program that you can build: a simulated coin toss.

We will go into more detail about the quantum coin toss in *Chapter 4, Starting at the Ground Level with Terra*, but I will use that program as an example here. It is very small, and not too complicated to understand.

As we discussed briefly in *Chapter 2, Quantum Computing and Qubits with Python*, a quantum computer, in contrast to a classical computer, provides you with probabilistic, or randomized, computation. In this case, we set up our qubit as a superposition that results in probabilities to get an outcome of 0 or 1, or heads or tails in coin toss nomenclature, when we measure the qubit.

## How to do it...

Build the quantum circuit and then run it. This is the circuit we will come back to later in the book, on the Qiskit® side of things:

1. Log in to IBM Quantum Experience® at https://quantum-computing.ibm. com/composer.

2. From IBM Quantum Experience®, select **Circuit Composer** from the left pane.

3. Create a new circuit.

4. Find the gates that you need.

   In this recipe, we will just use two quantum instructions, one of which we briefly discussed in *Chapter 2, Quantum Computing and Qubits with Python*, in the *Hadamard gate* recipe. Remember that the H gate takes the input qubit and creates a superposition.

   We will also use a measurement instruction to measure the qubit and write the result to the classical bit line at the bottom of the score.

5.  Build the circuit by dragging the H gate from the **Gates** section of the composer to the first qubit line. And then drag the **Measurement** instruction to the same line, placing it to the right of the H gate. Your quantum score is now done. Your circuit should look something like this:

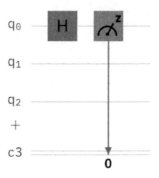

Figure 3.16 – Simple coin toss circuit

---

**But why do I have so many qubits that I do not use?**

The default number of qubits set by the composer is **3**. You can place your H gate on any qubit you want as long as you place the **Measure** instruction on the same qubit.

There is also nothing stopping you from placing an H gate on each of the qubits followed by a **Measure** gate. What you are then building is a set of five simultaneous coin tosses.

You can also change the number of qubits, by clicking on the + icon directly below the lowest qubit, or by hovering over a qubit and clicking the trashcan icon that appears.

---

6.  Save the circuit by first clicking **Untitled circuit** and giving the experiment a good name, then save it. Your circuit is now ready to run.

7.  Click the **Run on ibmq_qasm_simulator** button.

8.  Take a look at the results.

To see the results of your job, click the **Jobs** icon right beneath the **Run** button. Wait for the job to display the **Completed** result, then click the job results box to open the **Result** page. Your 1,024 runs of the same circuit have resulted in a statistical 50/50 spread of the two possible outcomes 0 and 1, as we expected in the *Quick introduction to quantum gates* recipe in *Chapter 2, Quantum Computing and Qubits with Python*. The results will look something like the following:

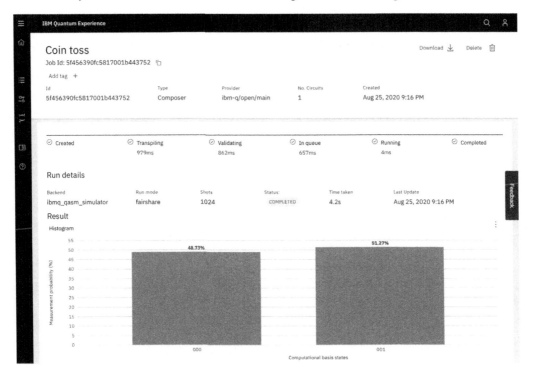

Figure 3.17 – The 50/50 result of our quantum coin toss, half heads and half tails

Here, the output is a roughly equal probability of getting a 0 or a 1, just like a physical coin, where the probability of heads or tails is roughly equal.

9.  Run your score on a real quantum computer.

    But really, running your scores on a simulator is a little disappointing perhaps. That is not why you started down the quantum computing path. But fear not, we can do better.

We will run the score one more time but select a non-simulator backend. For this simple quantum score, the result will be the same for a 1-qubit coin toss unless the backend is really out of tune. For more complex quantum programs, however, the results will differ between the simulator and the real quantum computer.

10. Click the **Run settings** button, and then select a *backend* other than **ibmq_qasm_ simulator**.

To get a feel for how long your wait time might be for each backend, you can go to the main **IBM Quantum Experience** dashboard and look at the individual queues for the backends.

11. Wait for the results.

To see the results of your job, click the **Jobs** icon right beneath the **Run** button. Wait for the job to display the **Completed** result, then click the job results box to open the **Results** page.

> **Get in line**
>
> By default, your quantum score will run on the online IBM Quantum® simulator that simulates a universal 32-qubit quantum computer. The simulator is a great way to test and tweak your quantum scores to make sure they run the way that you expect them to. Running on the simulator is usually very quick. Running on an actual quantum computer can take longer though, as you will be sharing those with other users.

12. The results might look something like the following:

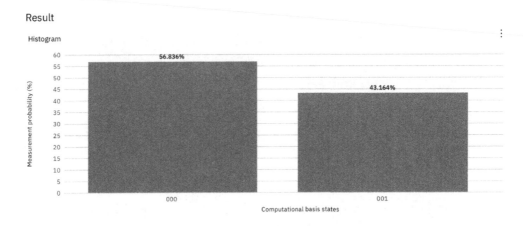

Figure 3.18 – The quantum coin toss results on a real quantum computer

Note how the result looks fairly similar to what you got on the simulator. This will generally be the case unless the physical quantum computer qubit on which you run your score is out of balance, and favors one outcome over the other. Remember, the actual qubits are physical things and not perfect mathematical abstracts. In *Chapter 5, Touring the IBM Quantum® Hardware with Qiskit®*, we will, among other things, take a look at how individual qubits behave, and what to expect when running your circuits on them.

## There's more

A non-simulator backend can only inherently run a set of basis gates, from which all other gates are constructed. When you run your quantum program, it gets interpreted by the software, and the fairly complex high-level gate architecture gets **transpiled** into a basic quantum program that consists of a set of basis gates only—u1, u2, u3, id, and cx. It turns out that all quantum programs that you write on Qiskit® can be expressed by using only these gates.

You can see the basis gates used by the quantum backend from the **Your backends** part of the IBM Quantum Experience® web console, by clicking the backend that you are interested in:

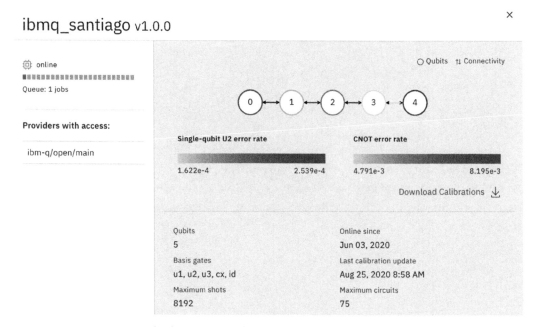

Figure 3.19 – The ibmq_santiago backend basis gates are u1, u2, u3, cx, and id

Why is this important? Well, the translation of the gates (in your score) to the basis gates that can be run on a backend is called **transpiling** and is done before you run the program. The transpiler takes your input score and converts it to the basis gates, which are then run on the backend.

Now, it turns out that the regular gates that you are using are not always directly translatable to a single basis gate. Sometimes the transpiler has to do a bit of work, reworking your circuit by replacing your gates with clusters of other gates.

For example, here are the original and transpiled versions of the simple quantum coin toss as run on one of IBM's 5-qubit machines:

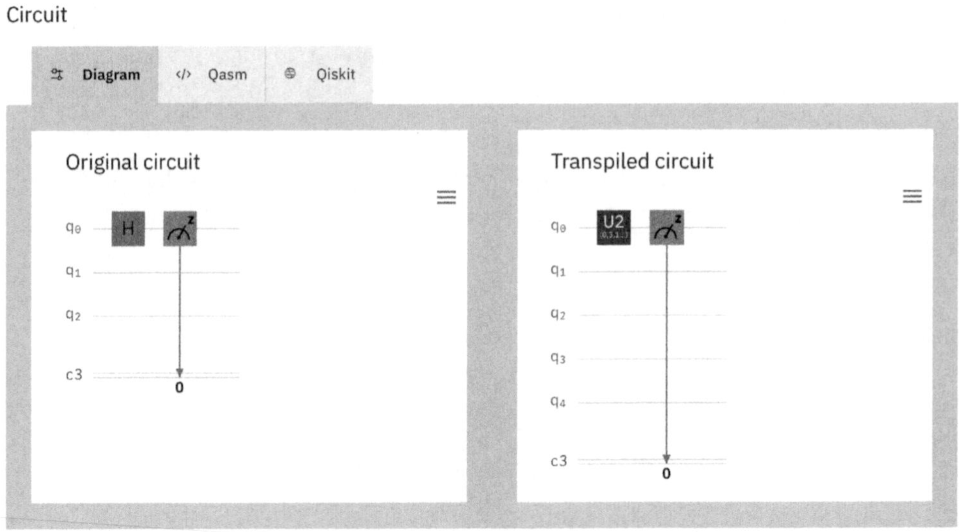

Figure 3.20 – Original and transpiled quantum coin toss

As you can see, not many changes have occurred. The **H** gate is now a **U2** gate with 0 and $\pi$ as input, and our simplified 3-qubit score is replaced by the actual five qubits of the backend. But the depth of the circuit stays the same – two gates long.

For more complicated circuits, things get more complex mainly because there are other gates in it. In the example that follows, which is from *Chapter 9, Grover's Search Algorithm*, in addition to X and H gates, there are more elaborate gates, such as the **controlled-controlled NOT (CCX)** gate with two inputs and one output. The original score has a depth of 22 gates:

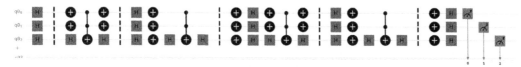

Figure 3.21 – Original Grover search algorithm for three qubits

Because the quantum computer backend cannot directly use the X, H, and CCX gates, these have to be transpiled into U and CX gates. The transpiled score is 49 gates deep:

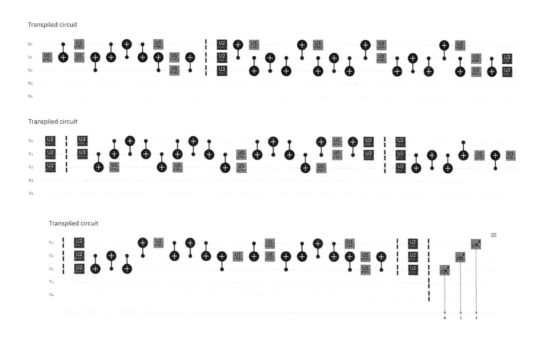

Figure 3.22 – Transpiled Grover search algorithm for three qubits

> **The importance of the barrier**
>
> If you take a closer look at the original Grover circuit, you will notice that in some locations, you see two of the same kind of gate immediately following each other. Remember from *Chapter 2, Quantum Computing and Qubits with Python*, that quantum gates are reversible, and that two identical gates following each other might simply cancel out. If we let the transpiler go to work, it would just remove the duplicated gates in order to simplify the circuit. This is usually not the best solution as the gates might be part of a bigger structure that needs to be kept intact.
>
> This is where the barrier component and the vertical gray bar in the score comes in. A **barrier** tells the transpiler to not simplify across it; if two identical gates are separated by a barrier, the transpiler will not remove them but transpile each of them into the correct gate type. Take a look at the transpiler version of the Grover score and you will see what I mean.

# Moving between worlds

Now you have seen how to create your quantum scores in Circuit Composer, and how to run them on a simulator, and on a real IBM quantum computer. But the rest of the book will be about working in Qiskit® with your programs. Do we just say farewell to IBM Quantum Experience® then?

Not so fast. IBM Quantum Experience® is a great environment for learning how to build quantum scores, and you do not have to troubleshoot Python code or worry about your environment being up to date (IBM takes care of that for you), and it is actually pretty easy to take what you create in IBM Quantum Experience® and just move it over to Qiskit®.

You have two options:

- **Qiskit®**: With Qiskit® code export, your quantum score is translated into Python code that you can paste directly into your Python interpreter and run. This is a one-way trip from IBM Quantum Experience® to Qiskit®.

- **QASM**: Underneath the covers, IBM Quantum Experience® runs **OpenQASM (Quantum Assembly Language)** code to keep track of your scores. You can export your quantum scores as QASM from the **Code Editor**. You can then use the `QuantumCircuit.from_qasm_str()` method in Qiskit® to import that code. To go the other way, use `<circuit>.qasm()` to export your circuit from Qiskit® and then paste into **Code Editor** to go the other way.

# Getting ready

The Python files for this recipe can be downloaded from here: `https://github.com/PacktPublishing/Quantum-Computing-in-Practice-with-Qiskit-and-IBM-Quantum-Experience/tree/master/Chapter03`.

# How to do it...

Let's start by importing the QASM code from your coin toss experiment:

1.  From your web browser, go to the following URL, and then log in with your IBM Quantum Experience® account: `https://quantum-computing.ibm.com/`.

2.  Select **Circuit Composer**, and in the breadcrumb click **Circuits**.

3.  On the **Circuit Composer** file page, click your **Coin toss** circuit.

4.  In the **Circuit Composer** window, in the left pane, select the <\> **Code** editor.

5.  To export your quantum score as Qiskit® code, in the dropdown select **Qiskit**, then copy the Python code you see into your Python interpreter. This will create a quantum circuit called **circuit** in your environment, which you can then continue working with, for example, by adding a `print(circuit)` line and running the code. This will result in an output something like this:

```
In [1]: from qiskit import QuantumRegister, ClassicalRegister, QuantumCircuit
   ...: from numpy import pi
   ...:
   ...: qreg_q = QuantumRegister(1, 'q')
   ...: creg_c = ClassicalRegister(1, 'c')
   ...: circuit = QuantumCircuit(qreg_q, creg_c)
   ...:
   ...: circuit.h(qreg_q[0])
   ...: circuit.measure(qreg_q[0], creg_c[0])
Out[1]: <qiskit.circuit.instructionset.InstructionSet at 0x7fb3bc16fd90>

In [2]: print(circuit)

q_0: ┤ H ├┤M├
c: 1/═══════
          0
```

Figure 3.23 – The exported coin toss Python code and its output

6.  To export your quantum score as QASM code, in the dropdown, select **QASM**, then copy the QASM code you see. It should look something like this:

```
OPENQASM 2.0;
include "qelib1.inc";

qreg q[1];
creg c[1];

h q[0];
measure q[0] -> c[0];
```

You can also click on **Export** to save the code as a .qasm file, and later import that file into Qiskit®.

7.  Now, move over to your Qiskit® environment and run the ch3_r1_import_qasm.py file. If you have forgotten how to get there, take a look at the *Open a recipe file* recipe in *Chapter 1, Preparing Your Environment*.

8.  For this simple recipe, we will only need the QuantumCircuit method, so we'll add that:

```
from qiskit import QuantumCircuit
```

9.  First, we import the QASM string from IBM Quantum Experience®, either as a pasted string or as a saved file:

```
qasm_string=input("Paste in a QASM string from IBM
    Quantum Experience (or enter the full path and file
    name of a .qasm file to import):\n")
if qasm_string[-5:] == ".qasm":
    circ=QuantumCircuit.from_qasm_file(qasm_string)
else:
    circ=QuantumCircuit.from_qasm_str(qasm_string)
```

10. If you paste in the QASM code at the prompt, you will end up with something similar to the following example. If you enter a filename, the file will get imported, with much the same end result:

```
Ch 3: Moving between worlds 1
-----------------------------
```

11. Paste in a QASM string from IBM Qx (or enter the full path and filename of a .qasm file to import):

```
OPENQASM 2.0;
include "qelib1.inc";

qreg q[1];
creg c[1];

h q[0];
measure q[0] -> c[0];
```

12. Hit *Enter* and the circuit is imported to Qiskit®, and can now be used for quantum computations. The added print(circuit) at the end should display something like the following:

Imported quantum circuit
------------------------------

Figure 3.24 – The imported coin toss quantum circuit

13. You have now imported your QASM code into Qiskit® and created a quantum circuit object named `circ`.

Now let's try creating and exporting OpenQASM code from Qiskit®:

> **But I don't know how to code in Qiskit® yet**
>
> Up until this point, you have not yet created any quantum circuits in Qiskit®. Not to worry, we will use the `random_circuit()` method to create random circuits that you can export and then import into IBM Quantum Experience® to take a look at.

1. In your Qiskit® environment, open the `ch3_r2_export_qasm.py` file.

2. The random circuit method to import is this:

```
from qiskit.circuit.random.utils import random_circuit
```

3. First, we create and print a random quantum circuit:

```
circ=random_circuit(2,2,measure=True)
```

The depth of the random circuit is set to 2 in this example, which means we will create a circuit with two gates maximum. The number of qubits is also set to 2, with obvious results. You can tweak these numbers to see what shows up.

The circuit might look something like this:

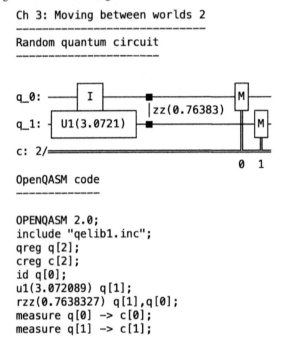

```
Ch 3: Moving between worlds 2
-----------------------------
Random quantum circuit
----------------------
```

```
OpenQASM code
-------------
```

```
OPENQASM 2.0;
include "qelib1.inc";
qreg q[2];
creg c[2];
id q[0];
u1(3.072089) q[1];
rzz(0.7638327) q[1],q[0];
measure q[0] -> c[0];
measure q[1] -> c[1];
```

Figure 3.25 – A randomly created circuit

4.  Next, we export the circuit as QASM code:

```
circ.qasm(formatted=True, filename="Circuit.qasm")
```

The QASM code is displayed and is also saved to a file in your local environment with the filename specified:

```
OPENQASM 2.0;
include "qelib1.inc";
qreg q[2];
creg c[2];
id q[0];
u1(3.072089) q[1];
rzz(0.7638327) q[1],q[0];measure q[0] -> c[0];
measure q[1] -> c[1];
```

5.  Back in IBM Quantum Experience®, you can now go to the circuit editor in the **Circuit Composer** window. Click **New** to open an empty circuit composer, then select the <\> **Code** editor and paste in the randomly generated circuit QASM code. Or, click **Import Code** to import the `Circuit.qasm` file that you just created.

6.  Watch your circuit instantly appear in Circuit Composer:

Figure 3.26 – Imported, randomly generated circuit

7.  You can now run the circuit, drag and drop new gates into the circuit, or just move or tweak the existing gates to see how your changes cause the circuit to behave differently. Don't forget to use the **Inspect** feature, **Measurement probabilities**, and **Q-sphere** displays to step through your circuit and see what it does.

## How it works...

When you use the `circ=QuantumCircuit.from_qasm_file()` method to import your quantum score, the `circ` object that you assign it to is now a `QuantumCircuit()` object, much in the same way that you will be creating quantum circuits in the chapters that follow.

Using Qiskit®, you can display the circuit, append gates to the circuit, and more.

We will not be doing anything elaborate with the circuit in this chapter, but put a bookmark here to return when you start creating your own circuits in *Chapter 4, Starting at the Ground Level with Terra*.

## There's more

As you work your way through this book, you will be running your experiments mainly in your Python Qiskit® environment. If you want to, you can pull the circuits that you build over from the IBM Quantum Experience® environment and run them here as well. Perhaps you like the graphical drag-and-drop environment better, and the option to edit your scores on the fly?

In the Qiskit® Python examples that follow, we will be creating `QuantumCircuit` objects that we give names such as `qc`, `circ`, `circuit`, and so on. You can export these to QASM and then import them to IBM Quantum Experience® using the `circ.qasm(formatted=True, filename="Circuit.qasm")` command.

If you want, you can use the `print(circ)` or `circ.draw()` functions to print out the circuit, and then manually recreate it in the composer.

### Our sample code from building quantum scores with IBM Quantum Experience®

If you remember, we displayed a fairly complex but random circuit in the second recipe of this chapter. Here is the QASM code for that circuit. Go ahead and import it and see if you get the same results:

```
OPENQASM 2.0;
include "qelib1.inc";
qreg q[5];
creg c[5];
h q[0];
y q[1];
y q[2];
ch q[3],q[4];
ccx q[2],q[0],q[1];
u3(2.1128893,1.9882648,5.5897911) q[3];
tdg q[4];
cu1(3.0287577) q[1],q[4];
cu3(5.1184948,2.0719417,1.8609727) q[3],q[0];
s q[4];
z q[0];
ry(3.6419028) q[1];
```

```
rz(0.402055) q[2];
cu3(1.5290482,3.844241,4.4343541) q[2],q[3];
ccx q[4],q[0],q[2];
ch q[1],q[3];
measure q[0] -> c[0];
measure q[1] -> c[1];
measure q[2] -> c[2];
measure q[3] -> c[3];
measure q[4] -> c[4];
```

## See also

For much more information about OpenQASM, see the following publications:

- *Open Quantum Assembly Language*, Andrew W. Cross, Lev S. Bishop, John A. Smolin, Jay M. Gambetta, https://arxiv.org/abs/1707.03429.

- *OpenQASM* GitHub project: https://github.com/Qiskit/openqasm.

# 4

# Starting at the Ground Level with Terra

After our brief exploration of the IBM Quantum Experience® composer, and installation of IBM's Qiskit®, we are now ready to start writing quantum programs with Qiskit®. We will let go of the user interface, expanding our quantum computing journey into Python – one of the world's most popular and widespread scientific programming languages.

This chapter covers the basic requirements for building a quantum circuit with Qiskit®. We will walk through the making of a few minimalistic quantum programs that run on a local Qiskit Aer simulator and that display the results of the program in numeric as well as diagrammatic form. We will then take the leap and run the programs on actual IBM Quantum® hardware.

The theme of this chapter is *quantum coin tossing*, based on the rudimentary quantum program that we built in IBM Quantum Experience®. These are arguably the simplest meaningful quantum programs that you can write, as they start you off with a few basic foundational quantum gates, but also demonstrate the difference between probabilistic quantum computing and deterministic classical computing.

We will also expand on the minimal program by adding more gates, run the program many times to gather statistics about the outcomes, and more. The topics that we will be learning about in this chapter will be applied from the next chapter onwards.

In this chapter, we will cover the following recipes:

- Building a Qiskit® quantum program

- Quantum coin toss revisited

- Getting some statistics – tossing many coins in a row

- Implementing an upside-down coin toss

- Tossing two coins simultaneously

- Quantum-cheating in a coin toss? – Introducing the Bell state

- More ways to quantum-cheat – tweaking the odds

- Adding more coins – straight and cheating

- Tossing some real coins

# Technical requirements

The quantum programs that we discuss in this chapter can be found here: `https://github.com/PacktPublishing/Quantum-Computing-in-Practice-with-Qiskit-and-IBM-Quantum-Experience/tree/master/Chapter04`.

You can run the recipes in this chapter in your local Qiskit® environment that you set up as part of *Chapter 1, Preparing Your Environment*, or you can run them in the notebook environment of the IBM Quantum Experience®.

If you run them in your local environment, I'd recommend using the built-in Spyder iPython editor from your Anaconda installation. That is the editor used to build and run the samples in this book.

In the code examples in this book, you will sometimes see the following line of code:

```
from IPython.core.display import display
```

Depending on your environment, iPython might not display graphical output directly in the output. If this is the case, you can use the `display()` method to force the output, like this:

```
display(qc.draw('mpl'))
```

This example prints the quantum circuit qc to the iPython console.

# Building a Qiskit® quantum program

Generally speaking, there are just a few required building blocks to create a quantum program using Qiskit®. First, you have to set up the required infrastructure and create the quantum circuit (what we call the **quantum score** in IBM Quantum Experience®). Then, you have to configure a backend to run your quantum program on, and finally execute and retrieve the results of your calculations.

The following section is a summary of the Python building blocks that are required to make up a quantum program.

## Listing the required classes, modules, and functions

Qiskit® includes a large number of Python classes, but for our initial foray, we just need the basic ones. These are used to configure each of the components that follow:

- QuantumCircuit: This is used to create the circuit—the program—that you will execute. You will add gates and other components to the circuit.

- QuantumRegister: This represents the qubits that you can use to build your quantum program.

- ClassicalRegister: This represents the classical bits that are used to store the output of your quantum program.

- Aer: This is the Qiskit® simulation layer, which we will discuss in greater detail in *Chapter 7, Simulating Quantum Computers with Aer.*

- IBMQ: This module is required to execute your quantum programs on actual IBMQ hardware. It includes the tools you need to interact with IBMQ.

- execute: This component lets you run your program by providing the circuit, a backend, and a number of shots.

## Working with quantum registers and classical registers

To be able to build your quantum program, you first need to decide how many qubits you want to work with, and how many classical bits you want to include to store your output. You can either set these up explicitly or use the QuantumCircuit class to automatically create the registers.

The registers make up two sets of information-carrying bits of your quantum system:

- One set of quantum registers to hold your qubits
- One set of classical registers to hold your regular bits

You will use measurement gates to read your qubits and then write the resulting classical bit to the classical registers.

For most of the recipes in this book, the number of quantum and classical registers will be the same, but this is not required.

## Understanding your quantum circuit

The quantum circuit instance that you create will hold the qubits and classical bits. You will manipulate each instance by adding gates.

A quantum program can be assembled by combining more than one quantum circuit. You can, for example, create a circuit that holds the quantum gates and one circuit that holds the measurement gates. You can then add these circuits together to create a main quantum circuit that makes up your quantum program.

## Selecting a backend to run on

To be able to execute your quantum program, you must define a backend. A backend can be a local simulator, an IBM Quantum® simulator in the cloud, or actual IBM Quantum® hardware accessed through the cloud.

Initially, we will use the `qasm_simulator` backend that is included with Qiskit Aer, but we will also run our quantum programs on some of the freely available IBM Quantum® backends.

## Running your circuit as a job

You run the quantum program as a job by providing the circuit, a backend, and a number of shots. If you run your quantum programs on IBM Quantum® hardware, you can also include a job monitor to keep track of your place in the queue.

## Receiving the results of your job

When your job has run, the results are returned. In these initial recipes, where we use the `qasm_simulator` backend or the IBM Quantum® hardware, the returned results will be Python dictionaries.

For a 1-qubit circuit, the result might look like this:

```
{'1': 1}
```

In this case, the returned result of one shot was a qubit in the state $|1\rangle$.

The results could also look like this:

```
{'0': 495, '1': 505}
```

Here, the returned result was 1,000 shots, where 495 shots resulted in the qubit being $|0\rangle$, and 505 shots that resulted in $|1\rangle$.

The returned results can be more complex. The following example is a possible result of a 3-qubit quantum program that was run 1,000 times:

```
{'100': 113, '111': 139, '001': 112, '101': 114, '010': 121,
'011': 133, '000': 134, '110': 134}
```

Here, the result $|100\rangle$ came up 113 times, $|111\rangle$ came up 139 times, and so on.

But, enough talk, let's write some quantum programs.

# Quantum coin toss revisited

In this recipe, we will take a closer look at the very first quantum program we created in IBM Quantum Experience® – the **quantum coin toss**. Again, this is arguably the simplest quantum program that still provides real quantum computing value. It demonstrates the probabilistic nature of quantum computing. For a refresher, see *Chapter 3, IBM Quantum Experience® – Quantum Drag and Drop*.

In IBM Quantum Experience®, the coin toss program looked like this:

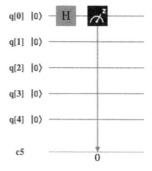

Figure 4.1 – Simple coin toss circuit in the IBM Quantum Experience® composer

With the quantum coin toss, we will again use the *Hadamard gate* to create a quantum superposition, and a measurement gate to force the superposition to collapse into one of the two qubit states $|0\rangle$ or $|1\rangle$, representing *heads* or *tails*. This time, however, we will create the circuit in Python with Qiskit®, which means that we need to also create the framework for the gates and measurement by defining and creating quantum circuits and classical circuits using Python commands.

This is a quantum circuit that simulates the probabilistic nature of a single qubit in superposition. The 1-qubit circuit initializes the qubit in the ground state – $|0\rangle$ – and then uses a Hadamard gate to put the qubit in superposition.

During our calculations, the statevector of the qubit looks like this:

$$|\psi\rangle = \frac{|0\rangle + |1\rangle}{\sqrt{2}}$$

Figure 4.2 – Formula for the statevector of the qubit

You can also write it in the vector form:

$$|\psi\rangle = \begin{bmatrix} \frac{1}{\sqrt{2}} \\ \frac{1}{\sqrt{2}} \end{bmatrix}$$

Figure 4.3 – Statevector of the qubit in the vector form

Another vector form is the Qiskit® statevector form that you will see in these examples:

```
[0.70710678+0.j  0.70710678+0.j]
```

Measuring the qubit causes it to collapse into one of the states $|0\rangle$ or $|1\rangle$ with a ~50% probability, that is, a coin toss. The result is displayed as a numeric readout, as a bar diagram, and as a Bloch sphere.

## Getting ready

The sample code for this recipe can be found here: `https://github.com/PacktPublishing/Quantum-Computing-in-Practice-with-Qiskit-and-IBM-Quantum-Experience/blob/master/Chapter04/ch4_r1_coin_toss.py`.

For a quick reminder of how to run the sample programs, see the *Downloading the code samples* recipe of *Chapter 1, Preparing Your Environment*.

You are ready to write your first quantum program.

## How to do it...

The following steps will—to a large extent—be repeated throughout the book, based on the basic required classes and steps for basic Qiskit® management. So, expect the *How to do it...* section's bullets to be somewhat briefer going forward.

There will, however, be differences depending on what program you are planning to run, and what Qiskit® components you will be using. Let's start the program now:

1.  Import the required Qiskit® classes.

    First, we import the Python classes that are required to create registers and circuits, set a backend, and so on. Please refer to the *Listing the required Qiskit® classes, modules, and functions* section of the *Building a Qiskit® quantum program* recipe:

    ```
    from qiskit import QuantumRegister, ClassicalRegister
    from qiskit import QuantumCircuit, Aer, execute
    from qiskit.tools.visualization import plot_histogram
    from IPython.core.display import display
    ```

    In addition, we also import the `display` method from `IPython.core.display`. This is used to correctly display the graphics output in our Anaconda Spyder IPython environment, and might not be required in your environment.

2.  Create the required registers and the quantum circuit.

    We create two registers, one for the quantum bit and one for the classic bit. We also create a quantum circuit that is made up of the quantum register and the classic register. The quantum register is initialized in the ground state, $|0\rangle$, and the classical register is set to 0:

    ```
    q = QuantumRegister(1)
    c = ClassicalRegister(1)
    qc = QuantumCircuit(q, c)
    ```

3.  Add gates to the quantum circuit.

    For our quantum program to actually do something, we now add a Hadamard gate that will put the qubit in a superposition, and also a measurement gate that we will use to read the value of the quantum bit at the end of our program. The Hadamard gate is one of the foundational gates. We will look much more closely at that gate, and others, in *Chapter 6, Understanding the Qiskit® Gate Library*:

    ```
    qc.h(q[0])
    qc.measure(q, c)
    display(qc.draw('mpl'))
    ```

    By visualizing the circuit with qc.draw('mpl'), we see that just like in the IBM Quantum Experience® composer, we have a quantum circuit with 1 qubit and 1 classical bit, with a Hadamard gate on the qubit, and a measurement gate that will write the state of the qubit q0_0 ($|0\rangle$ or $|1\rangle$) to the classical bit c0_0 as a 0 or 1:

    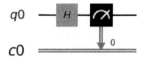

    Figure 4.4 – A simple quantum coin toss circuit

    In a strictly text-based Python environment, you can also print your circuit with the print(qc) command or use qc.draw('text'), both of which produce ASCII text output:

    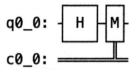

    Figure 4.5 – The circuit displayed as ASCII text

4.  Set the backend on which to run.

    For this initial recipe, we will use the built-in qasm_simulator backend. We create a backend variable and call on the Aer component to get us the required backend information:

    ```
    backend = Aer.get_backend('qasm_simulator')
    ```

5. Run the job.

Create a quantum job for the circuit and the selected backend that runs just one shot to simulate a coin toss. We then run the job and display the returned result; either $|0\rangle$ for heads or $|1\rangle$ for tails. The results are returned as a Python dictionary:

```
job = execute(qc, backend, shots=1)
result = job.result()
counts = result.get_counts(qc)
```

6. Print and visualize the results:

```
print(counts)
display(plot_histogram(counts))
```

First, we get a printout of the results:

```
{'0': 1}
```

Then, we get a printout of the result as a histogram:

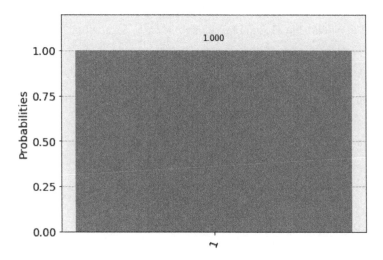

Figure 4.6 – The result of a single quantum "coin toss" as a histogram

Success! Your very first quantum coin toss program returned a tails, or $|1\rangle$ result.

## How it works...

We tossed a quantum coin that started out with *heads* up ( $|0\rangle$ ), *spun* in quantum space as a superposition of $|0\rangle$ and $|1\rangle$, and finally landed in a *tails* position when we measured it.

So, what happened?

Let's reiterate:

1.  We created a qubit and initialized it in the ground state, $|0\rangle$.

2.  We then applied a Hadamard gate to the qubit, which moved the statevector from the pole to the equator of the Bloch sphere.

    Mathematically, when you apply the Hadamard gate to your qubit, you run it through two rotations, first a $\frac{\pi}{2}$ rotation around the $y$ axis, and then a $\pi$ rotation around the $x$ axis. The qubit is now in a superposition of $|0\rangle$ and $|1\rangle$, halfway between the poles.

    For more detailed information about the Hadamard gate, see the *Creating superpositions with the H gate* recipe in *Chapter 6, Understanding the Qiskit® Gate Library*.

3.  Finally, we measured the qubit.

    By measuring, we destroyed the superposition, literally forcing nature to make up its mind, and the qubit will be either $|0\rangle$ or $|1\rangle$.

Now, go ahead and run your program a couple of times, noting if you get heads ( $|0\rangle$ ) or tails ( $|1\rangle$ ). If we have done this right, you should be simulating a coin toss pretty closely.

# Getting some statistics – tossing many coins in a row

Alright, so far, we have done a single coin toss at a time, much like you would do in real life.

But the power of quantum computing comes from running your quantum programs many times with the same initial conditions, letting the qubit superpositions play out their quantum mechanical advantages, and summarizing a large number of runs statistically.

With this recipe, we will do 1,000 coin tosses in the blink of an eye and take a look at the results to see how good the coin is. Will this coin be a fair way to start, say, a game of baseball? Let's see how that works.

## Getting ready

The sample code for this recipe can be found here: `https://github.com/PacktPublishing/Quantum-Computing-in-Practice-with-Qiskit-and-IBM-Quantum-Experience/blob/master/Chapter04/ch4_r2_coin_tosses.py`.

In this recipe, we will explore and expand on the `shots` job parameter. This parameter lets you control how many times you run the quantum job cycle – prepare, run, measure. So far, we have prepared our qubits in the $|0\rangle$ state, set the backend to a simulator, and then run one shot, which represents one full cycle.

In the IBM Quantum Experience® composer examples, we ran our scores 1,024 times, which is the default. We discovered that the output turned statistical. In this recipe, we will play with a different number of shots to see how the outcomes statistically change.

Generally speaking, you want to increase the number of shots to improve statistical accuracy.

## How to do it...

Much like in the previous recipe, the following steps are all you need:

> **Code reuse**
> And for the lazy coder, in this case, as you might have realized, the only real change to the circuit appears in *step 6*, where we set the number of shots. Feel free to reuse the previous recipe.

1. Import the required Qiskit® classes and methods:

```
from qiskit import QuantumRegister, ClassicalRegister
from qiskit import QuantumCircuit, Aer, execute
from qiskit.tools.visualization import plot_histogram
from IPython.core.display import display
```

2.  Create the required registers and the quantum circuit. Set up our quantum circuit with one qubit and one classical bit. Create the quantum circuit based on the registers:

```
q = QuantumRegister(1)
c = ClassicalRegister(1)
qc = QuantumCircuit(q, c)
```

3.  Add gates to the quantum circuit. Add the Hadamard and measurement gates:

```
qc.h(q[0])
qc.measure(q, c)
display(qc.draw('mpl'))
```

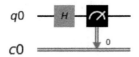

Figure 4.7 – The same simple quantum coin toss circuit

4.  Set the backend to our local simulator to run:

```
backend = Aer.get_backend('qasm_simulator')
```

5.  Run the job.

    Note that this time, we run it with *1,000 shots*. This means that we run our quantum circuit 1,000 times, collect the results, and provide the average output as our results:

```
job = execute(qc, backend, shots=1000)
result = job.result()
counts = result.get_counts(qc)
```

6.  Print and visualize the results:

```
print(counts)
display(plot_histogram(counts))
```

This time the output looks different:

```
{'0': 480, '1': 520}
```

And here is the output in the form of a histogram:

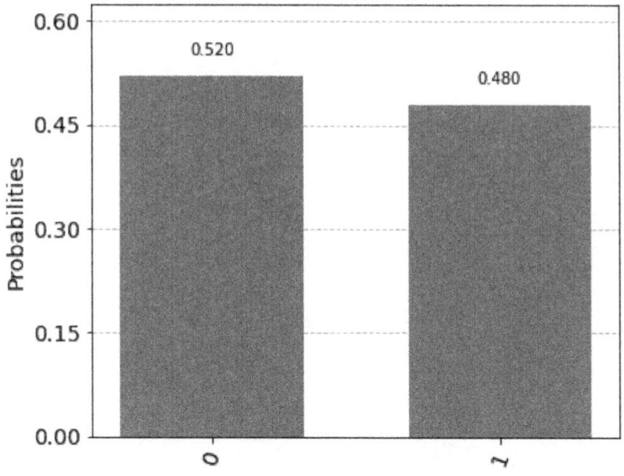

Figure 4.8 – The result of 1,000 shots, a roughly even distribution of 0 and 1

## How it works...

This time we used the underlying Qiskit® analytics to store and process the result of each individual shot and return it as a concatenated Python dictionary. The end result is a statistical view of all the actual outcomes of your quantum program. For the coin toss, you would expect to get heads and tails with roughly equal probability if you run it enough times.

Try adjusting the number of shots to 10,000 or 20,000, and see how your qubit behaves statistically.

In a more complex quantum program, the result will usually indicate a preference for a specific outcome, a specific combination of qubit statistics where certain solutions are amplified and show up much more often than others. This is one of the key tricks with writing good quantum algorithms, understanding how to get the circuits to point to the correct answer.

We will go into more detail on this later, starting with the *Exploring quantum phase kickback* recipe in *Chapter 9, Grover's Search Algorithm.*

# There's more...

Generally speaking, you are usually interested in getting the statistical result of your quantum program. In this case, we are looking at the probabilistic nature of a quantum coin toss – a random number generator. But sometimes, it might be interesting to see exactly what transpired, shot by shot.

You can achieve this by setting the `memory=True` parameter when you run your quantum program:

```
job = execute(circuit, backend, shots=10, memory=True)
```

This setting makes the quantum job save the individual results of each shot, and you can later retrieve these as a Python list by using the `result.get_memory()` command. For 10 shots on a 1-qubit circuit, the memory result might look like this:

```
['1', '1', '0', '0', '1', '1', '0', '1', '0', '0']
```

And for 10 shots on a 2-qubit circuit (which we will do in a later recipe), the memory result might look like this:

```
['10', '10', '10', '11', '11', '00', '10', '10', '01', '00']
```

You can then dig out any data you want from this list and process it further with other Python tools as needed.

# Implementing an upside-down coin toss

In this recipe, we will tweak our very first quantum program a little bit but still keep it relatively simple. An actual coin can be tossed starting with either heads or tails facing upward. Let's do another quantum coin toss but with a different starting point, the coin facing tails up. In Dirac notation, we start with our qubit in $|1\rangle$ instead of in $|0\rangle$.

## Getting ready

The sample code for this recipe can be found here: `https://github.com/PacktPublishing/Quantum-Computing-in-Practice-with-Qiskit-and-IBM-Quantum-Experience/blob/master/Chapter04/ch4_r3_coin_toss_tails.py`.

Just like the previous recipe, this one is almost identical to the first coin toss recipe. Feel free to reuse what you have already created. The only real difference is that we add a new quantum gate, the **X** (or **NOT**) gate.

## How to do it...

The following steps are to a large extent identical to the steps from the *Quantum coin toss revisited* recipe. There are, however, differences depending on the program you are creating, and what Qiskit® components you are using. I will describe these in detail.

Set up your code like the previous example and then add an X gate to flip the qubit:

1.  Import the required Qiskit® classes and methods:

    ```
    from qiskit import QuantumCircuit, Aer, execute
    from qiskit.visualization import plot_histogram
    from IPython.core.display import display
    ```

    Notice how we are not importing the QuantumRegister and ClassicalRegister methods here like we did before. In this recipe, we will take a look at a different way of creating your quantum circuit.

2.  Create the quantum circuit with 1 qubit and 1 classical bit:

    ```
    qc = QuantumCircuit(1, 1)
    ```

    Here, we are implicitly letting the QuantumCircuit method create the quantum and classical registers in the background; we do not have to explicitly create them. We will refer to these registers by numbers and lists going forward.

3.  Add the Hadamard gate, the X gate, and the measurement gates to the circuit:

    ```
    qc.x(0)
    qc.h(0)
    qc.measure(0, 0)
    ```

So, here is the first example of using just numbers to refer to the qubits. We add the X gate to the first qubit, here referred to as 0 as Python starts numbering at 0, not 1:

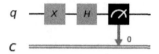

Figure 4.9 – The upside-down quantum coin toss circuit

4.  Set the backend to our local simulator:

```
backend = Aer.get_backend('qasm_simulator')
```

5.  To run the job, this time, we go back to 1 shot to do just a single coin toss:

```
counts = execute(qc, backend, shots=1).result().
    get_counts(qc)
```

Notice here how we have streamlined the code a bit and put all the execution in one row as we are only interested in the final counts.

6.  Visualize the results:

```
display(plot_histogram(counts))
```

The output looks like the following:

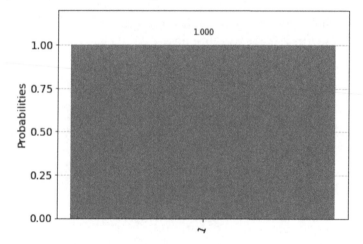

Figure 4.10 – The results of a single upside-down quantum coin toss

# How it works...

We are introducing a new gate in this recipe, the Pauli-X gate. The X gate works just like a NOT gate in classical computing – it flips the value of a qubit.

If the qubit is $|0\rangle$, then it is flipped to $|1\rangle$, and if it is in $|1\rangle$, then it is flipped to $|0\rangle$.

For simple situations like this, it is intuitively easy to understand exactly what the result will be, but for more complex qubit configurations, where the Bloch vector points at an arbitrary point on the Bloch sphere, it gets a little trickier. Essentially what happens is that the qubit is rotated around the $x$ axis through an angle of $\pi$ radians.

# There's more...

The X gate is handy for this, but there is another way to set your coin toss tails up. You can use the Qiskit Aer `initialize` method to set the initial state of a qubit to $|1\rangle$ before running your circuit.

The following is an example of how to do just that:

1. Create a Python vector that corresponds to an excited $|1\rangle$ state and initialize the quantum circuit:

```
initial_vector = [0.+0.j, 1.+0.j]
qc.initialize(initial_vector, 0)
```

2. Find the following code in your circuit, and replace it with the preceding initialize code snippet:

```
qc.x(0)
```

3. Now run the program as normal. The results should be similar, but your circuit printout will look like this:

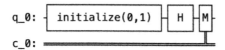

Figure 4.11 – Setting your qubit to $|1\rangle$ by using the initialize method

This way, you can initialize any number of qubits to any state you choose. The initialization vector needs to fulfill two main criteria:

1. It must include an entry for each of the $2^n$ possible states. In the preceding example, with 1 qubit, all we needed was a vector with length 2. For 2 qubits, the vector must have length 4, and so on.

2. The sum of the squares of the absolute value of the vector components must be equal to 1. Here's the initial vector from the preceding example that initialized the qubit to $|1\rangle$:

```
initial_vector = [0.+0.j, 1.+0.j]
```

This translates into the following:

$$|\psi\rangle = (0 + 0i)\,|0\rangle + (1 + 0i)\,|1\rangle$$

Figure 4.12 – Initial vector

This, in turn, gives the sum of probabilities:

$$Prob = |0|^2\,|0\rangle + |1|^2\,|1\rangle = 1$$

Figure 4.13 – Sum of probabilities

# Tossing two coins simultaneously

So far, we have only played with one coin at a time, but there is nothing stopping us from adding more coins. In this recipe, we will add a coin to the simulation, and toss two coins simultaneously. We will do this by adding a second qubit, expanding the number of qubits – two of everything.

## Getting ready

The sample code for this recipe can be found here: `https://github.com/PacktPublishing/Quantum-Computing-in-Practice-with-Qiskit-and-IBM-Quantum-Experience/blob/master/Chapter04/ch4_r4_two_coin_toss.py`.

# How to do it...

Set up your code like the previous example, but with a 2-qubit quantum circuit:

1.  Import the classes and methods that we need:

    ```
    from qiskit import QuantumCircuit, Aer, execute
    from qiskit.tools.visualization import plot_histogram
    from IPython.core.display import display
    ```

2.  Set up our quantum circuit with two qubits and two classical bits:

    ```
    qc = QuantumCircuit(2, 2)
    ```

3.  Add the Hadamard gates and the measurement gates to the circuit:

    ```
    qc.h([0,1])
    qc.measure([0,1],[0,1])
    display(qc.draw('mpl'))
    ```

    Note how we are now using lists to reference multiple qubits and multiple bits. For example, we apply the Hadamard gate to qubits 0 and 1 by using [0,1] as input:

    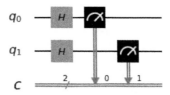

    Figure 4.14 – A 2-qubit quantum coin toss circuit

4.  Set the backend to our local simulator:

    ```
    backend = Aer.get_backend('qasm_simulator')
    ```

5.  Run the job with one shot:

    ```
    counts = execute(qc, backend, shots=1).result().
        get_counts(qc)
    ```

    Again, we are using streamlined code as we are only interested in the counts here.

6.  Visualize the results:

```
display(plot_histogram(counts))
```

The histogram looks like this:

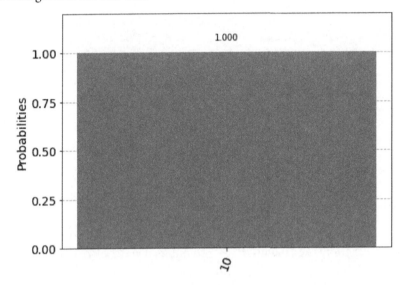

Figure 4.15 – The $|10\rangle$ result of a double quantum coin toss

## How it works...

You set the number of qubits when you create the quantum circuit.

When you ran the program, both qubits were supplied with Hadamard gates, creating two parallel qubits both in superposition.

In Qiskit®, qubit numbering starts with 0 for the first qubit and then counts upward. A 3-qubit circuit will contain the following qubits, referred to as the first, second, and third qubits:

- If you are using QuantumRegister notation, like in the *Quantum coin toss revisited* recipe: q[0], q[1], and q[2]

- If you are using the list notation: [0,1,2]

## There's more...

Do a little experimentation here by adding more qubits to your circuit. You will realize that you can use this simple method to create random numbers of any kind. The output will be a binary number of the same length as the number of qubits in your circuit.

For example, creating a circuit with 20 qubits and running it with one shot might result in the following output:

```
{'00101011101110011011': 1}
```

This translates into the following decimal number:

```
179099
```

So, you can use quantum programs to create any type of random number. For example, you can also use this setup to create dice of different sizes following the $2^n$ rule for a number of possible states (where n is the number of qubits). So, the calculation goes like this:

- One qubit = two possible states = coin
- Two qubits = four possible states = four-sided dice
- Three qubits = eight possible states = eight-sided dice

## Quantum-cheating in a coin toss? Introducing the Bell state

So, now you have the ability to toss one or more quantum coins and get a probabilistic outcome. That is all well and good, and we could picture ourselves doing some gambling with this new tool of ours, betting money against the outcome of a coin toss. But with a 50/50 outcome, the possibility of earning any real money is limited, unless, of course, we tweak the odds (that is, we cheat).

So how do you cheat in coin tossing? Well, knowing the outcome beforehand would be a clever way. And it turns out this is possible using a quantum phenomenon called **entanglement**.

By entangling two qubits, we connect them in a way so that they can no longer be described separately. In the most basic sense, if you have two entangled qubits and measure one of them as $|0\rangle$, the result of measuring the other one will be $|0\rangle$ as.

So, how do we use this to cheat in coin tossing? Well, we create two qubits, entangle them, and then we separate them (turns out this is the tricky part to do physically, but we will ignore that for now). You bring one qubit into the gambling den, and your friend keeps the other qubit outside the room.

When it is time to do a coin toss, you run your quantum circuit, entangle the qubits, and then your friend measures the qubit that they keep outside the room. They then sneakily, through some means (such as Bluetooth earphones, semaphoring, or telepathy), tell you what their measurement was, $|0\rangle$ or $|1\rangle$. You will then instantly know what your qubit is, before you measure it, and can bet money on that outcome. After measuring, you will find that you were indeed right, and cash in your winnings.

So, how is this done quantum programmatically? We will introduce a new gate, **controlled-NOT (CX)**.

## Getting ready

The sample code for this recipe can be found here: `https://github.com/ PacktPublishing/Quantum-Computing-in-Practice-with-Qiskit-and- IBM-Quantum-Experience/blob/master/Chapter04/ch4_r5_two_coin_ toss_bell.py`.

## How to do it...

Set up your code like the previous example, with 2 qubits and classical bits:

1. Import the classes and methods that we need:

   ```
   from qiskit import QuantumCircuit, Aer, execute
   from qiskit.tools.visualization import plot_histogram
   from IPython.core.display import display
   ```

2. Set up our quantum circuit with two qubits and two classical bits:

   ```
   qc = QuantumCircuit(2, 2)
   ```

3. Add the Hadamard gate, a controlled NOT gate, and the measurement gates to the circuit.

   For each circuit manipulation we do, such as adding a gate, we need to indicate which qubit to perform the manipulation on. For example, to add a Hadamard gate on the first qubit, you would use the code `qc.h(0)`:

   ```
   qc.h(0)
   qc.cx(0,1)
   qc.measure([0,1],[0,1])
   display(qc.draw('mpl'))
   ```

The preceding code gives the following output:

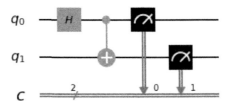

Figure 4.16 – 2-qubit quantum circuit with a controlled-NOT gate to entangle the qubits

4.  Set the backend to our local simulator:

```
backend = Aer.get_backend('qasm_simulator')
```

5.  Run the job with one shot:

```
counts = execute(qc, backend, shots=1).result().
    get_counts(qc)
```

6.  Visualize the results:

```
display(plot_histogram(counts))
```

The output for the histogram looks like this:

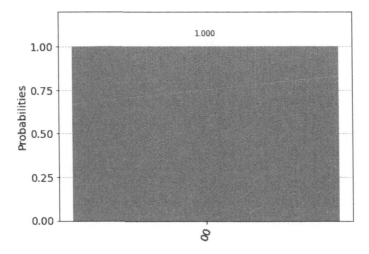

Figure 4.17 – The result of a 2-qubit entangled coin toss

7.   Run the circuit a couple of times and you will realize that the only result on this double quantum coin toss is $|00\rangle$ or $|11\rangle$. Now run the circuit again, but with 1,000 shots, and get the results:

```
counts = execute(qc, backend, shots=1000).result().get_
counts(qc)
```

You will see the following histogram as a result of your code:

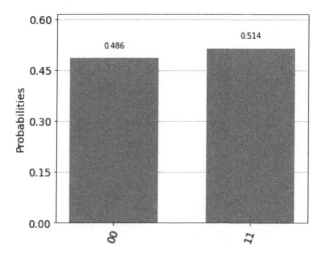

Figure 4.18 – Result of 1,000 shots. Only $|\mathbf{00}\rangle$ and $|\mathbf{11}\rangle$ appear!

## How it works...

Let's start with the new gate, CX. This gate takes as input the quantum state of the first qubit (as indicated by the dot on the first qubit score) and then executes a NOT gate (x) on the second qubit if the quantum state is $|1\rangle$. If the quantum state is $|0\rangle$, it does nothing to the second qubit.

So here's a really exciting part of this story. At a point where we expect the cx gate to act, we do not know the state of the first qubit yet. The Hadamard gate has put it in a nice superposition, hovering exactly between $|0\rangle$ and $|1\rangle$. Not until we measure the first qubit will we know what state the qubit is in. Not even nature will know the state because the qubit isn't in a specific state; it is in a superposition of two states.

So how would the CX gate know that it needed to flip the second qubit from $|0\rangle$ to $|1\rangle$ when we run the program? Well, that is the fascinating part of quantum computing, *it didn't*. Only when we measure the first qubit will the gate execution take place, and the entangled the second qubit will have flipped, or not. Einstein called this very real example of quantum mechanics *Spooky action at a distance* and wanted nothing to do with it.

So, the end result when running our little recipe is to get one of the two possible outcomes for these two qubits, $|00\rangle$ or $|11\rangle$ with roughly equal probability. If the first qubit reads $|0\rangle$, then so will the second qubit, giving you the $|00\rangle$ result. The same is true for the opposite reading of $|1\rangle$; both qubits will read the same, giving us $|11\rangle$. Once you have read 1 qubit, you immediately know what the second will be. This is how cheating is done in quantum coin tossing!

# There's more...

But the Bell state is not locked into just the two results $|00\rangle$ and $|11\rangle$. By using other gates, you can set this entanglement up to be $|01\rangle$ and $|10\rangle$ as well:

```
{'10': 542, '01': 458}
```

Which gate would you use, on which qubit would it act, and where in your circuit would you add it? In this case, you might want to start the qubits in different states to see what happens. Take a look at the *Implementing an upside-down coin toss* recipe for inspiration.

# See also

The results we got when running this Bell-state circuit on `qasm_simulator` (which simulates a perfect universal fault-tolerant quantum computer) gave us clear-cut results where both qubits were the same when measured all the time.

In the real world, where the existing physical quantum computers are still quite far from universal fault-tolerant quantum computers, the result will be somewhat different. For a quick look, see the *Tossing some real coins* recipe.

# More ways to quantum-cheat – tweaking the odds

In the previous recipe, we used a quantum phenomenon called entanglement to cheat with our coin tossing. Admittedly, this might be complicated to set up, and people do tend to get suspicious of coin tossers with an earpiece who are obviously listening for information before catching and revealing the coin (measuring the qubit).

But there are more ways to skin a cat. Remember our discussion of qubits and quantum gates. By manipulating the qubit using gates, we could adjust the state of the qubit before we measure it. The closer the vector is to either $|0\rangle$ or $|1\rangle$, the higher the probability of that specific outcome when you measure.

In this recipe, we will use a rotation gate, the **Ry** gate, to increase the probability of getting a tails outcome when we toss our coin.

## Getting ready

The sample code for this recipe can be found here: `https://github.com/PacktPublishing/Quantum-Computing-in-Practice-with-Qiskit-and-IBM-Quantum-Experience/blob/master/Chapter04/ch4_r6_coin_toss_rot.py`.

## How to do it...

Set up your code like the previous example and then add a **Ry** gate to rotate the qubit:

1.  Import the classes and methods that we need:

    ```
    from qiskit import QuantumCircuit, Aer, execute
    from qiskit.tools.visualization import plot_histogram
    from IPython.core.display import display
    from math import pi
    ```

2.  Set up our quantum circuit with one qubit and one classical bit and create the quantum circuit based on the registers:

    ```
    qc = QuantumCircuit(1, 1)
    ```

3. Add the Hadamard gate, the Ry gate, and the measurement gates to the circuit:

```
qc.h(0)
qc.ry(pi/8,0)
qc.measure(0, 0)
display(qc.draw('mpl'))
```

The preceding code should result in the following output:

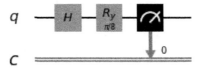

Figure 4.19 – Our cheating coin toss circuit with a Ry gate

4. Set the backend to our local simulator:

```
backend = Aer.get_backend('qasm_simulator')
```

5. Run the job with a thousand shots:

```
counts = execute(qc, backend, shots=1000).result().
    get_counts(qc)
```

6. Visualize the results:

```
display(plot_histogram(counts))
```

The histogram for the preceding code looks like the following:

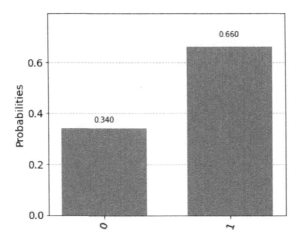

Figure 4.20 – A slightly skewed outcome for our cheating coin toss circuit

Alright, so the odds now seem to be much in your favor for tossing a $|1\rangle$ – almost 2 to 1.

## How it works...

So, what is going on here? By adding the Ry gate, we managed to tweak the odds mightily in our favor. Let's take a closer look at what that gate does.

Let's take a look at the Bloch vectors for the three different states that we are discussing here. In the sample code, there is this suspicious function that we have not touched upon yet. We will see more of it in *Chapter 6, Understanding the Qiskit® Gate Library*. By calling the get_psi() function and using the quantum circuit that you are building, you can see the behavior of the qubit at each stage of building the circuit. The function uses another simulator, statevector_simulator, that calculates the behavior of the qubit at a given location in your circuit, and then we use the plot_bloch_multivector() method to display it as a Bloch sphere:

```
# Function that returns the statevector (Psi) for the circuit
def get_psi(circuit):
    show_bloch=False
    if show_bloch:
        from qiskit.visualization import plot_bloch_multivector
        backend = Aer.get_backend('statevector_simulator')
        result = execute(circuit, backend).result()
        psi = result.get_statevector(circuit)
        print(title)
        display(qc.draw('mpl'))
        display(plot_bloch_multivector(psi))
```

When we call this function with a quantum circuit as an input, it will return the qubit statevector (psi or $\psi$) at the end of the circuit. If more than one qubit is included in the circuit, the function will include the complete statevector for all of them.

To run the circuit with the `get_psi()` function enabled, change the `show_bloch` variable from `False` to `True`, and run your circuit again. The output should now look something like the following:

1.  First, we show the qubit in the ground state:

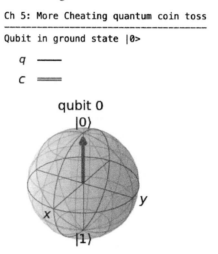

Figure 4.21 – In the initial ground state, the quantum vector is pointing straight up to $|0\rangle$ as we expect

2.  Then, we show the qubit after the Hadamard gate, now in a superposition of $|0\rangle$ and $|1\rangle$:

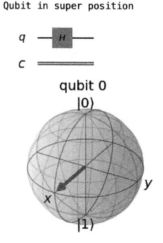

Figure 4.22 – After applying the Hadamard gate, the vector is now pointing along the x axis to the Bloch sphere equator

3.  We have seen this before. If we were to measure it now, we would get $|0\rangle$ and $|1\rangle$ with roughly 50% probability:

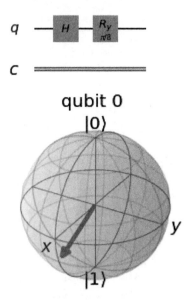

Figure 4.23 – Finally, after applying the Ry gate, the vector is now pointing below the Bloch sphere equator

Now, we apply the Ry gate, rotating the vector $\frac{\pi}{8}$ radians (0.3927 in our preceding circuit diagram) around the $y$ axis toward $|1\rangle$.

So, what happens here is that we have modified the angle $\theta$ by using the Ry gate.

Remember the formula from *Chapter 2, Quantum Computing and Qubits with Python*?

$$b = e^{i\varphi} \sin\left(\frac{\theta}{2}\right)$$

After applying the Hadamard gate, the angles were $\theta = \pi/2$ and $\Phi = 0$ (we haven't rotated around the $y$ axis yet).

The probability of measuring $|1\rangle$ was then:

$$|b|^2 = \left| e^i \sin\left(\frac{\pi}{4}\right) \right|^2 = 0.5$$

Now, if we change $\theta$ to $\frac{5\pi}{8}$ by adding $\frac{\pi}{8}$, we get this:

$$|b|^2 = \left| e^i \sin\left(\frac{5\pi}{16}\right) \right|^2 \approx 0.69$$

This corresponds very well with what we measured and shows us that we have indeed tweaked the probability of our quantum coin to land tails up.

## There's more...

There are three basic rotational gates—Rx, Ry, and Rz—that you can use to easily point the vector at any point on the Bloch sphere. These are described in more detail in *Chapter 6, Understanding the Qiskit® Gate Library*.

### Try your hand at these variations

Have a go at creating a couple of quantum circuits using these:

1.  Create a 1-qubit superposition without using the Hadamard gate.

2.  Measure the circuit to make sure that the result is the same as with a Hadamard gate.

3.  Create a 1-qubit superposition using the Hadamard gate, then use an R-gate to point the vector along the *y* axis.

    Which gate would that be, and what is the input? Can you get the same result by skipping the Hadamard gate and using only an R gate? Which one? Now, measure and see if that makes any difference to the expected outcome for a circuit in superposition.

4.  Look at the formula for calculating the probability of measuring $|1\rangle$ and see if you can use the Ry gate to set up a circuit that gives $|1\rangle$ as an outcome:

    99% of the time

    66% of the time

    33% of the time

Congratulations! Not only can you now cheat in quantum coin tossing, but you can also calculate your odds.

### More on the get_psi() function

We started out with this very small, 1-qubit quantum circuit as an example of how to use our home-made `get_psi()` function to step your way through your circuit to understand how your qubits behave at each stage. Remember that even though people sometimes talk about qubits being 0 and 1 at the same time, what they really are referring to is the superposition math we have looked at. The important thing is that during our calculations, we place our qubits in very well-known states by manipulating their statevectors.

For small circuits, it is fairly easy to envision what is going on at each step, but for larger circuits, you quickly run out of brainpower to mentally visualize how the little qubits behave.

You can use the `get_psi()` function and the statevector simulator for just this. Call it from any point in your circuit design to see what your qubits are up to. If your quantum programs do not behave the way you expect, use the statevector simulator and Bloch sphere visualization to troubleshoot.

As we move along through the book, we will tweak and modify the `get_psi()` function to suit our needs, and use it to display additional details about our circuits.

# Adding more coins – straight and cheating

Up until now, our recipes have been mainly of the 1- or 2-qubit sort. With our simulator, there is nothing stopping us from adding more qubits to our circuits at will, with the caveat that each additional qubit will require more and more processing power from the system on which your simulator runs. For example, the IBM Quantum Experience® `qasm_simulator` runs on an IBM POWER9™ server and maxes out at around 32 qubits.

In this recipe, we will create two 3-qubit quantum programs, one multi-coin toss, and one new entangled state called **GHZ** (for **Greenberger–Horne–Zeilinger** state).

Instead of doing this by creating two separate files, we will take a look at a new command, `reset()`. As the name implies, using the `reset()` command with a qubit sets it back to its original state of $|0\rangle$, ready to start a new quantum computing round. In this example, we use `reset()` to run two quantum programs in a row, writing to two sets of three classical registers, measuring twice per run.

# Getting ready

The sample code for this recipe can be found here: `https://github.com/` `PacktPublishing/Quantum-Computing-in-Practice-with-Qiskit-and-` `IBM-Quantum-Experience/blob/master/Chapter04/ch4_r7_three_` `coin_toss_ghz.py`.

# How to do it...

Set up your code like the previous examples, but with three qubits and classical bits:

1. Import the classes and methods that we need:

```
from qiskit import QuantumCircuit, Aer, execute
from qiskit.tools.visualization import plot_histogram
from IPython.core.display import display
```

2. Set up our quantum circuit with three qubits and six classical bits:

```
qc = QuantumCircuit(3, 6)
```

3. Add the Hadamard gates and the measurement gates to the circuit:

```
qc.h([0,1,2])
qc.measure([0,1,2],[0,1,2])
display(qc.draw('mpl'))
```

The output for the preceding code looks like this:

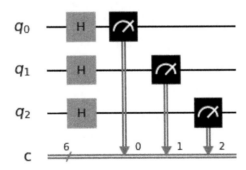

Figure 4.24 – A 3-qubit in superposition circuit, measuring to classical bits 0, 1, and 2

4.  Set the backend to our local simulator:

```
backend = Aer.get_backend('qasm_simulator')
```

5.  Run the job with a thousand shots:

```
counts = execute(qc, backend, shots=1000).result().
    get_counts(qc)
```

6.  Visualize the results:

```
display(plot_histogram(counts))
```

The histogram for the preceding code looks like the following:

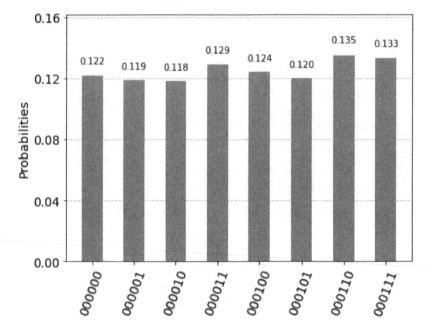

Figure 4.25 – Three qubits in superposition give random results

Notice here that we only see measurement results for the three first classical bits (0, 1, and 2). The three last classical bits are all 0.

7. Now modify the circuit by resetting the qubits, adding a Hadamard gate to qubit 0, then adding two CX (Controlled NOT) gates, one from qubit 0 to qubit 1, and one from qubit 0 to qubit 2.

We will use a new circuit command to reset the qubits of our circuit back to $|0\rangle$ and start over using `reset()`:

```
qc.barrier([0,1,2])
qc.reset([0,1,2])
qc.h(0)
qc.cx(0,1)
qc.cx(0,2)
qc.measure([0,1,2],[3,4,5])
display(qc.draw('mpl'))
```

Remember that when you modify just one qubit, you must specify which qubit to modify, like this `qc.h(0)`, to add a Hadamard gate to the first qubit:

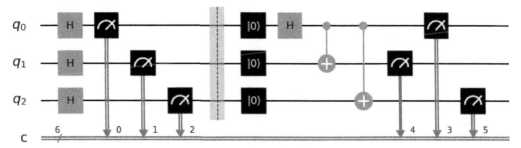

Figure 4.26 – Resetting the qubits of a quantum circuit back to $|0\rangle$ and starting over, writing to classical bits 3, 4, and 5 for the final measurement

8. Run the job with 1,000 shots:

```
counts = execute(qc, backend, shots=1000).result().
       get_counts(qc)
```

9. Display the results:

```
display(plot_histogram(counts))
```

The histogram presentation for the previous code looks like the following:

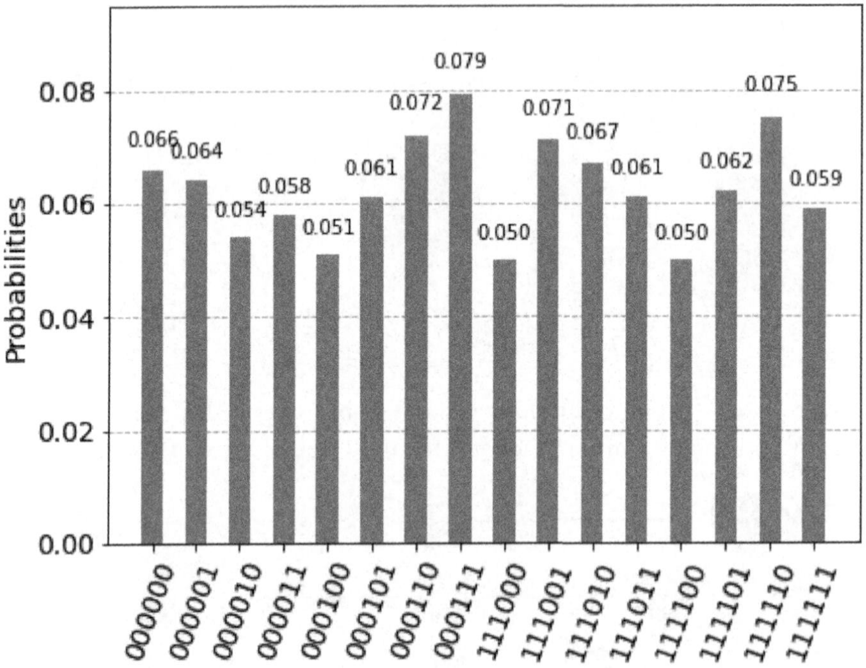

Figure 4.27 – The combined results of three coin toss qubits and of three entangled qubits, the GHZ state, in the first three and second three classical bits, respectively

## How it works...

There is nothing inherently new to the two circuits that we created, just more qubits, and two rounds of measurements. In the first one, we added all gates in parallel, and in the second one, we diligently specified which ones to add where. The end result was two 3-qubit circuits, one that represented even more coins tossed, and one that expanded on the Bell state we explored earlier.

That last one is interesting as it shows entanglement between several qubits; none of the qubits can now be treated separately. And this type of entanglement is key to more advanced quantum algorithms where a large number of qubits are set up, which are put in superposition and then entangled. They are finally acted on by other gates to produce specific outcomes.

Finally, we tested a new way of writing the outcomes to classical bits. We wrote the coin toss results to the first three classical bits and the GHZ state results to the three last ones.

# There's more...

Do a little experimentation to see how you can build larger circuits with more qubits, and how to add gates:

1.  Create a 5-qubit circuit, with Hadamard gates on all, but measurement gates on the first, third, and fifth qubits only. How many classical registers do you really need?

2.  Create a 5-qubit circuit where you entangle the first, second, fourth, and fifth qubits with the third qubit. On which qubit do you need to add the Hadamard gate?

3.  The GHZ circuit we built as a part of this recipe gives the entangled results $|000\rangle$ and $|111\rangle$ only. Build a circuit that gives you the result $|010\rangle$ or $|101\rangle$ instead.
    What gate other than H and CX do you use, and where do you put it, or them?

> **Tip**
> It might be easier to understand the workings of these circuits if you use one set of measurement commands only, and don't use the `reset()` command.

# Tossing some real coins

So, what do you say? Are you done simulating quantum coin tosses now, and want to do the real thing, running your Qiskit® quantum program on an actual IBM quantum computer? Let's finally get some use out of that IBM Quantum Experience® API key that you created.

In this recipe, you will run the cheating coin toss or Bell state on an actual IBM Quantum® machine by using Qiskit®. We know what the expected result is on a perfectly simulated quantum computer and will now take a look at what the results of a real so-called NISQ machine look like.

Finally, we will be getting some use out of that API key, introducing the IBMQ components, how to find the backends, how to select the best backend, and how to run the circuit against that backend.

## Getting ready

The sample code for this recipe can be found here: `https://github.com/ PacktPublishing/Quantum-Computing-in-Practice-with-Qiskit-and- IBM-Quantum-Experience/blob/master/Chapter04/ch4_r8_coin_toss_ IBMQ.py`.

To be able to run your quantum program on real IBM hardware, you need to use the API key that you are assigned with in your IBM Quantum Experience® account. If you are running Qiskit® from the IBM Quantum Experience® notebook environment, then your API key is already available to you and no further action is needed.

If, however, you are running Qiskit® on your own local machine, you must store the API key locally. You might have already carried out these required steps as part of the *Installing your API key and accessing your provider* recipe in *Chapter 1, Preparing Your Environment*. If not, go ahead and complete the task now. We'll wait for you here.

## How to do it

Set up your code as in the previous examples, with two qubits and classical bits:

1.  Import the classes and methods that we need:

    ```
    from qiskit import QuantumCircuit, execute
    from qiskit import IBMQ
    from qiskit.tools.monitor import job_monitor
    from IPython.core.display import display
    ```

2.  Retrieve the stored API key:

    ```
    IBMQ.load_account()
    provider = IBMQ.get_provider()
    ```

3.  Set up our quantum circuit with two qubits and two classical bits:

    ```
    qc = QuantumCircuit(2, 2)
    ```

4.  Add the Hadamard gate and the CX gate to prepare for a Bell state:

    ```
    qc.h(0)
    qc.cx(0,1)
    qc.measure([0,1],[0,1])
    display(qc.draw('mpl'))
    ```

The preceding code shows the following circuit:

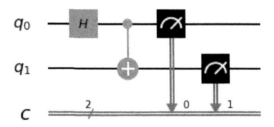

Figure 4.28 – 2-qubit Bell-state circuit

5.  Set the backend to the least busy IBM Quantum® machine available:

```
from qiskit.providers.ibmq import least_busy
backend = least_busy(provider.backends(n_qubits=5,
    operational=True, simulator=False))
print(backend.name())
ibmq_essex
```

We will revisit this way of picking an IBM Quantum® computer backend to run your circuit on in the *Finding the least busy backend* recipe of *Chapter 5, Touring the IBM Quantum Hardware® with Qiskit® Tools*. For now, just use the code as is.

6.  Run the job with 1,000 shots. Wait for the job to complete:

```
job = execute(qc, backend, shots=1000)
job_monitor(job)
Job Status: job has successfully run
```

7.  Get the results:

```
result = job.result()
counts = result.get_counts(qc)
from qiskit.tools.visualization import import plot_histogram
display(plot_histogram(counts))
```

The histogram presentation for the preceding code looks like the following:

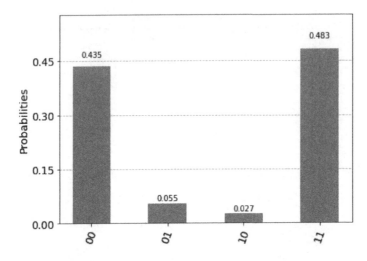

Figure 4.29 – The result of running the Bell-state circuit on an actual IBM Quantum® backend

Hold your horses! We were expecting results for only $|00\rangle$ and for $|11\rangle$ ... What is going on here?

## How it works...

Wow, look at those noisy qubits!

What you are seeing in the noisy results of your program is just that – noise. Even though the IBM Quantum® computers are running at temperatures colder than outer space (15 millikelvin), they still suffer from random noise both when executing gates on the qubits and when measuring them.

The local `qasm_simulator` that we have run our quantum programs on up until this point behaves like a perfect **universal quantum computer**. The real hardware, on the other hand, is what is called a **Noisy Intermediate-Scale Quantum (NISQ)** computer, which behaves less than perfectly.

We will explore the existing IBM Quantum® backends in more detail in *Chapter 5, Touring the IBM Quantum® Hardware with Qiskit® Tools*.

# There's more...

When running your job on an actual IBM Quantum® machine, things will generally differ from the controlled experience you had with your local simulator.

## Get in line

As soon as you start running one or two quantum programs on the IBM Quantum® machines, you will most likely realize that you are not the only one. As it happens, there are a limited number of quantum computers available to the general public to use for free. As of this writing, a steadily growing number of physical backends and one simulator can be used. Use the `provider.backends()` command to list the ones that are currently available:

```
from qiskit import IBMQ
IBMQ.load_account()
provider = IBMQ.get_provider()
provider.backends()
```

The preceding code might give a result similar to the following:

```
[<IBMQSimulator('ibmq_qasm_simulator') from IBMQ(hub='ibm-q',
group='open', project='main')>,
 <IBMQBackend('ibmqx2') from IBMQ(hub='ibm-q', group='open',
project='main')>,
 <IBMQBackend('ibmq_16_melbourne') from IBMQ(hub='ibm-q',
group='open', project='main')>,
 <IBMQBackend('ibmq_vigo') from IBMQ(hub='ibm-q', group='open',
project='main')>,
 <IBMQBackend('ibmq_ourense') from IBMQ(hub='ibm-q',
group='open', project='main')>,
 <IBMQBackend('ibmq_london') from IBMQ(hub='ibm-q',
group='open', project='main')>,
 <IBMQBackend('ibmq_burlington') from IBMQ(hub='ibm-q',
group='open', project='main')>,
 <IBMQBackend('ibmq_essex') from IBMQ(hub='ibm-q',
group='open', project='main')>,
 <IBMQBackend('ibmq_armonk') from IBMQ(hub='ibm-q',
group='open', project='main')>]
```

Remember that you are in a timeshare here, with everyone else simultaneously running on the same machine as you. In the next chapter, we will take a closer look at these machines and explore how to figure out which one is best to use at any given moment.

## Hardware details in the results

After your job is complete and you have looked at the results, you can take a quick peek at the complete returned results as well by using the `job.result()` command. It will look something like this:

```
namespace(backend_name='ibmq_burlington',
          backend_version='1.1.4',
          qobj_id='630c02ca-7d06-4430-91e8-8ef08b9f5a63',
          job_id='5f15dec89def8b001b437dfe',
          success=True,
          results=[namespace(shots=1000,
                    success=True,
                    data=namespace(counts=namespace(
                                        0x0=471,
                                        0x1=529)),
                    meas_level=2,
                    header=namespace(memory_slots=2,
                                     qreg_sizes=[['q', 5]],
                                     qubit_labels=[['q',0],
                                                   ['q',1],
                                                   ['q',2],
                                                   ['q',3],
                                                   ['q',4]],
                                     name='circuit58',
                                     n_qubits=5,
                                     creg_sizes=[['c', 2]],
                                     clbit_labels=[['c',0],
                                                   ['c',1]]),
                    memory=False)],
          status='Successful completion',
          header=namespace(backend_version='1.1.4',
                    backend_name='ibmq_burlington'),
          date=datetime.datetime(2020, 7, 20, 18, 13, 44,
   tzinfo=datetime.timezone.utc),
          time_taken=7.400392055511475,
          execution_id='bc4d19d0-cab4-11ea-b9ba-ac1f6b46a78e')
```

In this result set, you can see information about the quantum computer backend that was used, the results of the run, as well as the status and date and time for the run.

## What if the wait turns out to be long?

Sometimes there is just a really long queue ahead of you, and you have to wait your turn. In a sense, the IBM Quantum® machines work as a time-share setup from the early days of computing; only one program can run at the same time.

But no need to despair. Your job has been submitted, and you can take a step back and let the machines do their work, picking up the thread when it suits you.

This works the same as in the IBM Quantum Experience® Circuit Composer. Once submitted, your job will wait its turn, and then show up on the results page when returned. To do the same with your local Qiskit®, you first need your job ID.

You can use the job ID to get your most recent job, or even retrieve earlier jobs that you have executed. The job ID is unique for each executed job.

Use the `job.job_id()` command to get the job ID:

```
job.job_id()
Out[]: '5f15dec89def9b001b437dfe'
```

Now that you have a job ID, you can get back the `job` object by using the `retrieve_job()` command:

```
get_result=backend.retrieve_job(<jobid>)
```

And now you can get the job results just like you are used to, from the `job` object, for example:

```
counts = get_result.result().get_counts()
print(counts)
```

The preceding code might give the following output:

```
Out[]: {'11': 339, '10': 174, '00': 339, '01': 172}
```

You can also use the job ID to find the status of your job, and to see where in the queue it currently is:

```
print(backend.retrieve_job(<jobid>).status())
```

Here's an example:

```
Out []:  JobStatus.QUEUED
Out []:  JobStatus.RUNNING
Out []:  JobStatus.DONE
```

There are more features built in with the jobs that you can pull back from IBM Quantum Experience®. For a closer look at the backends and what you can learn about them, continue with *Chapter 5, Touring the IBM Quantum® Hardware with Qiskit® Tools.*

# 5

# Touring the IBM Quantum® Hardware with Qiskit®

In the previous chapters, we have mainly used built-in and local quantum computer simulators of various forms, but we also connected and ran some of our quantum programs on actual IBM quantum computers. In this chapter, we will take a closer look at these backends, down to the level of actual physical qubits.

We will take a quick tour of the IBM Quantum® lab by using both IBM Quantum Experience® and Qiskit® to access data about the available hardware. Among these things, we will look at the graphical view of the layout of the quantum chips, some physical aspects of quantum computers such as the T1 and T2 decoherence parameters, some basic and advanced error metrics, the way the available qubits can interact among themselves, and more.

In this chapter, we will cover the following recipes:

- What are the IBM Quantum® machines?
- Locating the available backends
- Comparing backends
- Finding the least busy backend
- Visualizing the backends
- Exploring a selected backend using Qiskit®

Throughout this chapter, we will generally use the Bell state program that we have used before, in *Chapter 4, Starting at the Ground Level with Terra*, as its ideal results, $|00\rangle$ and $|11\rangle$, are known to us, and we can use them to make comparisons between runs on different machines and different sets of qubits.

# Technical requirements

Before you begin working on the quantum programs in this chapter, make sure that you have completed all the steps in *Chapter 1, Preparing Your Environment*, especially the *Installing your API key and accessing your provider* recipe.

The quantum programs that we discuss in this chapter can be found here: `https://github.com/PacktPublishing/Quantum-Computing-in-Practice-with-Qiskit-and-IBM-Quantum-Experience/tree/master/Chapter05`.

# What are the IBM Quantum® machines?

This section is less of a recipe and rather more of a basic overview of the quantum components and processes that you will be encountering. If you'd rather jump ahead and start coding right away, then go to the next recipe.

With Qiskit®, you can run your quantum programs on two types of quantum computers: **simulators** and **IBM Quantum® hardware**. The simulators run either *locally* or in the *cloud* on IBM hardware. Generally speaking, running a simulator in the cloud gives you greater power and performance; `ibmq_qasm_simulator` – available online – lets you run fairly deep quantum programs on up to *32 qubits*. Your local simulator performance depends on your hardware; remember that simulating a quantum computer gets exponentially harder with each qubit added.

The actual IBM quantum computer hardware is located in an IBM lab and is accessed through the cloud. There are good reasons for this, so let's walk through this recipe on how to set up and run a quantum computer with the superconducting qubits that IBM Quantum® provides.

# Getting ready

Superconducting quantum computers are extremely sensitive to noise such as electromagnetic radiation, sound waves, and heat. An isolated environment equipped with cryogenic cooling provides a location with as little disturbance as possible.

Quantum computers may use so-called **Josephson junctions** kept at cryogenic temperatures and manipulated by microwave pulses. Ordinary people do not possess this kind of hardware, so, in this book, we will use the freely available IBM quantum computers in the cloud for our quantum programming.

# How to do it...

The following steps are a very high-level description of the process of running your quantum program on an actual IBM quantum computer:

1.  Write a quantum program in your local Qiskit® environment or on IBM Quantum Experience®.

2.  Send your program through the cloud to be queued at IBM Quantum®.

    The IBM cloud® model for quantum computing means that you will not have unrestricted access to the machines. This is a time-share system where everyone gets a some access sort of like a classical time-share system that used to be the norm in the early days of computing. The analogy is not too bad.

3.  Your program now gets **transpiled** into a program that can run on the machine you have chosen.

    When you run your quantum program, it gets interpreted by the software, and the fairly complex high-level gate architecture gets transpiled into a basic quantum program that consists of a set of basis gates only: u1, u2, u3, id, and cx. It turns out that all quantum programs that you write can be expressed using only these gates.

As a part of the transpiling, your circuit might change size and depth somewhat, as single gates are converted into sets of gates depending on the backend that you run your program on. Simply speaking, the size of a circuit is the raw number of gates that are used, and the depth is the length of the circuit from left to right, which roughly translates into how many parallel operations the quantum computer has to do to run your program. Your original program structure might have to change to accommodate the physical layout of the chip that you are running on.

4.   The gates of your transpiled program are coded into wave packages.

Now that your code has been converted into components that can be run on the chip, these components are translated into microwave packages that can be sent down to the quantum chip. Each gate can be seen as a rotation of the qubit Bloch vector around three axes, and each angle can be coded as a microwave pulse at different frequencies and durations.

5.   The quantum chip is reset.

Before we can do any quantum computing on the chip, its qubits need to be reset to their ground states. This is done by sending a specific microwave pulse to each qubit, much like when sending your gates to the qubits, which is described in the next step.

6.   Your coded gates are then sent to the qubits.

Each gate is sent to its corresponding qubit as a *wave package* on top of a GHz carrier wave tuned exactly to the frequency of the receiving qubit. We now leave behind what is called the **room temperature electronics** and enter the cryogenic environment. The signal that encodes the gate travels down into the innards of the quantum computer through successively cooler layers, finally reaching the quantum chip at 15 millikelvin – much colder than outer space. By the end of the journey, the wave package finally ends up impinging the qubit through a microwave resonator to change the state of the qubit.

This is repeated for each gate that you apply to each qubit and is what constitutes running the quantum program on the backend.

7.  The qubit is now read.

    And by the end of the program, a certain type of wave package interferes with the resonator, and the resulting package interference is then sent back up the stack, through successively warmer layers and then out into the room-temperature electronics.

    The interference is interpreted as a 0 or 1, and thus the result of your program is registered. At this state, the delicate balance of your resonating qubit has been destroyed – the qubit no longer behaves quantum mechanically and needs to be reset to ground state before we can use it again.

This whole process is repeated by the number of shots that you have ordered, and all results are stored in the cloud. Finally, your complete run is packaged and sent back to you, if you had the patience to wait, as well as being stored for later retrieval.

## How it works...

Most of the steps mentioned earlier are highly automated. You only have to write your quantum programs and send them off, then IBM Quantum® will do the rest and your qubit measurements are returned as ones or zeros.

As you can see, there are several steps where you can step in and dictate how things are done, for example, selecting the backend, picking the qubits to use based on qubit parameters, deciding the number of shots to run, and more. In this chapter, we will walk through how to dig out the hardware information and configuration parameters from the IBM Quantum® machines.

## See also

- For more information about the IBM Quantum® hardware, see `https://www.research.ibm.com/ibm-q/technology/devices/`

- You can also read this article on *Superconducting Qubits and the Physics of Josephson Junctions* by John M. Martinis and Kevin Osborne at NIST: `https://web.physics.ucsb.edu/~martinisgroup/classnotes/finland/LesHouchesJunctionPhysics.pdf`

- Also, here is a delightful Medium article on *QC – How to build a Quantum Computer with Superconducting Circuit?* by Jonathan Hui: `https://medium.com/@jonathan_hui/qc-how-to-build-a-quantum-computer-with-superconducting-circuit-4c30b1b296cd`

# Locating the available backends

In Qiskit®, a backend represents the system on which you run your quantum program. A **backend** can be a simulator, like the local Aer simulator that we have used earlier. If you want to run your quantum programs on real quantum computers instead of on your local simulator, you must identify an IBM Quantum® machine as a backend to use, and then configure your quantum program to use it.

Let's see the steps of what we'll be doing:

1.  Start by importing the required classes and methods and load your account information. In this case, we use the IBMQ class, which contains the main hardware-related functions.
2.  Take a look at the machines that are available to your account.
3.  Select a generally available backend.
4.  Create and run a Bell state quantum program on the selected backend.
5.  Select a simulator backend and run the Bell state quantum program again for comparison.

## Getting ready

In this recipe, we will use the IBMQ `provider.backends()` method to identify and filter available backends to run your programs and then use the `provider.get_backend()` method to select the backend. In the example that follows, we will use the `ibmqx2` and `ibmq_qasm_simulator` backends. We will then run a small quantum program on one of the hardware backends, and then on the simulator backend.

The Python file in the following recipe can be downloaded from here: `https://github.com/PacktPublishing/Quantum-Computing-in-Practice-with-Qiskit-and-IBM-Quantum-Experience/blob/master/Chapter05/ch5_r1_identifying_backends.py`.

## How to do it...

1.  As always, we start by importing the Qiskit® classes and methods to use:

```
from qiskit import IBMQ, QuantumCircuit, execute
from qiskit.tools.monitor import job_monitor
```

2.  Before you can start using the IBMQ class and the backend methods (if not already set), you must set the provider that is associated with your account:

```
if not IBMQ.active_account():
    IBMQ.load_account()
provider = IBMQ.get_provider()
```

3.  The provider.backends() method is used to locate the IBM Quantum® backends that are available to your IBM Quantum® account. With that information, you can later set the backend that you want to run your quantum program on by using the provider.get_backend() method:

```
print(provider.backends(operational=True,
    simulator=False))
```

4.  The preceding code might give an output similar to the following:

```
Available backends:
[<IBMQBackend('ibmqx2') from IBMQ(hub='ibm-q',
group='open', project='main')>, <IBMQBackend('ibmq_16_
melbourne') from IBMQ(hub='ibm-q', group='open',
project='main')>, <IBMQBackend('ibmq_vigo') from
IBMQ(hub='ibm-q', group='open', project='main')>,
<IBMQBackend('ibmq_ourense') from IBMQ(hub='ibm-q',
group='open', project='main')>, <IBMQBackend('ibmq_
valencia') from IBMQ(hub='ibm-q', group='open',
project='main')>, <IBMQBackend('ibmq_london') from
IBMQ(hub='ibm-q', group='open', project='main')>,
<IBMQBackend('ibmq_burlington') from IBMQ(hub='ibm-q',
group='open', project='main')>, <IBMQBackend('ibmq_
essex') from IBMQ(hub='ibm-q', group='open',
project='main')>, <IBMQBackend('ibmq_armonk') from
IBMQ(hub='ibm-q', group='open', project='main')>,
<IBMQBackend('ibmq_santiago') from IBMQ(hub='ibm-q',
group='open', project='main')>]
```

> **The IBM Quantum® simulator**
>
> See how the list also includes a simulator. This simulator runs on powerful IBM hardware and will be able to manage both more qubits and more complex quantum programs than both your local simulator and the IBM Quantum® backends that you have access to.

We are using filtering here to get only the backends that we are interested in. For example, as we are only interested in physical machines, we will filter by the `simulator` parameter:

```
>>> provider.backends(simulator=False)
```

Alternatively, you can use complex filtering such as lambda functions:

```
>>> provider.backends(filters=lambda x: not
x.configuration().simulator)
```

We are also only interested in backends that are not down for maintenance. To do this, we filter by the `operational` parameter:

```
>>> provider.backends(operational=True, simulator=False)
```

Or else, you can use the following code:

```
>>> provider.backends(filters=lambda x: not
x.configuration().simulator and x.status().operational)
```

5. So, with this in mind, when you want to run your quantum program on an IBM Quantum® machine, you need to specify the backend to run on, and for this, you can use the `get_backend()` method. Let's manually select a backend from our previous list, for example, `ibmqx2`:

```
backend = provider.get_backend('ibmqx2')
print("\nSelected backend:", backend.name())
```

6. The preceding code should give the following result:

```
Out[]: Selected backend: ibmqx2
```

7. Now, with a backend selected, you can execute jobs on the backend with the command `job = execute(<your_quantum_circuit>, backend)`. In this case, we will use the following command:

```
job = execute(qc, backend, shots=1000)
```

8. We can now create the circuit to test:

```
qc = QuantumCircuit(2,2)
qc.h(0)
qc.cx(0,1)
qc.measure([0,1],[0,1])
print("\nQuantum circuit:")
print(qc)
```

```
job = execute(qc, backend, shots=1000)
job_monitor(job)
result = job.result()
counts = result.get_counts(qc)
print("\nResults:", counts)
```

9.  The sample code should give a result similar to this:

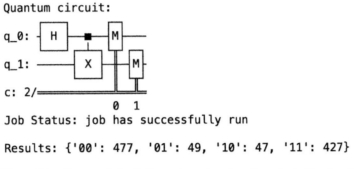

Figure 5.1 – Output of the Bell quantum circuit on the selected backend

10. To select the IBM Quantum® simulator as the backend, and run the circuit on that one, you can do the following:

```
print(provider.backends(operational=True,
    simulator=True))
backend = provider.get_backend('ibmq_qasm_simulator')
job = execute(qc, backend, shots=1000)
job_monitor(job)
result = job.result()
counts = result.get_counts(qc)
print("\nSimulator results:", counts)
```

11. The preceding code should give the following result:

```
Available simulator backends:
[<IBMQSimulator('ibmq_qasm_simulator') from IBMQ(hub='ibm-q', group='open', project='main')>]
Job Status: job has successfully run

Simulator results: {'00': 494, '11': 506}
```

Figure 5.2 – Output of the Bell quantum circuit on the ibmq_qasm_simulator backend

So, we have now identified the IBM Quantum® backends that are available to us and run a quantum program on a backend that we selected, and on a simulator backend. In the next recipe, *Comparing backends*, we will do a simple performance comparison of the available backends.

## There's more...

You can also use the `backends()` method to look at the simulator backends that you have at your disposal on your locally installed Qiskit® environment. First, start by importing the `Aer` simulator class and then use the `backends()` method to take a look at the available backends:

```
from qiskit import Aer
Aer.backends()
```

The preceding code should give the following result:

```
Out[]: [<QasmSimulator('qasm_simulator') from AerProvider()>,
 <StatevectorSimulator('statevector_simulator') from
 AerProvider()>,
 <UnitarySimulator('unitary_simulator') from AerProvider()>,
 <PulseSimulator('pulse_simulator') from AerProvider()>]
```

These are all simulators:

- `'qasm_simulator'`: This simulator lets you run your quantum programs and get results returned as if you were running on a perfect quantum computer with no errors and no noise.

- `'statevector_simulator'`: With this one, you can simulate what the statevector for your qubits looks like throughout your circuit.

- `'unitary_simulator'`: This simulator lets you create the unitary matrix for your circuit.

- `'pulse_simulator'`: This simulator lets you simulate sending discrete pulses to a qubit.

We have already seen `'qasm_simulator'` and `'statevector_simulator'` used in *Chapter 4*, *Starting at the Ground Level with Terra*, and we will take a closer look at `'unitary_simulator'` as a part of *Chapter 6*, *Understanding the Qiskit® Gate Library*.

## See also

- For more information about the available IBM Quantum® systems: `https://www.ibm.com/quantum-computing/technology/systems/`.

- You can also use Python help using `help(IBMQ)` and `help(provider.backends)` to find more information about these Qiskit® methods.

# Comparing backends

The IBM Quantum® backends are all slightly different, from the number of qubits to the individual behavior and interaction between these. Depending on how you write your quantum program, you might want to run the code on a machine with certain characteristics.

The backend information that is returned by IBMQ is just a plain Python list and you can juggle the returned data with any other list. For example, you can write a Python script that finds the available IBM Quantum® backends, then run a quantum program on each of the backends and compare the results in a diagram that shows a rough measure of the *quality* of the backends' qubits.

In this recipe, we will use a simple Python loop to run a succession of identical Bell-state quantum programs on the available IBM Quantum® backends to get a rough estimate of the performance of the backends.

## Getting ready

The file required for this recipe can be downloaded from here: `https://github.com/PacktPublishing/Quantum-Computing-in-Practice-with-Qiskit-and-IBM-Quantum-Experience/blob/master/Chapter05/ch5_r2_comparing_backends.py`.

## How to do it...

Let's take a look at how to compare backends:

1. First, we import the required classes and methods.

   In this case, we use the IBMQ library, which contains the main hardware-related functions. We also import the classes to build quantum circuits, monitor jobs, and display results. And then load the stored account API key and get the provider:

   ```
   from qiskit import IBMQ, QuantumCircuit, execute
   from qiskit.tools.monitor import import job_monitor
   ```

```
from qiskit.visualization import plot_histogram

if not IBMQ.active_account():
    IBMQ.load_account()
provider = IBMQ.get_provider()
```

2.  Now, we will create the quantum program for which we know the expected results.

    For example, a Bell state program, which will give the results |00⟩ and |11⟩ only on a perfect quantum computer:

```
qc = QuantumCircuit(2,2)
qc.h(0)
qc.cx(0,1)
qc.measure([0,1],[0,1])
```

3.  The preceding code should give the following result:

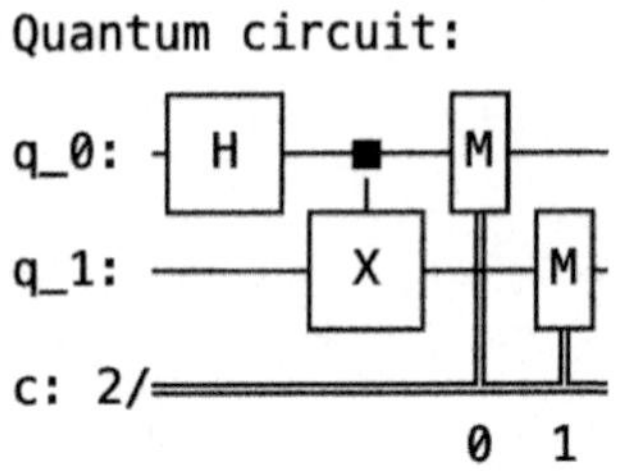

**Quantum circuit:**

Figure 5.3 – A Bell state quantum circuit

4.  Now, we will get all available and operational backends, including the IBM Quantum® simulator to use as a benchmark:

```
backends = provider.backends(filters=lambda b:
    b.configuration().n_qubits > 1 and
        b.status().operational)
print("\nAvailable backends:", backends)
```

---

**Filtering out single-qubit backends**

See how we are using a filter here, to only include backends with more than 1 qubit. The reason for this is that our code requires two operational qubits and the code will fail if we run it on a backend with just one. One of the available IBM Quantum® machines—ibmq_armonk—is a quantum computer with just 1 qubit; we do not want to use that one and use the filter to remove it from our list of backends. The purpose of the ibmq_armonk backend is to experiment with qubit pulse programming, which is beyond the scope of this book.

5.  The preceding code might give the following result:

```
Available backends:
[<IBMQSimulator('ibmq_qasm_simulator') from
IBMQ(hub='ibm-q', group='open', project='main')>,
<IBMQBackend('ibmqx2') from IBMQ(hub='ibm-q',
group='open', project='main')>, <IBMQBackend('ibmq_16_
melbourne') from IBMQ(hub='ibm-q', group='open',
project='main')>, <IBMQBackend('ibmq_vigo') from
IBMQ(hub='ibm-q', group='open', project='main')>,
<IBMQBackend('ibmq_ourense') from IBMQ(hub='ibm-q',
group='open', project='main')>, <IBMQBackend('ibmq_
valencia') from IBMQ(hub='ibm-q', group='open',
project='main')>, <IBMQBackend('ibmq_london') from
IBMQ(hub='ibm-q', group='open', project='main')>,
<IBMQBackend('ibmq_burlington') from IBMQ(hub='ibm-q',
group='open', project='main')>, <IBMQBackend('ibmq_
essex') from IBMQ(hub='ibm-q', group='open',
project='main')>, <IBMQBackend('ibmq_santiago') from
IBMQ(hub='ibm-q', group='open', project='main')>]
```

6.  Then, we will run the simple quantum program on these backends in order. The resulting counts are stored in a dictionary that we call counts:

```
counts = {}
for n in range(0, len(backends)):
    print('Run on:', backends[n])
    job = execute(qc, backends[n], shots=1000)
    job_monitor(job)
    result = job.result()
    counts[backends[n].name()] = result.get_counts(qc)
```

> **Get in line**
>
> Running four quantum programs on several different machines might take a while, depending on the number of other users actively using the backends, and the number of jobs that are queued up. For example, running this program on eight backends and one simulator might take about an hour on a typical Sunday evening.

7.    The preceding code might give the following result:

```
Run on: ibmq_qasm_simulator
Job Status: job has successfully run
Run on: ibmqx2
Job Status: job has successfully run
Run on: ibmq_16_melbourne
Job Status: job has successfully run

. . .

Run on: ibmq_essex
Job Status: job has successfully run
Run on: ibmq_santiago
Job Status: job has successfully run
```

8.    Now that the jobs are running, we can print out and then plot the results using the following code:

```
print("\nRaw results:", counts)
#Optionally define the histogram colors.
colors = ['green','darkgreen','red','darkred','orange',
    'yellow','blue','darkblue','purple']
#Plot the counts dictionary values in a histogram, using
#the counts dictionary keys as legend.
display(plot_histogram(list(counts.values()),
    title = "Bell results on all available backends
    legend=list(counts), color = colors[0:len(backends)],
    bar_labels = True)
```

9.    The preceding code might give the following result:

```
Raw results: {'ibmq_qasm_simulator': {'00': 510, '11':
490}, 'ibmqx2': {'00': 434, '01': 77, '10': 39, '11':
450}, 'ibmq_16_melbourne': {'00': 474, '01': 42, '10':
48, '11': 436}, 'ibmq_vigo': {'00': 512, '01': 18, '10':
42, '11': 428}, 'ibmq_ourense': {'00': 494, '01': 26,
'10': 19, '11': 461}, 'ibmq_valencia': {'00': 482, '01':
31, '10': 30, '11': 457}, 'ibmq_london': {'00': 463,
'01': 48, '10': 39, '11': 450}, 'ibmq_burlington': {'00':
385, '01': 182, '10': 84, '11': 349}, 'ibmq_essex':
{'00': 482, '01': 46, '10': 24, '11': 448}, 'ibmq_
santiago': {'00': 514, '01': 17, '10': 17, '11': 452}}
```

These raw results show how well each backend ran the program. The `ibmq-qasm-simulator` represents the ideal results on a simulated universal quantum computer; the other results show how the program ran on actual IBM Quantum® backends. A perfect quantum computer would get results similar to the simulator, resulting in values for |00⟩ and |11⟩ only:

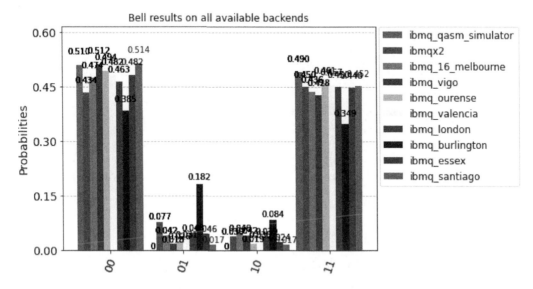

Figure 5.4 – Graphical view of the Bell results

What we have created here is a simple comparison of the available IBM Quantum® backends using a *basic 2-qubit Bell state quantum program*. On a perfect quantum computer, we only expect the results – |00⟩ and |11⟩ – which is indeed what we see for `ibmq_qasm_simulator`. Like we discussed in *Chapter 4*, *Starting at the Ground Level with Terra*, for real **Noisy Intermediate-Scale Quantum (NISQ)** machines, we expect some noise and a mixed result, consisting of |00⟩, |01⟩, |10⟩, and |11⟩ for the IBM Quantum® hardware.

Generally speaking, the smaller the |01⟩ and |10⟩ bars are, the better the backends perform, but there are many factors at play. These will be explored later in this chapter and in *Chapter 8*, *Cleaning Up Your Quantum Act with Ignis*.

Also, keep in mind that we are only comparing the default execution of your quantum programs here. Different qubit configurations, readout errors, qubit connection issues, and other errors that occur with real hardware play a part and make the results somewhat random.

# There's more

In this recipe, we ran our quantum program on almost all available backends. As you saw in the *Locating the available backends* recipe, you can also filter the backends. This recipe required at least two qubits to run, so we added a filter to include backends with more than one qubit:

```
backends = provider.backends(filters=lambda b:
b.configuration().n_qubits > 1 and b.status().operational)
```

You can use the filter capability for other reasons; for example, to run on only 5-qubit machines, filter by the number of qubits:

```
# Get all available and operational backends.
backends = provider.backends(n_qubits=5)
```

You can now see how the available backends behave, and how busy some of them might be. Time to figure out a way to speed up your quantum program executions by finding the backend with the shortest queue.

# Finding the least busy backend

When you run your quantum program on an IBM Quantum® backend, you will quickly realize that you might not be the only one attempting to use that same backend at the same time. Depending on the time and day of the week, and the type and purpose of the quantum programs being run, not all IBM Quantum® machines are used to the same degree.

If you are not concerned with which machine you should run the code on, you can use the least_busy method to automatically find the best backend to run your programs on. The least busy status of a backend generally means that you have the least wait time, but this is not necessarily true. Some programs run longer than others, and queues (just like in the supermarket) might move at different speeds.

Let's take a look at the following steps:

1. Start by importing the required IBMQ and least_busy methods and load our account.

2. Use the least_busy method to automatically select the generally available least busy backend, and the least busy backend with 5 qubits.

3. Finally, let's display the overview data for all backends to verify that the backends that we selected are indeed the least busy backends.

The least_busy method is convenient if we do not want to wait for our execution but might not be the best option. Qiskit® has given us the name of the least busy backend. We can now trust Qiskit® and run our quantum code on that backend, or, depending on our purposes, we might choose another backend to run on. It might turn out that the least busy backend is a machine with noisy qubits or short T1 or T2 that doesn't suit our purposes.

## Getting ready

The file required in the following recipe can be downloaded from here: https://github.com/PacktPublishing/Quantum-Computing-in-Practice-with-Qiskit-and-IBM-Quantum-Experience/blob/master/Chapter05/ch5_r3_least_busy.py.

## How to do it...

What least_busy is looking for are backends that include a pending_jobs parameter. If you add additional filtering features that exclude the actual least busy backend, the method will return the backend with the least pending jobs that meet the filtering criteria.

Let's take a look:

1.  Start by importing the required IBMQ and least_busy methods, and load our account:

    ```
    from qiskit import IBMQ
    from qiskit.providers.ibmq import least_busy
    if not IBMQ.active_account():
        IBMQ.load_account()
    provider = IBMQ.get_provider()
    ```

2.  Now we can ask IBM Quantum® which backend is least busy, and set our backend parameter accordingly:

    ```
    backend = least_busy(provider.backends(simulator=False))
    print("Least busy backend:", backend.name())
    ```

    The preceding code might give the following result:
    ```
    Out []:
    Least busy backend: ibmq_armonk
    ```

In this example, the least busy backend turned out to be ibmq_armonk, which is a 1-qubit machine designed for pulse testing. This is not the backend that you want to run your multi-qubit circuits on.

3. Filter the least busy results.

   You can feed the least_busy method a filtered list of backends, for example, to only include 5-qubit machines, or just call the method with the unfiltered provider.backends() function, like in the following example:

```
filtered_backend = least_busy(provider.backends(
    n_qubits=5, operational=True, simulator=False))
print("\nLeast busy 5-qubit backend:",
    filtered_backend.name())
```

   The preceding code might give the following output:

```
Out []:
Least busy 5-qubit backend: ibmq_santiago
```

   There we go – this is the least busy backend with five qubits.

4. To check that the method selected the best backend, we can use the backend_overview() method to take a look at the number of pending jobs for the available backends:

```
from qiskit.tools.monitor import backend_overview
print("\nAll backends overview:\n")
backend_overview()
```

   The preceding code might give the following result:

```
All backends overview:

ibmq_santiago              ibmq_armonk               ibmq_essex
---------------            -------------             -----------
Num. Qubits:  5            Num. Qubits:  1           Num. Qubits:  5
Pending Jobs: 1            Pending Jobs: 0           Pending Jobs: 5
Least busy:   False        Least busy:   True        Least busy:   False
Operational:  True         Operational:  True        Operational:  True
Avg. T1:      144.5        Avg. T1:      168.5       Avg. T1:      86.2
Avg. T2:      141.2        Avg. T2:      184.9       Avg. T2:      122.9


ibmq_burlington            ibmq_london               ibmq_valencia
-----------------          -------------             -------------
Num. Qubits:  5            Num. Qubits:  5           Num. Qubits:  5
Pending Jobs: 4            Pending Jobs: 8           Pending Jobs: 32
Least busy:   False        Least busy:   False       Least busy:   False
Operational:  True         Operational:  True        Operational:  True
Avg. T1:      83.9         Avg. T1:      67.9        Avg. T1:      70.9
Avg. T2:      72.2         Avg. T2:      76.4        Avg. T2:      62.0


ibmq_ourense               ibmq_vigo                 ibmq_16_melbourne
-------------              ---------                 -----------------
Num. Qubits:  5            Num. Qubits:  5           Num. Qubits:  15
Pending Jobs: 29           Pending Jobs: 26          Pending Jobs: 8
Least busy:   False        Least busy:   False       Least busy:   False
Operational:  True         Operational:  True        Operational:  True
Avg. T1:      93.7         Avg. T1:      104.8       Avg. T1:      54.2
Avg. T2:      64.9         Avg. T2:      84.6        Avg. T2:      55.4


ibmqx2
------
Num. Qubits:  5
Pending Jobs: 4
Least busy:   False
Operational:  True
Avg. T1:      65.3
Avg. T2:      45.5
```

Figure 5.5 – All available backends with no filtering

Keep an eye on the **Least busy** parameter. As you can see, the number of pending jobs is the smallest for the least busy backend.

So, the takeaway of this recipe is that you can automate which backend you run your quantum programs on, but that the returned backend might not be what you want if you need to run your program on a specific number of qubits. If this is the case, filter the search by the number of qubits to get the backend with the shortest queue.

# Visualizing the backends

Now that we have started poking at various parameters of the IBM Quantum® backends, it would be helpful to have a simple way of getting a visual overview of the quantum chips and various important parameters, such as how the qubits are interconnected, which connections are better than others, what the quality of each qubit is, and so on. Qiskit® comes with visualizations built in.

## Getting ready

The file required in the following recipe can be downloaded from here: `https://github.com/PacktPublishing/Quantum-Computing-in-Practice-with-Qiskit-and-IBM-Quantum-Experience/blob/master/Chapter05/ch5_r4_backend_vis.py`.

## How to do it...

We will use three methods of the `qiskit.visualization` package to look over the backends: `plot_gate_map()`, `plot_error_map()`, and `plot_circuit_layout()`. For the last one, we also need to *transpile* a quantum circuit using the `transpile()` method to then display which qubits Qiskit® is mapping your gates to on the backend.

Let's look at the following steps:

1. Start by importing the required `qiskit` and `qiskit.visualization` methods, and load our account:

```
from qiskit import IBMQ, QuantumCircuit, transpile
from qiskit.providers.ibmq import least_busy
# Import the backend visualization methods
from qiskit.visualization import plot_gate_map,
plot_error_map, plot_circuit_layout
if not IBMQ.active_account():
    IBMQ.load_account()
provider = IBMQ.get_provider()
```

2. Grab and get all available IBM Quantum® backends that have more than 1 qubit and that are not simulators:

```
available_backends = provider.backends(filters=lambda b:
    b.configuration().n_qubits > 1 and b.status().
        operational)
print("{0:20} {1:<10}".format("Name","#Qubits"))
print("{0:20} {1:<10}".format("----","-------"))
for n in range(0, len(available_backends)):
    backend = provider.get_backend(str(available_
        backends[n]))
    print("{0:20} {1:<10}".format(backend.name(),
        backend.configuration().n_qubits))
```

3.  Select the backend that you want to take a look at:

```
backend_input = input("Enter the name of a backend, or X
    for the least busy:")
if backend_input not in ["X","x"]:
    backend = provider.get_backend(backend_input)
else:
    backend = least_busy(provider.backends(
        filters=lambda b: b.configuration().n_qubits > 1
            and b.status().operational))
```

4.  Now, let's display the gate map and the error map for the backend:

```
print("\nQubit data for backend:",backend.status().
    backend_name)
display(plot_gate_map(backend, plot_directed=True))
display(plot_error_map(backend))
```

This first visualization shows the logical layout of the backend, optionally with the permitted direction of communication between the qubits displayed (plot_directed=True).

Consider this example: display(plot_gate_map(backend, plot_directed=True)).

The preceding code might give the following output for ibmq_burlington:

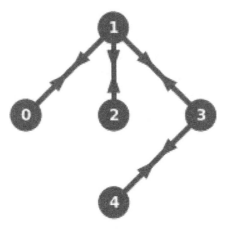

Figure 5.6 – The gate map for ibmq_burlington

With the error map visualization, you get a view of the readout error and CX error rates for the backend. This map gives you an indication of the quality of the qubits for providing accurate readout results, and for correctly executing on the **controlled-NOT (CX)** gates between two qubits:

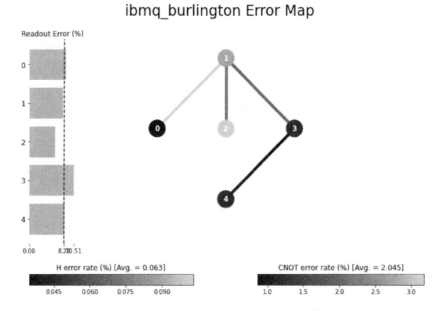

Figure 5.7 – The error map form ibmq_burlington

5. And finally, create a Bell circuit, transpile it, and use it to display the circuit layout:

```
# Create and transpile a 2 qubit Bell circuit
qc = QuantumCircuit(2)
qc.h(0)
qc.cx(0,1)
display(qc.draw('mpl'))
qc_transpiled = transpile(qc, backend=backend,
    optimization_level=3)
display(qc_transpiled.draw('mpl'))
# Display the circuit layout for the backend.
display(plot_circuit_layout(qc_transpiled, backend,
    view='physical'))
```

The circuit layout is a little bit more complex, as it not only takes a backend as input, but you must also feed it the transpiled quantum circuit that you want to run on it.

For example, still on ibmq_burlington, we might want to run a Bell circuit.

The preceding code might give the following result:

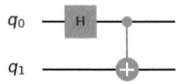

Figure 5.8 – A Bell quantum circuit with two qubits

The transpiled circuit tells us that we will run the circuit on qubits 0 and 1. As we started out with a 2-qubit circuit, we gave the transpiler the option to assign any two qubits to our circuit:

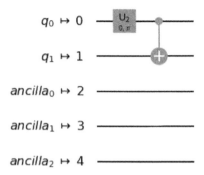

Figure 5.9 – The transpiled Bell circuit

The circuit layout shows us the expected qubit assignment:

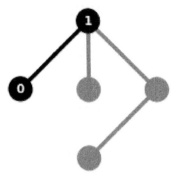

Figure 5.10 – The CX gate in the Bell circuit is mapped from qubit 0 to qubit 1

The view illustrates what the physical chip looks like, in a symbolic way with no technical details.

# There's more...

We have seen the visualization steps in Qiskit®. You can also get the same information in IBM Quantum Experience®.

Let's take a look:

1.  Log in to IBM Quantum Experience® at `https://quantum-computing.ibm.com`.

2.  On the **Welcome** page, on the right-hand side, you'll see a list of the available backends:

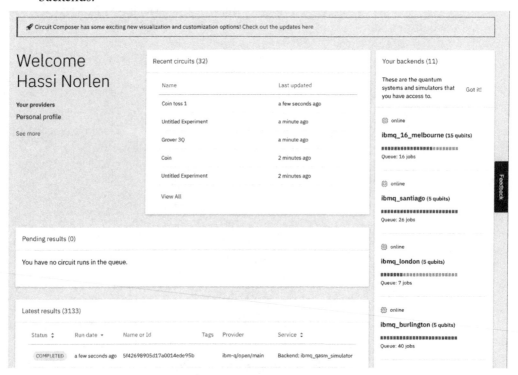

Figure 5.11 – The IBM Quantum Experience® home page

3.  Click on the backend that you are interested in, for example, `ibmq_burlington`, to see the chip layout and additional information:

# ibmq_burlington v1.1.4

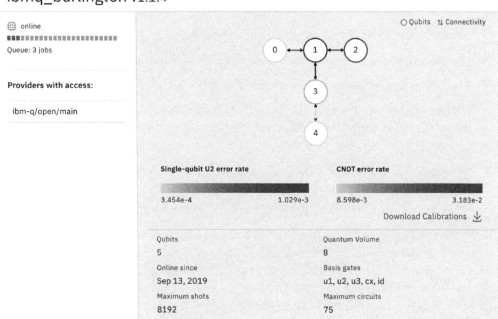

Figure 5.12 – Details of the ibmq_burlington chip

Here's a short list of the different pieces of data that you can see for the selected chip:

- **Online or offline**: Is the backend currently available?

- **The current queue**: How many people are using the backend at the moment? This number gives you a rough estimate of how busy the backend is, and how long it might take before your program will run.

- **Providers**: This will be **open** for the freely available backends.

- **A blueprint view of the actual quantum chip**: The view illustrates what the physical chip looks like, in a symbolic way with no technical details.

- **A connectivity map**: The arrows between the qubits illustrate how they can be connected using 2-qubit gates such as the **CNOT** (also known as **controlled-NOT**, or **CX**) gate. The connection can be made from the qubit where the arrow starts to the qubit where it ends.

- **Single-qubit error rate**: This is a measure of the quality of the qubit. It is a summary of the error rate of the qubit itself and the readout error. Basically, this is the probability that a qubit in one state will be read as the other state.

- **CNOT error rate**: This is the measure of the quality of the qubit connection. It is the probability that two entangled qubits will read the opposite of the entanglement.

- **Number of qubits**: The number of available qubits.

- **Online since**: The date and time that the machine came online.

- **Maximum shots**: The maximum number of shots you can run on the backend.

- **Quantum volume**: The measured quantum volume for the backend. The quantum volume is IBM's suggested benchmark for measuring the performance of today's quantum computers.

- **Basis gates**: These are the generic gates that are used to build quantum programs on the chip. Generally speaking, these are `u1`, `u2`, `u3`, `cx`, and `id`. With these gates, you can build all other quantum gates that are supported by Qiskit®.

You can use the visualized IBM Quantum® information as guidance for writing and executing your quantum programs, and also include aspects such as the qubit properties and error map to fine-tune your programs for a specific backend. However, in a pure, non-user interface Qiskit® environment, you might want to access this data without having to resort to a user interface. This is all covered in the next recipe, where we dig out this data directly in Qiskit®.

## See also

For a good overview and explanation of the quantum volume concept, see the Medium article: *What Is Quantum Volume, Anyway?* by Ryan F. Mandelbaum, senior technical writer, IBM Quantum® and Qiskit®: `https://medium.com/qiskit/what-is-quantum-volume-anyway-a4dff801c36f`

# Exploring a selected backend using Qiskit®

Exploring backend data visually is a handy but strictly manual process. Sometimes you might want to include backend information in your program logic when running your programs, for example, to select the appropriate backend or dynamically apply your gates on the best qubits. To do this, we can pull this data directly from the available backend information by using Qiskit®.

In this recipe, we will use the `backend.configuration()`, `backend.status()`, and `backend.properties()` methods to retrieve and list the available and operational backends, with some important configuration data such as the number of qubits, the maximum number of experiments you can run, and the number of pending jobs in the queue. We will also dig out some important qubit parameters such as T1, T2, frequency, and readout error for a selected backend.

Okay, let's take a look at how it is done:

1.  Start by importing the IBMQ class and load our account.

2.  Get all available and operational backends.

3.  Fish out and print the backend criteria, such as the name, number of qubits, max number of experiments, and pending jobs to compare.

4.  Select the least busy backend with five qubits.

5.  Print out qubit properties for the selected backend.

You can now take a closer look at the selected properties of the backend and, for example, use this information to decide which backend you want to run your programs on.

## Getting ready

The file required in the following recipe can be downloaded from here: `https://github.com/PacktPublishing/Quantum-Computing-in-Practice-with-Qiskit-and-IBM-Quantum-Experience/blob/master/Chapter05/ch5_r5_explore.py`.

## How to do it...

Depending on the type of quantum program that you are writing, certain aspects of the backend might be important to you, and you might want to include these directly when you code your program. For example, you might be interested in the qubits with the smallest gate errors and readout errors, or if you are running deep circuits, you might be interested in long T1 and T2 times:

1.  Like always, let's start by importing the IBMQ class and load our account:

```
from qiskit import IBMQ
from qiskit.providers.ibmq import least_busy
if not IBMQ.active_account():
    IBMQ.load_account()
provider = IBMQ.get_provider()
```

2.  Get all available backends.

    We will use simple Python scripting to compare the available backends based
    on different criteria – the name, number of qubits, maximum allowed number
    of experiments per day, and number of pending jobs. First, we need a list of the
    available backends:

    ```
    available_backends = provider.backends(operational=True)
    ```

3.  Fish out some backend parameters to compare.

    To find the parameters, we loop through the list and print out four selected
    parameters for each backend – name, n_qubits, max_experiments, and
    pending_jobs:

    ```
    print("{0:20} {1:<10} {2:<10} {3:<10}".format("Name",
        "#Qubits","Max exp.","Pending jobs"))
    print("{0:20} {1:<10} {2:<10} {3:<10}".format("----","---
        ----","--------","------------"))
    for n in range(0, len(available_backends)):
        backend = provider.get_backend(str(
            available_backends[n]))
        print("{0:20} {1:<10} {2:<10} {3:<10}".
            format(backend.name(),
            backend.configuration().n_qubits,
                backend.configuration().
            max_experiments,backend.status().pending_jobs))
    ```

    The preceding code might give the following result:

| Name | #Qubits | Max exp. | Pending jobs |
|------|---------|----------|--------------|
| ibmq_qasm_simulator | 32 | 300 | 0 |
| ibmqx2 | 5 | 75 | 4 |
| ibmq_16_melbourne | 15 | 75 | 9 |
| ibmq_vigo | 5 | 75 | 26 |
| ibmq_ourense | 5 | 75 | 30 |
| ibmq_valencia | 5 | 75 | 31 |
| ibmq_london | 5 | 75 | 7 |
| ibmq_burlington | 5 | 75 | 5 |
| ibmq_essex | 5 | 75 | 6 |
| ibmq_armonk | 1 | 75 | 1 |
| ibmq_santiago | 5 | 75 | 1 |

Figure 5.13 – The available backends with selected parameters displayed

4. Now, we can dig in and take a look at some of the available qubit data for the least busy backend with five qubits, such as the T1 and T2 decoherence values, the frequency, and the readout error for the qubits.

For this exercise, we can write another simple Python `for` loop that prints the properties of the backend's qubits, such as name, value, and unit for the relevant data entry.

We will loop through the number of qubits of the backend (`least_busy_backend.configuration().n_qubits`) and then the number of property parameters for each qubit (`len(least_busy_backend.properties().qubits[0])`):

```
least_busy_backend = least_busy(provider.backends(
    n_qubits=5,operational=True, simulator=False))
print("\nQubit data for backend:",
    least_busy_backend.status().backend_name)
for q in range (0,
    least_busy_backend.configuration().n_qubits):
    print("\nQubit",q,":")
    for n in range (0, len(least_busy_backend.
        properties().qubits[0])):
        print(least_busy_backend.properties().qubits[q]
            [n].name,"=",least_busy_backend.properties().
            qubits[q][n].value,
            least_busy_backend.properties()
            .qubits[q][n].unit)
```

The preceding code should give a result similar to the following:

```
Qubit data for backend: ibmq_santiago

Qubit 0 :
T1 = 155.66702846003767 us
T2 = 213.9817460296015 us
frequency = 4.833428942479864 GHz
anharmonicity = 0 GHz
readout_error = 0.024499999999999966
prob_meas0_prep1 = 0.0316
prob_meas1_prep0 = 0.01739999999999997

Qubit 1 :
T1 = 167.16669714408508 us
T2 = 119.95932781265637 us
frequency = 4.623642178144719 GHz
anharmonicity = 0 GHz
readout_error = 0.012599999999999945
prob_meas0_prep1 = 0.0198
prob_meas1_prep0 = 0.00539999999999996

Qubit 2 :
T1 = 120.82422878269975 us
T2 = 86.8999241784768 us
frequency = 4.820532843939097 GHz
anharmonicity = 0 GHz
readout_error = 0.00869999999999993
prob_meas0_prep1 = 0.012599999999999945
prob_meas1_prep0 = 0.0048

Qubit 3 :
T1 = 158.97337859643895 us
T2 = 136.1602802946587 us
frequency = 4.7423153531828355 GHz
anharmonicity = 0 GHz
readout_error = 0.013700000000000045
prob_meas0_prep1 = 0.017000000000000015
prob_meas1_prep0 = 0.0104

Qubit 4 :
T1 = 119.67022511348239 us
T2 = 149.2204924000382 us
frequency = 4.816323579676691 GHz
anharmonicity = 0 GHz
readout_error = 0.017299999999999982
prob_meas0_prep1 = 0.02839999999999998
prob_meas1_prep0 = 0.0062
```

Figure 5.14 – Qubit details for a selected backend

With that, we all of a sudden know much more about our qubits. They are not just logical entities anymore, but concrete physical objects, albeit physical objects behaving quantum mechanically. In the *Comparing qubits on a chip* recipe of *Chapter 8, Cleaning Up Your Quantum Act with Ignis,* we will take a look at how you can use the backend. properties().gates information in your own programs.

# There's more...

In this recipe, we have looked at a selected subset of backend and qubit properties. With Qiskit®, you can dig out a lot more information by using the following methods:

- `backend.configuration()`

  `backend_name`

  `backend_version`

  `n_qubits`

  `basis_gates`

  `gates`

  `local`

  `simulator`

  `conditional`

  `open_pulse`

  `memory`

  `max_shots`
- `backend.status()`

  `backend_name`

  `backend_version`

  `operational`

  `pending_jobs`

  `status_msg`
- `backend.properties()`

  `backend_name`

  `backend_version`

  `last_update_date`

  `qubits`

  `gates`

  `general`

> **Tip**
>
> To print out the full list of value for each method, use the `to_dict()` parameter. For example: `backend.configuration().to_dict()`

Try to modify the sample code to look up specific parameters such as the following:

- The backend name
- The basis gates available for the backend
- The qubit coupling map that specifies how the individual qubits can communicate
- A list of the gates and their properties for the backend

# 6
# Understanding the Qiskit® Gate Library

In this chapter, we will explore the quantum gates that are offered out of the Qiskit® box. By including a quantum gate library that features the most common gates, Qiskit® makes coding your circuits easy.

Among the gates that we will look at are the Pauli X, Y, and Z gates used for basic qubit flips, the H (or Hadamard) gate used to create qubit superpositions, and the CX (controlled-NOT) gate used to create quantum entanglement. For a quick refresher, take a look at *Chapter 4, Starting at the Ground Level with Terra*.

We will also look at the specialized S and T gates, spin our qubits with R gates, and then show how just a minimal set of U1, U2, U3, ID, and CX basis gates are used to translate the other gates for direct use with a quantum computer.

We will stop by the multi-qubit gates and finally end our tour with a short look beneath the covers to see how the simple gates that we string out in the Qiskit® programs get translated into much more complex sets of basis gates by the transpiler before we can run them on a real quantum computer.

In this chapter, we will cover the following recipes:

- Visualizing quantum gates
- Flipping with the Pauli X, Y, and Z gates

- Creating superpositions with the H gate

- Fixed Z rotations with phase shift gates S, S†, T, and T†

- Free rotation around the axes with Rx, Ry, and Rz

- Building our circuits with the basis gates – U1, U2, U3, and ID

- Using gates on 2 qubits

- Using gates on more than 2 qubits

- What your quantum circuit really looks like

In these recipes, you will be exposed to quantum gate unitary matrixes and qubit state vectors, both of which we discussed mathematically in the *A quick introduction to quantum gates* recipe in *Chapter 2, Quantum Computing and Qubits with Python*. Feel free to jump back and test the math again if needed.

# Technical requirements

The quantum programs that we discuss in this chapter can be found here: https://github.com/PacktPublishing/Quantum-Computing-in-Practice-with-Qiskit-and-IBM-Quantum-Experience/tree/master/Chapter06.

# Visualizing quantum gates

To help us understand quantum gates, we can use the ch6_r1_quantum_gate_ui.py sample program.

This recipe differs a bit from the ones that we have seen so far. Up until now, we have mainly just used Qiskit® commands inside a Python wrapper, with no actual coding beyond that. This time, we start out by building a rudimentary Python implementation to create a very basic *before-after gate exploration UI*. When you run the program, it prompts you to select an initial qubit state and a gate to apply to your qubit; then it creates a visualization to show you the gate action on the qubit.

The script builds your circuit for you and then shows the basic minimum circuit that supports the gate, the state vector, and a Bloch sphere or Q-sphere visualization that corresponds to the gate action. The visualization highlights the qubit's state before the gate, and how the state changes after the gate.

> **Hybrid classical/quantum programs**
>
> So, what we are doing here is building a hybrid classical/quantum program, where we use Python to drive user input control, general logic, and presentation, and the Qiskit® components to access the quantum-related features. This is what we will be doing going forward in the following chapters.

# Getting ready

Before we step into the visualizer, let's spend a second discussing a few basic qubit states that we can initialize our qubit in. You know two of them ($|0\rangle$ and $|1\rangle$) well, but for an understanding of where on the Bloch sphere our qubit state vector points, here's a quick introduction of the rest with their Dirac ket description and a Bloch sphere reference:

- $|0\rangle = |0\rangle$: Straight up along the $z$ axis

- $|1\rangle = |1\rangle$: Straight down along the $z$ axis

- $|+\rangle = \frac{|0\rangle + |1\rangle}{\sqrt{2}}$: Out along the $+ x$ axis

- $|-\rangle = \frac{|0\rangle - |1\rangle}{\sqrt{2}}$: In along the $- x$ axis

- $|R\rangle = \frac{|0\rangle + i|1\rangle}{\sqrt{2}}$: Right along the $+ y$ axis

- $|L\rangle = \frac{|0\rangle - i|1\rangle}{\sqrt{2}}$: Left along the $- y$ axis

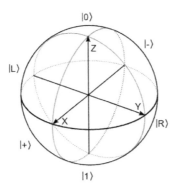

Figure 6.1 – The initial qubit states mapped on the Bloch sphere

In this recipe, we will explore several interesting Qiskit® features:

- **Visualization**: The `qiskit.visualization` class includes various methods to visualize your qubits and your circuits. In this recipe, we will use the following:

  **Bloch sphere**: Displays a single qubit as a Bloch sphere:

  ```
  plot_bloch_multivector(state_vector)
  ```

  **Q-sphere**: Displays 1 or more qubits as a state probability vector on a sphere:

  ```
  plot_state_qsphere(state_vector)
  ```

- **Initialize**: Used to initialize a qubit to specific initial states:

  ```
  circuit.initialize(initial_vector,qubit)
  ```

- **Statevector simulator**: An **Aer** quantum simulator that is used to calculate the state vector of a qubit:

  ```
  Aer.get_backend('statevector_simulator')
  ```

- **Unitary simulator**: An **Aer** quantum simulator that lets you calculate the unitary matrix of a quantum circuit. If you use this simulator on a circuit that contains only a single gate, you can in essence pull out the matrix representation of that quantum gate:

  ```
  Aer.get_backend('unitary_simulator')
  ```

- **QASM input**: To build the circuits, we take a shortcut by creating and importing QASM strings using the `QuantumCircuit.from_qasm_str(qasm_string)` method that we explored in the *Moving between worlds* recipe in *Chapter 3, IBM Quantum® Experience – Drag and Drop Quantum Computing*.

The code for the sample program is available here: `https://github.com/PacktPublishing/Quantum-Computing-in-Practice-with-Qiskit-and-IBM-Quantum-Experience/blob/master/Chapter06/ch6_r1_quantum_gate_ui.py`.

# How to do it...

The sample program is a little convoluted but running it is straightforward. Each step is separated by an input step to select start states and gates, or by a simple *Hit Enter* before the next step rolls along:

1.  Run the `ch6_r1_quantum_gate_ui.py` sample file in your Python environment.

    At the first prompt, enter the starting state for your first qubit. If you pick a gate that uses more than 1 qubit, such as the CX gate, the qubit state that you select here is for the controlling qubit. Your options are the following:

    ```
    Start state:
    0.  |0⟩
    1.  |1⟩
    +.  |+⟩
    -.  |-⟩
    R.  |R⟩
    L.  |L⟩
    r.  Random (a|0⟩ + b|1⟩)
    d.  Define (θ and φ)
    ```

    Figure 6.2 – The first prompt: Select a start state

    The first six options let you pick one of the basic states that we discussed earlier: $|0⟩, |1⟩$, or $\frac{|0⟩ + |1⟩}{\sqrt{2}}, \frac{|0⟩ - |1⟩}{\sqrt{2}}, \frac{|0⟩ + i|1⟩}{\sqrt{2}}$, or $\frac{|0⟩ - i|1⟩}{\sqrt{2}}$. The r option will create a random qubit state, and the d option lets you create your state by entering the two angles **theta** (θ) and **phi** (ψ), which are then used to create the qubit state using the following formula:

    $$|\psi⟩ = \cos\left(\frac{\theta}{2}\right)|0⟩ + e^{i\varphi} \sin\left(\frac{\theta}{2}\right)|1⟩$$

    Note that the angles are in radians. The available start states are defined in the `start_states` list that is defined at the beginning of our program:

    ```
    # List our start states
    start_states=["1","+","-","R","L","r","d"]
    valid_start=["0"]+start_states
    ```

2.  At the second prompt, enter the gate that you want to explore, for example X:

    ```
    Enter a gate:
    Available gates:
     ['id', 'x', 'y', 'z', 't', 'tdg', 's', 'sdg',
    'h', 'rx', 'ry', 'rz', 'u1', 'u2', 'u3', 'cx',
    'cy', 'cz', 'ch', 'swap', 'rx', 'ry', 'rz',
    'u1', 'u2', 'u3']
    ```

    Figure 6.3 – The second prompt: Select a gate

The available gates are printed from the **all gates** list. This list is one of the first things that we define at the beginning of the program to bring order to our gate zoo:

```
# List our gates
rot_gates=["rx","ry","rz"]
unitary_gates=["u1","u2","u3"]
single_gates=["id","x","y","z","t","tdg","s","sdg","h"]
    +rot_gates
oneq_gates=single_gates+unitary_gates
control_gates=["cx","cy","cz","ch"]
twoq_gates=control_gates+["swap"]
all_gates=oneq_gates+twoq_gates+rot_gates+unitary_gates
```

The program now uses the get unitary() function from the sample code on a blank circuit to retrieve and print the unitary matrix for the gate that you selected.

For an X gate, the output will look something like this:

### Unitary for the x gate:

```
[[0.+0.j 1.+0.j]
 [1.+0.j 0.+0.j]]
```

Figure 6.4 – First output: The unitary for the gate

Compare this to the matrix version of the X gate that we calculated in *Chapter 2, Quantum Computing and Qubits with Python*:

$$X: \begin{bmatrix} 0 & 1 \\ 1 & 0 \end{bmatrix}$$

We are now ready for the meat of the program.

3.  Press *Enter* to create the initial setup.

    The program calls the qgate(gate,start) function to set up the circuit based on your input. It uses the gate input with create_circuit(n_qubits,start) to set up a 1-qubit or 2-qubit circuit, and then uses the qgate_out(circuit,start) function to display the empty circuit. At this point, the circuit will only include an initialized qubit set to the starting state you selected, and if the input state is |0⟩, then we do not need to initialize the circuit at all.

The `initialize()` method takes a vector of complex amplitudes and a target qubit as input and adds a circuit instruction that looks much like a gate. The complex amplitudes must be normalized, and in the program, we use the following to create the vector: `[a * complex(1, 0), b * complex(1, 0)]`.

The output should be something like the following:

```
Circuit:
--------

q_0:

State vector:
-------------
[1.+0.j 0.+0.j]
```

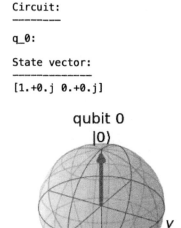

Figure 6.5 – Second output: Initial circuit, state vector, and Bloch-sphere

4.  Press *Enter* again to add the gate you selected and display the end results after the gate.

    The end result of the call to the `qgate(gate,start)` function was to return the complete circuit. We now use the `qgate_out(circuit,start)` function to display the final results, after the gate is applied.

Here is the expected output for an X gate, acting on a qubit initialized to $|0\rangle$:

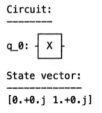

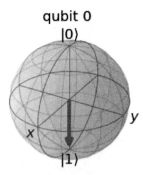

Figure 6.6 – Third output: Circuit, state vector, and Bloch sphere after the gate

The result of the initial run is the qubit started out in the $|0\rangle$ state, pointing straight up, and was then flipped by the X gate to $|1\rangle$, pointing straight down.

## How it works...

In the program, we defined several functions that run the Qiskit® specific functionality of the program:

- get_psi(circuit): This is the same function that we introduced in *Chapter 4, Starting at the Ground Level with Terra*, with a slight twist. Instead of using it to directly plot the Bloch vector, we set it up to return the state vector so that we can use it elsewhere. The function takes as input a quantum circuit and returns the state vector of that circuit by using the statevector_simulator backend that is provided by Qiskit Aer:

```
def get_psi(circuit):
    global psi
    backend = Aer.get_backend('statevector_simulator')
    result = execute(circuit, backend).result()
    psi = result.get_statevector(circuit)
    return(psi)
```

- `get_unitary(circuit)`: This function takes as input a quantum circuit and returns the unitary matrix for that circuit by using the `unitary_simulator` Aer backend:

```
def get_unitary(circuit):
    simulator = Aer.get_backend('unitary_simulator')
    result = execute(circuit, simulator).result()
    unitary = result.get_unitary(circuit)
    return(unitary)
```

- `create_circuit(n_qubits,start)`: This function creates a quantum circuit and initializes it to the start state that you selected.

We start by setting up the start vector based on the user input: 1, +, -, R, L, r, or d:

```
def create_circuit(n_qubits,start):
    if start=="1":
        initial_vector = [0,complex(1,0)]
    elif start=="+":
        # Create |+> state
        initial_vector = [1/sqrt(2) * complex(1, 0),
            1/sqrt(2) * complex(1, 0)]
    elif start=="-":
        # Create |-> state
        initial_vector = [1/sqrt(2) * complex(1, 0),
            -1/sqrt(2) * complex(1, 0)]
    elif start=="R":
        # Create |R> state
        initial_vector = [1/sqrt(2) * complex(1, 0),
            1*1.j/sqrt(2) * complex(1, 0)]
    elif start=="L":
        # Create |L> state
        initial_vector = [1/sqrt(2) * complex(1, 0),
            -1*1.j/sqrt(2) * complex(1, 0)]
    elif start=="r":
        # Create random initial vector
        theta=random.random()*pi
        phi=random.random()*2*pi
        a = cos(theta/2)
        b = cmath.exp(phi*1j)*sin(theta/2)
        initial_vector = [a * complex(1, 0),
            b * complex(1, 0)]
    elif start=="d":
        a = cos(start_theta/2)
        b = cmath.exp(start_phi*1j)*sin(start_theta/2)
```

```
        initial_vector = [a * complex(1, 0),
            b * complex(1, 0)]
    else:
        initial_vector = [complex(1,0),0]
    if start!="n":
        print("\nInitial vector for |"+start+"\u232A:")
        print(np.around(initial_vector, decimals = 3))
```

We then create the circuit for the specified number of qubits and initialize the qubit if the start state is not $|0\rangle$:

```
circuit = QuantumCircuit(n_qubits)
if start in start_states:
    circuit.initialize(initial_vector,n_qubits-1)
return(circuit)
```

- qgate_out(circuit,start): In addition, we use the print functionality with some of the Qiskit® methods to create and save images of our circuits and the Bloch-sphere representations of the qubits:

```
def qgate_out(circuit,start):
    # Print the circuit
    psi=get_psi(circuit)
    if start!="n":
        print("\nCircuit:")
        print("--------")
        print(circuit)
        print("\nState vector:")
        print("------------")
        print(np.around(psi, decimals = 3))
        display(plot_bloch_multivector(psi))
        if circuit.num_qubits>1 and gate
            in control_gates:
            display(plot_state_qsphere(psi))
    return(psi)
```

- qgate(gate,start): This function takes as input a gate and a start state, and then creates a quantum circuit from these. For single-qubit gates, the gate is added to the first qubit, and for 2-qubit gates, the second qubit is the controller qubit and the first qubit is the controlled qubit.

It then compares the input gate to the `oneq_gates` list, and promptly calls the `create_circuit()` function to create a 1-qubit or 2-qubit circuit. At this point, we also create the correct 1-qubit or 2-qubit QASM string that we use to append the selected gate to the circuit using the `from_qasm_str()` method that we started looking at in the *Moving between worlds* recipe in *Chapter 3, IBM Quantum Experience® – Quantum Drag and Drop*. As luck would have it, the QASM code for our gates corresponds one-to-one with the names of the gates. To add an `x` gate, we use the following command:

```
circuit+=QuantumCircuit.from_qasm_str(qasm_string+gate+"
    q[0];")
```

Where the string addition is in the `from_qasm_string()` command:

```
qasm_string+gate+" q[0];"
```

This translates into the following code and appends the `x gate` to the circuit:

```
OPENQASM 2.0; include "qelib1.inc";
qreg q[1];
x q[0];
```

The `qgate()` function then returns the circuit and we can move on:

```
def qgate(gate,start):
    # If the gates require angles, add those to the QASM
    # code
    qasm_angle_gates={"rx":"rx("+str(theta)+") q[0];",
        "ry":"ry("+str(theta)+") q[0];",
        "rz":"rz("+str(phi)+") q[0];",
        "u1":"u1("+str(phi)+") q[0];",
        "u2":"u2("+str(phi)+",
        "+str(lam)+") q[0];",
        "u3":"u3("+str(theta)+",
        "+str(phi)+","+str(lam)+") q[0];"}
    # Create the circuits and then add the gate using
    # QASM import
    if gate in oneq_gates:
        circuit=create_circuit(1,start)
        qasm_string='OPENQASM 2.0; include "qelib1.inc";
            qreg q[1];'
    else:
        circuit=create_circuit(2,start)
        qasm_string='OPENQASM 2.0; include "qelib1.inc";
            qreg q[2];'
    qgate_out(circuit,start)
```

```
        if gate in oneq_gates:
            if gate in rot_gates+unitary_gates:
                circuit+=QuantumCircuit.from_qasm_str(
                    qasm_string+qasm_angle_gates[gate])
            else:
                circuit+=QuantumCircuit.from_qasm_str(
                    qasm_string+gate+" q[0];")
        else:
            circuit+=QuantumCircuit.from_qasm_str(
                qasm_string+gate+" q[1],q[0];")
    return(circuit)
```

So, now you are equipped with a little program that lets you set up very basic one-gate circuits and study the initial and final state vectors, see the unitary matrixes of the selected gates, and view how the gates make the Bloch vector move around, and visualize on a **Q-sphere** where the **Bloch sphere** is no longer enough.

Now take this program for a spin by working your way through the rest of the recipes in this chapter to explore the base set of quantum gates that Qiskit® provides.

## See also

For a quick interactive look at a single-qubit Bloch sphere representation and what certain gate operations do to it, take a look at the **grok-bloch** application by Qiskit Advocate James Weaver: `https://github.com/JavaFXpert/grok-bloch`. You can install and run it from your own Python environment or run it online here: `https://javafxpert.github.io/grok-bloch/`.

# Flipping with the Pauli X, Y, and Z gates

The Pauli X, Y, and Z gates all act on a single qubit, and perform an action similar to a classical NOT gate, which flips the value of a classical bit. For example, the X gate sends $|0\rangle$ to $|1\rangle$ and vice versa.

As we shall see, the X gate is actually a rotation around the $x$ axis of $\pi$ radians. The same is true for the Pauli Y and Z gates, but along the $y$ and $z$ axes correspondingly.

Mathematically, the X, Y, and Z gates can be expressed as the following unitary matrixes:

$$X = \begin{bmatrix} 0 & 1 \\ 1 & 0 \end{bmatrix} Y = \begin{bmatrix} 0 & -i \\ i & 0 \end{bmatrix} Z = \begin{bmatrix} 1 & 0 \\ 0 & -1 \end{bmatrix}$$

This recipe will serve as a sort of template for how to use the sample code that is provided in the chapter. The remaining recipes will largely gloss over the deeper details.

Let's take a look at the Pauli X, Y, and Z gates by running the Quantum Gate UI sample program. It starts by setting up a plain quantum circuit with a single qubit initiated in a state that you select. The gate selected is then added to the circuit, and then the unitary simulator and state vector simulators are run to display the results in the form of a qubit state vector and the gate unitary matrix.

The sample script is available at: `https://github.com/PacktPublishing/ Quantum-Computing-in-Practice-with-Qiskit-and-IBM-Quantum- Experience/blob/master/Chapter06/ch6_r1_quantum_qate_ui.py`.

## How to do it...

1.   Run the `ch6_r1_quantum_gate_ui.py` sample program.

2.   Select a start state for your qubit.

     The X and Y gates work well with $|0\rangle$ and $|1\rangle$, essentially acting as a NOT gate. With $|+\rangle (\frac{|0\rangle + |1\rangle}{\sqrt{2}})$, the X gate will do nothing, but the Y and Z gate will create a phase shift of $\pi$, creating $|-\rangle (\frac{|0\rangle - |1\rangle}{\sqrt{2}})$.

     Also test $|L\rangle$ and $|R\rangle$ to see what they do. If you use the **r (random)** or **d (define)** inputs, then you can explore the gate rotations in more detail.

3.   When prompted, enter x, y, or z to select the gate to test.

     We tested the X gate in the *Visualizing the quantum gates* recipe. Now take a look at the others.

     The Z gate with a random start state might produce the following output:

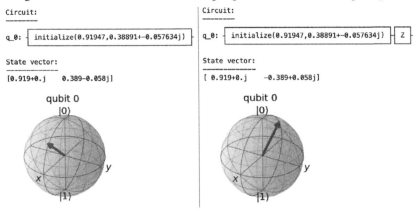

Figure 6.7 – The Z gate with a random start state

## There's more...

The Pauli gates cannot run directly on a quantum backend, but are automatically transpiled to the following unitary basis gates before you run your program:

```
x(qubit) = u3(3.141,0,3.141,qubit)
y(qubit) = u3(3.141,1.571,1.571,qubit)
z(qubit) = u1(3.141,qubit)
```

For more information, see the *Building our circuits with the basis gates – U1,U2, U3, and ID* and *What your quantum circuit really looks like* recipes in this chapter.

# Creating superpositions with the H gate

Now, let's revisit our old friend from *Chapter 4, Starting at the Ground Level with Terra*, the **Hadamard** or **H** gate. This is a fairly specialized gate that we can use to make a generic qubit superposition. But there's more to it than that; we can also make use of the H gate to change the axis of measurement from the generic *z* (or computational) axis to the *x* axis to gain additional insights into the qubit behavior. More on that in the *There's more* section.

The H gate can be expressed as the following unitary matrix:

$$H = \frac{1}{\sqrt{2}}\begin{bmatrix} 1 & 1 \\ 1 & -1 \end{bmatrix}$$

Unless you are really good at interpreting matrix operations, it might not be entirely clear just what this gate will do with your qubits. If we describe the behavior as a combination of 2 qubit rotations instead, things might become clearer. When you apply the Hadamard gate to your qubit, you run it through two rotations: first a $\frac{\pi}{2}$ rotation around the *y* axis, and then a $\pi$ rotation around the *x* axis.

For a qubit in state $|0\rangle$, this means that we start at the North Pole, and then travel down to the equator, ending up at the $|+\rangle$ location on the Bloch sphere, and finally just rotate around the *x* axis. Similarly, if you start at the South Pole at $|1\rangle$, you first move up to the equator but at the other extreme on the *x* axis, ending up at $|-\rangle$.

If we do the matrix math for $|0\rangle$, we get the following:

$$\frac{1}{\sqrt{2}}\begin{bmatrix} 1 & 1 \\ 1 & -1 \end{bmatrix}\begin{bmatrix} 1 \\ 0 \end{bmatrix} = \frac{1}{\sqrt{2}}\begin{bmatrix} 1 \\ 1 \end{bmatrix}$$

Now we can use the following Dirac ket notation:

$$|\psi\rangle = a\,|0\rangle + b|1\rangle$$

$$\text{where, } a = \cos\left(\frac{\theta}{2}\right), b = e^{i\varphi}\sin\left(\frac{\theta}{2}\right)$$

If we replace $a$ and $b$ with $1/\sqrt{2}$ from above, we get: $\theta = \pi/2$ and $\varphi = 0$, which corresponds to $|+\rangle$.

If we apply the Hadamard gate to qubits in states other than pure $|0\rangle$ and $|1\rangle$, we rotate the qubit to a new position.

The sample script is available at: `https://github.com/PacktPublishing/` `Quantum-Computing-in-Practice-with-Qiskit-and-IBM-Quantum-` `Experience/blob/master/Chapter06/ch6_r1_quantum_qate_ui.py`.

## How to do it...

To explore the Hadamard gate, we run the Quantum Gate program that is described in the *Visualizing quantum gates* recipe:

1. Run the `ch6_r1_quantum_gate_ui.py` sample program.

2. Select a start state for your qubit.

   The H gate works well with $|0\rangle$ and $|1\rangle$, placing you on the equator in an equal superposition. With $|+\rangle(\frac{|0\rangle + |1\rangle}{\sqrt{2}})$ and $|-\rangle(\frac{|0\rangle - |1\rangle}{\sqrt{2}})$, the H gate will return the equal superposition to the corresponding computational states, $|0\rangle$ and $|1\rangle$. Try the $|L\rangle$, $|R\rangle$, Random or Define inputs to explore the gate rotations in more detail.

3.  When prompted, enter *h* to select the gate to test. The H gate applied to |0⟩ will produce the following output:

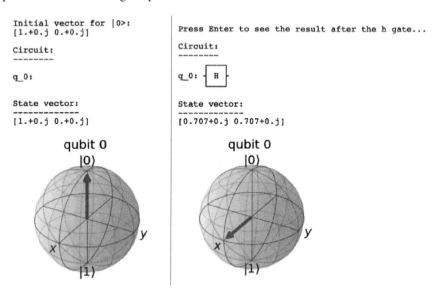

Figure 6.8 – The H gate with |0> start state

## There's more...

The Hadamard gate cannot run directly on a quantum backend, but is automatically transpiled to the following unitary basis gate before you run your program:

```
h(qubit)=u2(0,3.141,qubit)
```

For more information, see the *Building our circuits with the basis gates – U1,U2, U3, and ID* and *What your quantum circuit really looks like* recipes in this chapter.

The Hadamard gate is also commonly used to change your measurement axis from the default (computational) *z* axis to the *x* axis. By measuring in the *x* axis, you can detect the qubit phase.

To figure out the value of the phase, you must add one more measurement, this time along the *y* axis. To achieve this, you use the Hadamard gate in combination with the S dagger gate to shift over to Y.

The way you can visualize the changing of the measurement basis is to picture us rotating the qubit to match up with the axis we want to measure, and then do a standard Z measurement. When we measure along the $x$ axis, we rotate the qubit to face in the $|+\rangle$ direction, and for the $y$ axis to point, in the $|R\rangle$ direction.

Here are the gate combinations that you need to apply to measure along the three Bloch sphere axes:

**Measure along z (computational basis):**

Figure 6.9 - Measure along z

**Measure along x:**

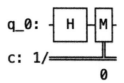

Figure6.10 - Measure along x

**Measure along y:**

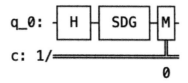

Figure 6.11 - Measure along y

# See also

For an example of measuring along different axes to measure the phase of a qubit, see the *Exploring quantum phase kickback* recipe of *Chapter 9, Grover's Search Algorithm.*

# Fixed z rotations with phase shift gates S, S†, T, and T†

The S, S†, T, and T† gates all perform rotations around the $z$ axis of the qubit. This means that when you measure the qubit, there is no change in the probability of measuring the outcome as 1 or 0. What does change is the phase of the qubit.

> **The S-gate and T-gate are not their own inverses**
>
> As the S and T gates perform set rotations around the $z$ axis, they are not reversible. Adding two of these gates in a row does not negate them. Instead, Qiskit includes the S† and T† gates which serve as the reverse S and T gates. For a quick reminder, see the *A quick introduction to quantum gates* recipe in *Chapter 2, Quantum Computing and Qubits with Python.*

Mathematically, the S and T gates can be expressed as the following unitary matrixes:

$$S = \begin{bmatrix} 1 & 0 \\ 0 & i \end{bmatrix} S^\dagger = \begin{bmatrix} 1 & 0 \\ 0 & -i \end{bmatrix} T = \begin{bmatrix} 1 & 0 \\ 0 & e^{i\frac{\pi}{4}} \end{bmatrix} T^\dagger = \begin{bmatrix} 1 & 0 \\ 0 & e^{-i\frac{\pi}{4}} \end{bmatrix}$$

The sample script is available at: `https://github.com/PacktPublishing/Quantum-Computing-in-Practice-with-Qiskit-and-IBM-Quantum-Experience/blob/master/Chapter06/ch6_r1_quantum_qate_ui.py`.

## How to do it...

To explore the phase shift gates, we run the Quantum Gate UI program that is described in the *Visualizing quantum gates* recipe:

1.  Run the `ch6_r1_quantum_gate_ui.py` sample program.

2.  Select a start state for your qubit.

    As these phase shift gates perform rotations around the $z$ axis, there is very little point in using the default $|0\rangle$ or $|1\rangle$ qubits, which are phaseless. Instead, pick a superposition state qubit such as **+, -, L, R, r,** or **d**.

3.  When prompted, enter s, sdg, t, or tdg to select the gate to test. The S gate on | + ⟩ should produce the following output:

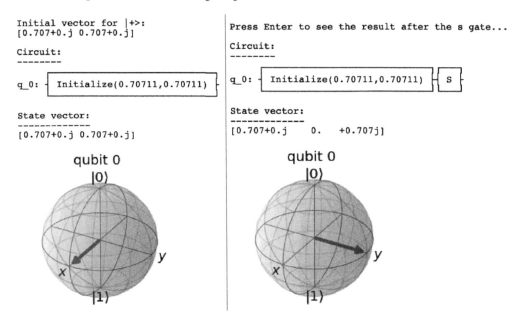

Figure 6.12 – The S gate with the | + ⟩ start state

# There's more...

The phase shift gates cannot run directly on a quantum backend, but are automatically transpiled to the following unitary basis gates before you run your program:

```
s(qubit)   = u1(1.570,qubit)
sdg(qubit) = u1(-1.570,qubit)
t(qubit)   = u1(0.785,qubit)
tdg(qubit) = u1(-0.785,qubit)
```

For more information, see the *Building our circuits with the basis gates – U1, U2, U3, and ID* and *What your quantum circuit really looks like* recipes in this chapter.

# Free rotation around the axes with Rx, Ry, and Rz

While all the phase gates rotate around the $z$ axis to change the phase of the qubit, the rotation gates perform rotations around the respective axes of the Bloch sphere. Rx and Ry rotate the qubit $\theta$ angle at the phase angle ($\varphi$) 0 and $\frac{\pi}{2}$, and Rz rotates around Z, with the special case of $\varphi = \frac{\pi}{4}$ and $\varphi = \frac{\pi}{2}$, corresponding to the S and T gates.

> **The R-gates are not their own inverses**
>
> As the R-gates perform free rotations around the X, Y, or Z axes, they are not reversible. Adding two of these gates in a row does not negate them. For a quick reminder, see the *A quick introduction to quantum gates* recipe in *Chapter 2, Quantum Computing and Qubits with Python*.

Mathematically, the R gates can be expressed as unitary matrixes:

$$Rx = \begin{bmatrix} \cos\frac{\theta}{2} & -i\sin\frac{\theta}{2} \\ -i\sin\frac{\theta}{2} & \cos\frac{\theta}{2} \end{bmatrix}$$

$$Ry = \begin{bmatrix} \cos\frac{\theta}{2} & -\sin\frac{\theta}{2} \\ \sin\frac{\theta}{2} & \cos\frac{\theta}{2} \end{bmatrix}$$

$$Rz = \begin{bmatrix} e^{-i\frac{\varphi}{2}} & 0 \\ 0 & e^{i\frac{\varphi}{2}} \end{bmatrix}$$

The sample script is available at: `https://github.com/PacktPublishing/Quantum-Computing-in-Practice-with-Qiskit-and-IBM-Quantum-Experience/blob/master/Chapter06/ch6_r1_quantum_qate_ui.py`.

## How to do it...

To explore the phase shift gates, we run the Quantum Gate program that is described in the *Visualizing the quantum gates* recipe:

1.  Run the `ch6_r1_quantum_gate_ui.py` sample program.

2.  Select a start state for your qubit.

The R gates perform arbitrary rotations around the corresponding axes.

As all these gates perform rotations around the corresponding axes, play around with $|0\rangle, |1\rangle, |+\rangle, |-\rangle, |L\rangle,$ or $|R\rangle$ to get a feel for what rotates where. Then test with Random or Define to explore more exotic rotations.

3. When prompted, enter rx, ry, or rz to select the gate to test.

4. Enter the angle ($\theta$ or $\varphi$) with which to rotate. The Rx gate, set to $\frac{\pi}{3}$ rotation on $|L\rangle$, should produce the following output:

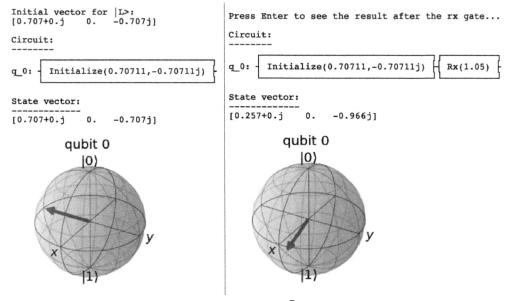

Figure 6.13 – The Rx gate rotating $\frac{\pi}{3}$ with the $|L\rangle$ start state

Now, test again using various rotation angles to see the behavior by entering the following values for the $\theta$ and/or $\varphi$ angles:

$$\pm\pi/3 \text{ (enter } \pm1.0472)$$

$$\pm\pi/4 \text{ (enter } \pm0.7854)$$

$$\pm\pi/2 \text{ (enter } \pm1.5708)$$

## There's more...

The Pauli gates cannot run directly on a quantum backend, but are automatically transpiled to the following unitary basis gates before you run your program:

```
rx(θ,qubit)  = u3(θ,-1.507,1.507,qubit)
ry(θ,qubit)  = u3(θ,0,0,qubit)
rz(φ,qubit)  = u1(φ,qubit)
```

For more information, see the *Building our circuits with the basis gates – U1,U2, U3, and ID* and *What your quantum circuit really looks like* recipes in this chapter.

# Building our circuits with the basis gates – U1, U2, U3, and ID

Let's begin by exploring three of the gates that we recognize from *Chapter 5, Touring the IBM Quantum® Hardware with Qiskit®*. You will not be using these three basis gates, U1, U2, and U3, in your quantum programs. However, they serve as building blocks for all other single-qubit gates when you run your circuits on a quantum computer. In fact, every other single-qubit gate can be written using just the U3 gate. There is nothing explicitly stopping you from using them, but the gate collection that we will go through in the rest of the recipes covers all the ground that we need.

> **The U gates are not their own inverses**
>
> As the U gates perform free rotations around the $x$, $y$, and $z$ axes, they are generally not reversible. Adding two of these gates in a row does not negate them unless the rotations add up to complete rotations. For a quick reminder, see the *A quick introduction to quantum gates* recipe in *Chapter 2, Quantum Computing and Qubits with Python*.

If you remember back when we explored the IBM Quantum® backends in *Chapter 5, Touring the IBM Quantum® Hardware with Qiskit®*, we took a look at the so-called **basis gates** available for the hardware backend using the following command:

```
backend.configuration().basis_gates
```

It returned something like this:

```
['u1', 'u2', 'u3', 'cx', 'id']
```

The CX and ID gates are ordinary gates that you use in your programs, UX (Controlled NOT) to create entanglements, and ID to run a gate that leaves the qubit untouched (more on these later). The U1, U2, and U3 gates are different though.

Remember from *Chapter 2, Quantum Computing and Qubits with Python,* how we can see a quantum gate as a rotation around the θ and φ angles. This is exactly what the U gates do, with one, two, and three inputs respectively. In fact, single-qubit U-gate rotations and CNOT gates constitute a universal gate set for quantum computing. And here, the Id gate is a special case of rotation, with no rotation at all.

The key thing with the basis gates is that you can program your qubits directly on the hardware using them. All other gates are translated into basis gates and then executed as you will see when we discuss the transpiler.

## The U3 gate

The U3 gate is really the Swiss Army knife of quantum gates. It is the foundational unitary matrix for qubit manipulation. Every single-qubit manipulation that can be done can be done with the U3 gate, which can be expressed as the following unitary matrix:

$$U3\,(\theta,\lambda,\phi) = \begin{bmatrix} \cos\left(\dfrac{\theta}{2}\right) & -e^{i\phi}\sin\left(\dfrac{\theta}{2}\right) \\ e^{i\lambda}\sin\left(\dfrac{\theta}{2}\right) & e^{i(\lambda+\phi)}\cos\left(\dfrac{\theta}{2}\right) \end{bmatrix}$$

The three angles are as follows:

- $\theta$ = The polar angle between $|0\rangle$ and the state vector
- $\phi$ = The longitudinal angle from the $x$ axis $(|+\rangle)$
- $\lambda$ = The overall qubit phase angle (not visible on the Bloch sphere)

The U2 and U1 gates are basically specializations of U3, just like the other quantum gates are specializations of the U gates in general.

## The U2 gate

With the U2 gate, you can manipulate two angles at the same time. The U2 gate is the same as the U3 gate with $\theta = \dfrac{\pi}{2}$.

The U2 gate can be expressed as the following unitary matrix:

$$U2\,(\lambda, \phi) = U3\left(\frac{\pi}{2}, \lambda, \phi\right) = \frac{1}{\sqrt{2}}\begin{bmatrix} 1 & e^{-i\phi} \\ e^{i\phi} & e^{i(\lambda+\phi)} \end{bmatrix}$$

## The U1 gate

With the U1 gate, you can rotate the phase of the qubit around the $z$ axis. A special case of the U1 is the Rz gate, which has the same input. The U1 gate is the same as the U3 gate with $\theta = 0$ and $\lambda = 0$.

The U1 gate can be expressed as the following unitary matrix:

$$U1(\phi) = U3\,(0, 0, \phi) = \begin{bmatrix} 1 & 0 \\ 0 & e^{i\phi} \end{bmatrix}$$

With these three gates, you can perform all possible single-qubit manipulations. They are not that user-friendly to read through and therefore Qiskit® includes translations of all relevant quantum gates for your programming ease. When you run your circuits, however, all the gates are translated into the collection of basis gates supported by the selected backend.

The Pauli Id gate is a special gate that leaves the qubit in the same state as it was found. The gate can be expressed using the following matrix:

$$Id = \begin{bmatrix} 1 & 0 \\ 0 & 1 \end{bmatrix} = U3\,(0, 0, 0).$$

## Getting ready

The code for the sample program is available here: `https://github.com/PacktPublishing/Quantum-Computing-in-Practice-with-Qiskit-and-IBM-Quantum-Experience/blob/master/Chapter06/ch6_r2_u_animation.py`.

In this recipe, we use the Pillow package to create, save, and merge images. For more information about Pillow, see `https://pypi.org/project/Pillow/`.

> **Installing Pillow**
>
> If you need to install Pillow in your environment, you can use the following commands:
>
> ```
> (environment_name) … $  pip install --upgrade pip
>
> (environment_name) … $  pip install --upgrade
> Pillow
> ```

# How to do it...

In this recipe, we will visualize the rotations of the U gates on a Bloch sphere. As you already know, we can use the `plot_bloch_multivector()` and `plot_state_qsphere()` methods to visualize how our state vectors behave and what the possible outcomes are. These both provide static views of the qubit at one moment and of the U gates for a specific set of angles.

In the sample program, you enter the angles input for your U gates, after which the program takes snapshots between 0 and the angle at a given resolution and produces an animated GIF that shows the movement of the qubit state vector on the Bloch sphere.

Note that this animation doesn't really show you how a qubit vector moves when you apply the gate, but rather gives a view of how you can use the U gates to position your qubit state vector wherever you want:

1.  Start by running the `ch6_r2_u_animation.py` script in your Python environment.

2.  At the prompts, enter the type of gate that you want to test, and then enter the required input angles for the gate. For the U3 gate, your input might look like this for $\theta = \frac{\pi}{2}, \phi = \pi,$ and $\lambda = 0$:

```
Animating the U gates
---------------------
Enter u3, u2, or u3:
u3
Enter θ:
1.57
Enter φ:
3.14
Enter λ:
0
Building animation...
```

In the background, we are now calling the `create_images()` function, which takes the input you provided and then iteratively creates a set of circuits that iteratively apply the U gate you selected with the input angles divided into smaller angles as dictated by the *steps* parameter. Each circuit is then run through the statevector simulator in the `get_psi()` function that we created in the first recipe, *Visualizing the quantum gates*, and is finally saved as a Bloch sphere image and a Q-sphere image using `plot_bloch_multivector()` and `plot_state_qsphere()`. The images are continuously appended to two lists that will later be merged into an animation.

Here's how we build the function.

Start by setting the input parameters and all internal function variables:

```
def create_images(gate,theta=0.0,phi=0.0,lam=0.0):
    steps=20.0
    theta_steps=theta/steps
    phi_steps=phi/steps
    lam_steps=lam/steps
    n, theta,phi,lam=0,0.0,0.0,0.0
```

Then create the image and animation tools:

```
global q_images, b_images, q_filename, b_filename
b_images=[]
q_images=[]
b_filename="animated_qubit"
q_filename="animated_qsphere"
```

Finally, run the image creation loop based on the input parameters:

```
while n < steps+1:
    qc=QuantumCircuit(1)
    if gate=="u3":
        qc.u3(theta,phi,lam,0)
        title="U3: \u03B8 = "+str(round(theta,2))+"
            \u03D5 = "+str(round(phi,2))+" \u03BB =
            "+str(round(lam,2))
    elif gate=="u2":
        qc.u2(phi,lam,0)
        title="U2: \u03D5 = "+str(round(phi,2))+"
            \u03BB = "+str(round(lam,2))
    else:
        qc.h(0)
        qc.u1(phi,0)
        title="U1: \u03D5 = "+str(round(phi,2))
```

```
# Get the statevector of the qubit
# Create Bloch sphere images
plot_bloch_multivector(get_psi(qc),title).
    savefig('images/bloch'+str(n)+'.png')
imb = Image.open('images/bloch'+str(n)+'.png')
b_images.append(imb)
# Create Q-sphere images
plot_state_qsphere(psi).savefig(
    'images/qsphere'+str(n)+'.png')
imq = Image.open('images/qsphere'+str(n)+'.png')
q_images.append(imq)
# Rev our loop
n+=1
theta+=theta_steps
phi+=phi_steps
lam+=lam_steps
```

3.  Create and save the animated GIFs.

    The final step is to create the GIFs. Here we use the `save_gif(gate)` function to iterate through the image lists we created and let Pillow build the GIFs with our initial parameters. This is what we do:

```
def save_gif(gate):
    duration=100
    b_images[0].save(gate+'_'+b_filename+'.gif',
            save_all=True,
            append_images=b_images[1:],
            duration=duration,
            loop=0)
    q_images[0].save(gate+'_'+q_filename+'.gif',
            save_all=True,
            append_images=q_images[1:],
            duration=duration,
            loop=0)
    print("Bloch sphere animation saved as: \n"+os.
        getcwd()+"/"+gate+"_"+b_filename+".
        gif"+"\nQsphere animation saved as: \n"+os.
        getcwd()+"/"+gate+"_"+q_filename+".gif")
```

The final Python output might look like this:

```
Bloch sphere animation saved as:
/<path_to_your_directory>/ch6/Recipes/u3_animated_qubit.
```

```
gif
Qsphere animation saved as:
/<path_to_your_directory>/ch6/Recipes/u3_animated_
qsphere.gif
```

4.  The final result will be two animated GIFs saved in the same directory as where you run your script.

    You can now open the GIFs in an image viewer or web browser to take a look:

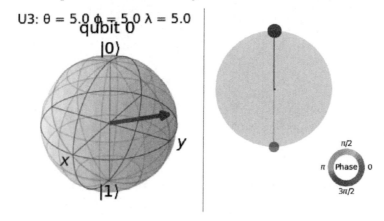

Figure 6.14 – Still of animated GIFs of a Bloch sphere and a Q-sphere

If you view the animated GIFs side by side and synchronized, the Q-sphere representation shows the relative probabilities and phase angle of the qubit as the U gate is applied to it. Play around with different angles and different loop parameters to see how you can make the animations work for you.

If you set the angles in the range of 0 to $2\pi$ and set your steps to a reasonably high number, you can create nice smooth looping effects. There is nothing stopping you from setting the angles really high though, which will result in fairly chaotic behavior in the animations. Have fun!

When you test the U gates with the script, remember the following:

-   U3 lets you point the qubit vector anywhere on the Bloch sphere using two angles, $\theta$ and $\phi$. The third angle, $\lambda$, has no effect on the Bloch sphere representation.

-   U2 is the same as U3 but with $\theta$ set to $\frac{\pi}{2}$, which places the qubit vector on the equator.

-   U1 is the same as U3 but with both $\theta$ and $\lambda$ set to 0. A special case of U1 is Rz.

# There's more...

Well, in this case, there's less not more. The sample script in this recipe will work in your local environment, but not very well in your IBM Quantum Experience® notebook environment as you do not have access to the underlying filesystem.

# Using gates on 2 qubits

Two-qubit gates such as controlled gates are slightly different from ordinary 1-qubit gates; they let you create interaction between your qubits. In general, this translates into using 1 qubit as the control qubit, and the other as the acted-on qubit. Mathematically, this is not super complex, but intuitively you might have to think once or twice about what is going on.

## Getting ready

The first 2-qubit gate that we'll touch on is the Controlled-NOT gate that we saw in *Chapter 4, Starting at the Ground Level with Terra*. The CX gate is generally used to create entanglement between qubits if the control qubit is in a superposition.

A CX gate where the controlling qubit is the second qubit and the controlled qubit the first can be expressed as the following matrix:

$$CX = \begin{bmatrix} 1 & 0 & 0 & 0 \\ 0 & 1 & 0 & 0 \\ 0 & 0 & 0 & 1 \\ 0 & 0 & 1 & 0 \end{bmatrix}$$

This corresponds to the following circuit:

Figure 6.15 – CX gate from q_1 to q_0

The way you interpret this is to run the first or controlling qubit through an Id gate, leaving it untouched. The second, or controlled, qubit applies an X gate if the first qubit is 1.

Here are two matrix calculations to demonstrate:

$$\begin{bmatrix} 1 & 0 & 0 & 0 \\ 0 & 1 & 0 & 0 \\ 0 & 0 & 0 & 1 \\ 0 & 0 & 1 & 0 \end{bmatrix} \begin{bmatrix} 0 \\ 0 \\ 1 \\ 0 \end{bmatrix} = \begin{bmatrix} 0 \\ 0 \\ 0 \\ 1 \end{bmatrix}$$

Here, the first qubit is 1 and the second 0. The result is both qubits in 1:

$$\begin{bmatrix} 1 & 0 & 0 & 0 \\ 0 & 1 & 0 & 0 \\ 0 & 0 & 0 & 1 \\ 0 & 0 & 1 & 0 \end{bmatrix} \begin{bmatrix} 0 \\ 0 \\ 0 \\ 1 \end{bmatrix} = \begin{bmatrix} 0 \\ 0 \\ 1 \\ 0 \end{bmatrix}$$

Here, both qubits are 1. The result is the first qubit is 1 and the second is 0.

The CX gate is one of the basis gates of the IBM Quantum® backends.

> **Other CX matrices**
>
> If the CX gate points the other way, with the first qubit as the controlling qubit, the matrix will look like this instead:
>
> $$CX = \begin{bmatrix} 1 & 0 & 0 & 0 \\ 0 & 0 & 0 & 1 \\ 0 & 0 & 1 & 0 \\ 0 & 1 & 0 & 0 \end{bmatrix}$$
>
> To convince yourself, do the calculation. For a quick refresher, see the *A quick introduction to quantum gates* recipe in *Chapter 2, Quantum Computing and Qubits with Python.*

The sample script is available at: `https://github.com/PacktPublishing/Quantum-Computing-in-Practice-with-Qiskit-and-IBM-Quantum-Experience/blob/master/Chapter06/ch6_r1_quantum_gate_ui.py`.

## How to do it...

Earlier, for the single-qubit gates, the Quantum Gate program set up a plain quantum circuit with one qubit initiated in the ground state $|0\rangle$. When we start playing with multi-qubit gates, the program will initialize with both qubits in $|0\rangle$. The gate selected is then run on the circuit, and results in the form of a qubit state vector and the gate unitary matrix are displayed.

To explore the control gates, we run the Quantum Gate program that is described in the *Visualizing quantum gates* recipe:

1.  Run the ch6_r1_quantum_gate_ui.py sample program.

2.  Select a start state for your controlling qubit.

    The Cn gates use a single qubit as the controlling qubit and the other qubit as the controlled qubit. If the state of the controlling qubit is anything other than |0⟩, some action will be performed on the controlled qubit.

    If you want to, then you can start by testing with |0⟩—just to verify that no action is performed and that the 2-qubit state doesn't change. Then test with start state |1⟩ to create a Bell state, as we did in *Chapter 4*, *Starting at the Ground Level with Terra*. After you are done with this, play around with | + ⟩, | − ⟩, |L⟩, |R⟩, Random or Define to explore other control states.

3.  When prompted, enter cx, cy, cz, or ch to select the gate to test. For example, a CX gate with the controlling qubit state | + ⟩ will generate the following output:

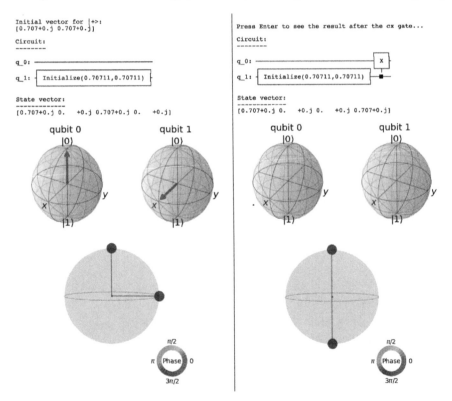

Figure 6.16 – CX gate with the start state |+>

Here, notice that the Bloch sphere representation makes no sense after the CX gate has been applied. The qubits are now entangled, and we can get no further individual information from them. In this case, we display the Q-sphere interpretation for clarification, where the initial Q-sphere indicates equal probabilities of getting states $|00\rangle$ and $|01\rangle$, and after the X gate, equal probabilities of getting $|00\rangle$ and $|11\rangle$, as expected for a Bell state.

## How it works...

The CX gate is just one of many possible two-qubit control gates. Among the others built into Qiskit® are the CY and CZ gates:

$$CY = \begin{bmatrix} 1 & 0 & 0 & 0 \\ 0 & 1 & 0 & 0 \\ 0 & 0 & 0 & -i \\ 0 & 0 & i & 0 \end{bmatrix}$$

$$CZ = \begin{bmatrix} 1 & 0 & 0 & 0 \\ 0 & 1 & 0 & 0 \\ 0 & 0 & 1 & 0 \\ 0 & 0 & 0 & -1 \end{bmatrix}$$

Or why not a controlled Hadamard gate?

$$CH = \begin{bmatrix} 1 & 0 & 0 & 0 \\ 0 & 1 & 0 & 0 \\ 0 & 0 & \frac{1}{\sqrt{2}} & \frac{1}{\sqrt{2}} \\ 0 & 0 & \frac{1}{\sqrt{2}} & -\frac{1}{\sqrt{2}} \end{bmatrix}$$

Another handy 2-qubit gate is the SWAP gate that swaps the value of the first and second qubit. In this case, there is no entanglement and the individual qubits remain individuals:

$$SWAP = \begin{bmatrix} 1 & 0 & 0 & 0 \\ 0 & 0 & 1 & 0 \\ 0 & 1 & 0 & 0 \\ 0 & 0 & 0 & 1 \end{bmatrix}$$

## There's more...

The two-qubit gates can also be written as a combination of basis gates. For example, this is how you can code the CY gate:

```
qc.u1(-1.507,0)
qc.cx(1,0)
qc.u1(1.507,0)
```

For more information, and to test-transpile the other Cn gates, see the *What your quantum circuit really looks like* recipe.

## See also

*Quantum Computation and Quantum Information*, 10th Anniversary Edition, Michael A. Nielsen & Isaac L. Chuang, *Chapter 4.3 Controlled operations*.

# Using gates on more than 2 qubits

In addition to the single-qubit and two-qubit gates, Qiskit® also supports 3- and more qubit gates. We will use one of them, the Toffoli gate when we build the 3-qubit Grover search algorithm circuit in *Chapter 9, Grover's Search Algorithm*. We are including the Fredkin gate for completeness and will not be using it in any other examples; feel free to try it out.

The multi-qubit gates in this recipe use 2, more, and 1 controlling qubit respectively:

- **Toffoli**: Controlled-controlled NOT (**CCX**), which takes 2 qubits as input and flips the third if both controlling qubits are set.

- **MCX**: Multi-controlled NOT takes a number of qubits (controlling) as input and flips the controlled qubit if all are set.

  There is (in principle) no limit to the number of controlling qubits that you can use with your gates. In the 4- and more qubit Grover search algorithm circuit in *Chapter 9, Grover's Search Algorithm*, we build a 4-qubit **CCCX controlled-controlled-controlled** gate by using the **MCX** gate.

- **Fredkin**: Controlled SWAP, (**CSWAP**), which takes a single qubit as input and swaps the other two if the controlling qubit is set.

## How to do it...

In your quantum programs, use the following sample code to implement these 3-qubit gates.

## Toffoli

The Toffoli or **CCX** gate is represented by the following unitary matrix with the second and third qubits controlling the first qubit:

$$CCX = \begin{bmatrix} 1 & 0 & 0 & 0 & 0 & 0 & 0 & 0 \\ 0 & 1 & 0 & 0 & 0 & 0 & 0 & 0 \\ 0 & 0 & 1 & 0 & 0 & 0 & 0 & 0 \\ 0 & 0 & 0 & 1 & 0 & 0 & 0 & 0 \\ 0 & 0 & 0 & 0 & 1 & 0 & 0 & 0 \\ 0 & 0 & 0 & 0 & 0 & 1 & 0 & 0 \\ 0 & 0 & 0 & 0 & 0 & 0 & 0 & 1 \\ 0 & 0 & 0 & 0 & 0 & 0 & 1 & 0 \end{bmatrix}$$

The following code implements the CCX gate:

```
from qiskit import QuantumCircuit
qc=QuantumCircuit(3)
qc.ccx(2,1,0)
print(qc)
```

And the circuit looks like this:

Figure 6.17 – The Toffoli gate

---

**Other CCX matrixes**

Just like for the CX gate, the matrix will look different depending on which qubits you should use to control. For example, here is the matrix for a CCX gate where the first and second qubits control the third:

$$CCX_{0,1,2} = \begin{bmatrix} 1 & 0 & 0 & 0 & 0 & 0 & 0 & 0 \\ 0 & 1 & 0 & 0 & 0 & 0 & 0 & 0 \\ 0 & 0 & 1 & 0 & 0 & 0 & 0 & 0 \\ 0 & 0 & 0 & 0 & 0 & 0 & 0 & 1 \\ 0 & 0 & 0 & 0 & 1 & 0 & 0 & 0 \\ 0 & 0 & 0 & 0 & 0 & 1 & 0 & 0 \\ 0 & 0 & 0 & 0 & 0 & 0 & 1 & 0 \\ 0 & 0 & 0 & 1 & 0 & 0 & 0 & 0 \end{bmatrix}$$

To convince yourself, do the calculation.

---

## MCX

The MCX gate is used to build general controlled-NOT gates with more than one controlling gate. The Toffoli (CCX) gate is a special example where this is an already coded gate. For controlled-NOT gates with more than 2 controlling qubits, you can use the MCX gate.

The following code implements the MCX gate as a CCCX gate with second, third, and fourth qubits controlling the first qubit:

```
from qiskit import QuantumCircuit
qc=QuantumCircuit(4)
qc.mcx([1,2,3],0)
print(qc)
```

And the circuit looks like this:

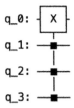

Figure 6.18 – The MCX gate for 3 controlling qubits (CCCX)

## Fredkin

The Fredkin or **CSWAP** gate is represented by the following unitary matrix with the controlling third qubit swapping the first and second qubits:

$$CSWAP = \begin{bmatrix} 1 & 0 & 0 & 0 & 0 & 0 & 0 & 0 \\ 0 & 1 & 0 & 0 & 0 & 0 & 0 & 0 \\ 0 & 0 & 1 & 0 & 0 & 0 & 0 & 0 \\ 0 & 0 & 0 & 1 & 0 & 0 & 0 & 0 \\ 0 & 0 & 0 & 0 & 1 & 0 & 0 & 0 \\ 0 & 0 & 0 & 0 & 0 & 0 & 1 & 0 \\ 0 & 0 & 0 & 0 & 0 & 1 & 0 & 0 \\ 0 & 0 & 0 & 0 & 0 & 0 & 0 & 1 \end{bmatrix}$$

The following code implements the CSWAP gate:

```
from qiskit import QuantumCircuit
qc=QuantumCircuit(3)
qc.cswap(2,1,0)
print(qc)
```

And the circuit looks like this:

Figure 6.19 – The Fredkin gate

## There's more...

Just like the other gates that we have looked at in this chapter, the Toffoli and Fredkin gates are included with the basic set of Qiskit® gates. However, they are not basis gates, which means that they need to be rewritten using a set of basis gates, such as **u1**, **u2**, **u3**, **id**, and **cx**. This is called **transpiling** and is what we will be doing in the next recipe, *What your quantum circuit really looks like*. But we're jumping ahead just a little here and displaying the complexity of constructing these alluringly simple gates. Do try them out in the next recipe.

## Toffoli constructed from basis gates

The Toffoli gate can be entered as a single gate in Qiskit®, which leads you to believe that the execution of the gate will correspond to *a single time step* just like the other gates:

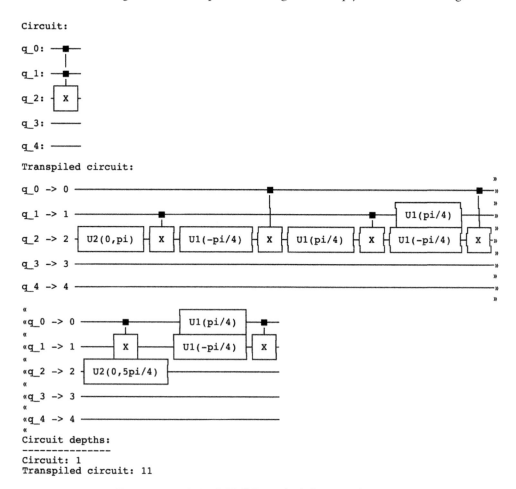

Figure 6.20 – A single Toffoli gate built from 10+ basis gates

When we unravel the CCX like this, we see that the truth is slightly worse than just one time step; the single gate is translated into a circuit depth of 11.

## Fredkin constructed from basis gates

Much like the Toffoli gate, Fredkin might be transpiled into a large number of basis gates when executed on a hardware backend:

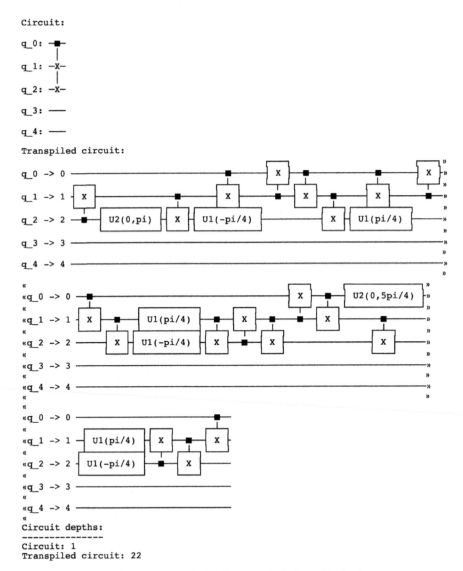

Figure 6.21 – A single Fredkin gate built from 20+ basis gates

For a single Fredkin gate, the circuit depth goes from 1 to 22. Not everything is easy to do on a quantum computer.

# What your quantum circuit really looks like

In *Chapter 3, IBM Quantum Experience® – Quantum Drag and Drop*, and *Chapter 5, Touring the IBM Quantum® Hardware with Qiskit®*, we touched on the concept of **transpiling**, and the fact that a physical quantum computer cannot natively run all the various quantum gates that we throw at it. Instead, each backend comes with a set of basis gates, such as u1, u2, u3, id, and cx. We discussed these gates in the previous recipes of this chapter and even listed how the other gates can be written as implementations or combinations of these.

In this recipe, we will take a look at some other aspects of the transpiling of circuits, such as the following:

- Simple transpiling of common gates to basis gates

- Transpiling for a simulator

- Transpiling your circuit if it doesn't match the physical layout of the backend

> **One-qubit backend basis gates**
>
> Most IBM Quantum® backends have the following basis gates: u1, u2, u3, id, and cx. One-qubit backends such as ibmq_armonk have no use for multi-qubit gates such as CX, which is not included. If you set your backend to ibmq_armonk and run the following command, you will get the corresponding output:
> ```
> >>> backend.configuration().basis_gates
> Out: ['id', 'u1', 'u2', 'u3'].
> ```

When we execute a quantum program on an IBM quantum computer, our code is first transpiled down to the core basis gates (u1, u2, u3, id, and cx) that we can execute directly on the hardware.

## Getting ready

The file required in the following recipe can be downloaded from here: https://github.com/PacktPublishing/Quantum-Computing-in-Practice-with-Qiskit-and-IBM-Quantum-Experience/blob/master/Chapter06/ch6_r3_transpiler.py.

This is how we build our Python sample:

1. First, we import the needed classes and methods, including `transpile`:

```
from qiskit import QuantumCircuit, IBMQ
from qiskit.compiler import transpile
from qiskit.providers.ibmq import least_busy
```

We also load our account, if needed, and set up a backend with 5 qubits:

```
if not IBMQ.active_account():
    IBMQ.load_account()
provider = IBMQ.get_provider()
backend = least_busy(provider.backends(n_qubits=5,
    operational=True, simulator=False))
```

2. Let's take a look at the basis gates and coupling map for the selected backend. The coupling map specifies the possible qubit connections for two-qubit circuits:

```
print("Basis gates for:", backend)
print(backend.configuration().basis_gates)
print("Coupling map for:", backend)
print(backend.configuration().coupling_map)
```

The preceding code should result in an output similar to the following:

```
Basis gates for: ibmqx2
['id', 'u1', 'u2', 'u3', 'cx']
Coupling map for: ibmqx2
[[0, 1], [0, 2], [1, 0], [1, 2], [2, 0], [2, 1], [2, 3],
 [2, 4], [3, 2], [3, 4], [4, 2], [4, 3]]
```

Figure 6.22 – Basis gates and CX coupling map for a backend

For a single qubit gates transpiling, the coupling map is not important. This changes when we write quantum programs that use two-qubit gates.

3. We then set up the `build_circuit()` function to create a basic circuit, and selectively add gates to it depending on what circuit we want to explore:

```
def build_circuit(choice):
    # Create the circuit
    qc = QuantumCircuit(5,5)

    if choice=="1":
        # Simple X
        qc.x(0)
    elif choice=="2":
```

```
        # H + Barrier
        #'''
        qc.x(0)
        qc.barrier(0)
        qc.h(0)
    elif choice=="3":
        # Controlled Y (CY)
        qc.cy(0,1)
    elif choice=="4":
        # Non-conforming CX
        qc.cx(0,4)
    else:
        # Multi qubit circuit
        qc.h(0)
        qc.h(3)
        qc.cx(0,4)
        qc.cswap(3,1,2)

    # Show measurement targets
    #qc.barrier([0,1,2,3,4])
    #qc.measure([0,1,2,3,4],[0,1,2,3,4])

    return(qc)
```

4.  Finally, we set up the `main()` function to run the circuit.

The main function prompts for a circuit to test, calls the `build_circuit()` function, transpiles the returned circuit using the `transpile()` class, and then displays the results:

```
def main():
    choice="1"
    while choice !="0":
        choice=input("Pick a circuit: 1. Simple,
            2. H + Barrier, 3. Controlled-Y,
            4. Non-conforming CX, 5. Multi\n")
        qc=build_circuit(choice)
        trans_qc = transpile(qc, backend)
        print("Circuit:")
        display(qc.draw())
        print("Transpiled circuit:")
        display(trans_qc.draw())
        print("Circuit depth:")
        print("---------------")
```

```
print("Circuit:", qc.depth())
print("Transpiled circuit:", trans_qc.depth())
print("\nCircuit size:")
print("---------------")
print("Circuit:", qc.size())
print("Transpiled circuit:", trans_qc.size())


if __name__ == '__main__':
    main()
```

## How to do it...

Let's build and transpile a simple X circuit:

1.  In your Python environment, run ch6_r3_transpiler.py.

2.  When prompted, enter 1 to pick the Simple X circuit:

```
Ch 6: Transpiling circuits
--------------------------
Basis gates for: ibmq_ourense
['id', 'u1', 'u2', 'u3', 'cx']
Coupling map for: ibmq_ourense
[[0, 1], [1, 0], [1, 2], [1, 3], [2, 1], [3, 1], [3, 4], [4, 3]]

Pick a circuit:
1. Simple X
2. Add H
3. H + Barrier
4. Controlled-Y
5. Non-conforming CX
6. Multi-gate
```

Figure 6.23 – First, select the Simple X circuit

3.  The code should result in an output similar to this:

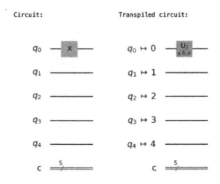

Figure 6.24 – The output of the simple, single X gate circuit

The resulting circuit looks pretty similar. The only real change is that the X gate is now a U3 gate, one of the basis gates.

4. We can get a numerical result as well, by pulling out the circuit depths and sizes for the circuit and the transpiled circuit.

This code should result in the following circuit depths and sizes:

```
Circuit depth:
----------------
Circuit: 1
Transpiled circuit: 1

Circuit size:
----------------
Circuit: 1
Transpiled circuit: 1
```

Figure 6.25 – Circuit depth and size

Here, depth means the number of end-to-end steps that the quantum computer has to execute. Each step might include one or more gates, depending on the layout of the circuit. The size is just the total number of gates that are executed.

For this very simple circuit transpiling, there isn't much of a change. The U3 gate performs the required rotation around the $x$ axis, and the circuit depth and size are the same. Technically, you could use the U3 gate instead of the X gate in your code, but it would be much less transparent.

---

**Transpiling for a simulator?**

So, what happens if you try transpiling your circuits for a simulator backend? As it turns out, the simulator includes many more basis gates than the hardware backends, so the transpiling will be different. To test this, simply uncomment the following line in the script to set the backend to a simulator and run the program again:

```
backend = provider.get_backend('ibmq_qasm_
simulator')
```

The `ibmq_qasm_simulator` supports the following basis gates:

```
['u1', 'u2', 'u3', 'cx', 'cz', 'id', 'x', 'y',
'z', 'h', 's', 'sdg', 't', 'tdg', 'ccx', 'swap',
'unitary', 'initialize', 'kraus']
```

That said, you can provide additional parameters when running the transpiler, such as `basis_gates` and `coupling_map` to define the basis gates that you want to use and specify how the qubits are connected for use when transpiling for multi-qubit gates. We will not go into any details about that in this chapter, but take a look at the Qiskit® help for more info:

```
>>> from qiskit.compiler import transpile

>>> help(transpile)
```

Now take a look at the *There's more* section for a short showcase of how things can get much more complicated, quickly.

## There's more...

This quick recipe gave a quick taste of what the transpiler does for a very simple quantum program, and illustrated how the transpiler translates your generic circuits into circuits that can be directly executed on the quantum chip.

The following quick examples illustrate the complexities that might befall the poor transpiler if you ask it to build circuits that do not at all match the physical layout of the backend. You can test these circuits in the sample code to see if you get similar results.

Test the following inputs when running the sample code:

### Adding H and H + Barrier – Multiple gates and the barrier circuit element

The transpiling of one gate doesn't leave the transpiler with a lot to do, but as soon as you add more gates, things quickly get more complex. Remember that quantum gates generically are rotations around the three axes $x$, $y$, and $z$. If two gates are added in a row, the transpiler seeks to simplify the circuit (and thus make it shorter; less deep) by combining multiple gates into single basis gate.

In the sample code, we extended the quantum circuit by adding a Hadamard gate after the X gate:

```
# Add H
qc.x(0)
qc.h(0)
```

When you run the circuit now, you should see something like this:

Circuit:

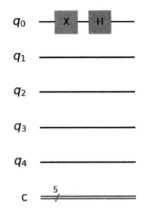

Transpiled circuit:

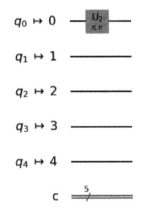

```
Circuit depth:
----------------
Circuit: 2
Transpiled circuit: 1

Circuit size:
----------------
Circuit: 2
Transpiled circuit: 1
```

Figure 6.26 – Simplified transpiled circuit

As you can see, the transpiler combined the two gates into one, simplifying and shortening the circuit by looking ahead at what the gate combination would result in, and coding that as a U gate. However, it is not always that you want this simplification. For example, as we saw in the *A quick introduction to quantum gates* recipe in *Chapter 2, Quantum Computing and Qubits with Python*, two identical quantum gates in a row might effectively cancel each other out. In some instances, a quantum circuit will end up being constructed out of repeating gates, and if those repeating gates are removed, the circuit will not work as expected.

The solution is the `barrier()` circuit component, which stops the transpiler from simplifying by combining gates. By using the *H + Barrier* option, we add a barrier between the X and H gates like this:

```
# H + Barrier
qc.x(0)
qc.barrier(0)
qc.h(0)
```

When you use the *H + Barrier* option, you should see something similar to this:

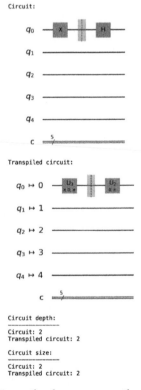

Figure 6.27 – Transpiler does not transpile past the barriers

The gates are now transpiled one by one, and the circuit depth is retained. So, no problem there, right? Well, these were pretty simple gates. What happens when we complicate our circuit a bit? Take a look at the next section.

## Controlled Y

The **controlled X gate (CX)** is a basis gate for the IBM Quantum® backends, but the **controlled Y (CY)** is not. To create a CY gate that can run on the backend, the transpiler adds some additional basis gates.

By using the *Controlled-Y* option, we add a `cy()` gate like this:

```
# Controlled Y (CY)
qc.cy(0,1)
```

To create a CY gate that can run on the backend, the transpiler adds some additional basis gates:

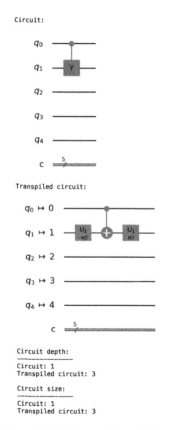

Figure 6.28 – Transpiling a CY gate

Here we have the transpiler do a quick trick, adding Z rotations before and after the X in the CX gate. If the control qubit is 0, we will just get a rotation back and forth around the z axis. If the control qubit is 1, we get a negative quarter rotation around Z, a half-turn rotation around X, and then a quarter rotation back around Z, effectively landing us where we would have been with a half-turn Y rotation. Granted, a Y rotation would have been easily done with $Y(qubit) = U3(\frac{\pi}{2}, \frac{\pi}{2}, \frac{\pi}{2}, qubit)$, but as the control functionality of the CX cannot be attached to the Y gate, we have to do this rework instead.

Let's look at some other examples. These will illustrate how the transpiler works to convert your seemingly simple quantum circuits to circuits made out of basis gates that can be run on the actual IBM Quantum® hardware.

## Non-conforming CX

In this example, we set up a CX gate between two qubits that are not physically connected. As you have seen, CX is a base gate, so this should not require any transpiling, right? Well, in this case, we force the transpiler to attempt to build your circuit across two qubits that are not directly connected. In this case, the transpiler must map your CX gate across several intermediate qubits, which will add complexity to your circuit. In our sample code, we build this circuit:

```
# Non-conforming CX
qc.cx(0,4)
```

Running the sample code with the non-conforming CX input should result in something similar to the following:

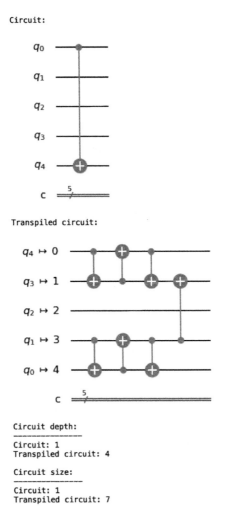

Figure 6.29 – Transpiling a CX gate across non-connected qubits

Notice how this simple, one-CX circuit all of a sudden ballooned to a circuit with seven CX gates. This is not the most efficient coding example. The reason for this is clear if you look at the coupling map for the quantum computer that we are transpiling for, IBM Quantum® Ourense. Qubit 4 cannot directly communicate with qubit 0, but has to go through 3 and 1 first:

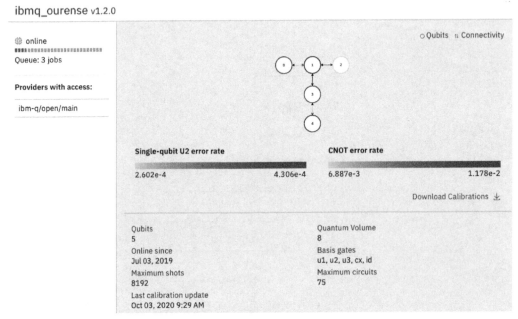

Figure 6.30 – The physical layout of one of the IBM Quantum® 5-qubit backends

For simple circuits, there is no big difference between the original and transpiled circuits; try having the CX gate go from qubit 0 to qubit 1 and see what you get. But for more elaborate ones, the circuits quickly diverge.

But hang on!

For those nitpickers of you that, like me, have looked over the circuit and walked through what happens if qubit 0 is set to 1 to trigger the CX, you will have noticed that the result of the original circuit ought to be **10001**. However, the transpiled circuit seems to give the result **01010**. This is correct! The transpiler has moved your circuit around to optimize it for the backend configuration. But won't the results be wrong if you run the circuit then? Well, no... and to see why, uncomment the `barrier` and `measure` lines in the code and run it again:

```
# Show measurement targets
qc.barrier([0,1,2,3,4])
qc.measure([0,1,2,3,4],[0,1,2,3,4])
```

This ought to result in the following output:

Circuit:

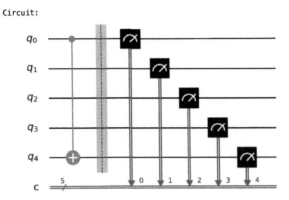

Transpiled circuit:

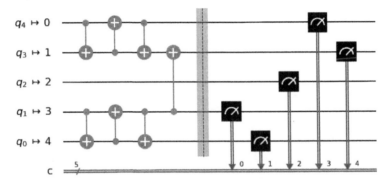

Circuit depth:

Circuit: 2
Transpiled circuit: 5

Circuit size:
--------------------
Circuit: 6
Transpiled circuit: 12

Figure 6.31 – The transpiler also moves the measurement instructions around

As you can see from the new mapping, qubits 1 and 3 are now measured to classical bits 0 and 4, just as we expected. The final measurement output will be correct.

## Multi-gate – Combined Bell and CSWAP circuit

This last example illustrates the complexity that occurs when you try to achieve something reasonably simple but run out of pathways to achieve it. We are creating a Bell state over qubits 0 and 4 and adding a controlled-SWAP gate from qubit 3 to qubits 1 and 2 to have those qubits just swap values:

```
# Multi qubit circuit
qc.h(0)
qc.h(3)
qc.cx(0,4)
qc.cswap(3,1,2)
```

The multi-gate input should give the following result:

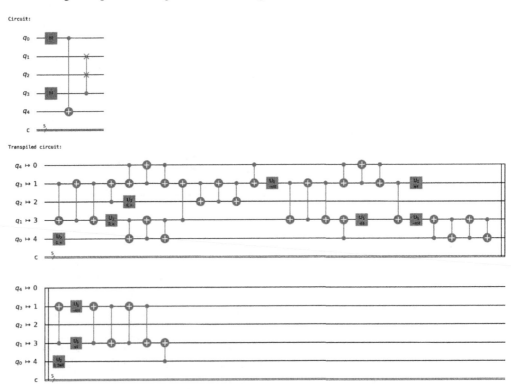

Figure 6.32 – A complex transpiling of a reasonably simple Bell + CSWAP circuit

Well, trying this relatively simple circuit quickly took a turn for the worse. It ballooned from a depth of 2 to 32. The circuit size also went up from the original 4 gates to an astounding 43. Look at all those CX gates!

```
Circuit depth:
-------------------
Circuit: 2
Transpiled circuit: 32

Circuit size:
-------------------
Circuit: 4
Transpiled circuit: 43
```

Figure 6.33 – Depth and size of the multi-gate circuit

Again, if you take a look at *Figure 6.33*, you can see why this happens. The simple act on our part of connecting qubit 0 and 4 is physically impossible as the quantum chip is laid out. Instead, this connection requires a chain of intermediate qubit connections across qubits 1, 2, and 3. These additional connections caused the number of individual gates to explode.

Now try the following circuit instead and see how that changes the counts. You should expect both depth and size to shrink significantly as you are now coding for qubits that can directly communicate with each other. Apparently, coding for the backend that you want to run your program on is still important in this **Noisy Intermediate-Scale Quantum (NISQ)** era:

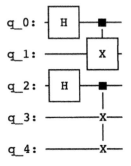

Figure 6.34 – A better conforming Bell + CSWAP circuit

As we have seen in this chapter, good quality programming is as important in quantum computing as it is in classical computing, if not more. The transpiler, left to its own devices, will do its best to translate your circuits to the backend where you plan to run them.

If it gets crowded, and you utilize all the qubits extensively, the rewriting of your circuit might extend the execution time beyond the T1 and T2 times, making your circuit produce junk results on today's **NISQ computer** even though it otherwise is very nicely constructed.

Quantum programming is definitely an art!

# 7

# Simulating Quantum Computers with Aer

So far, we have mainly been running our quantum programs on our local QASM simulator, which out of the box simulates a **universal error-correcting quantum computer**—the type of machine that the quantum computing world expects, or at least hopes, will be a reality within the next few years.

But these amazing machines are not available yet, so in this chapter, we will explore quantum simulators both locally with **Qiskit Aer** and in the cloud with **IBM Quantum®** simulators. We will understand how to run your quantum circuits on these simulated perfect backends.

However, you can also use Qiskit Aer to simulate today's **Noisy Intermediate-Scale Quantum (NISQ)** computers by setting up noise profiles for the simulator to emulate the real IBM Quantum® hardware, with gate errors and noise. So, we will take a look at that as well.

We will also look at two other local simulator types and what you can use them for: the **unitary simulator** and the **state vector simulator**.

In this chapter, we will cover the following recipes:

- Understanding the usage of quantum simulators
- Comparing the Qiskit Aer simulator with an IBM quantum computer
- Adding noise profiles of IBM Quantum® backends to local simulators
- Understanding your circuits by using the unitary simulator
- Running diagnostics with the state vector simulator

The goal of the chapter is to get equipped with the tools to use the simulators when you develop and test your quantum programs so that you do not have to wait in line for your IBM Quantum® backends to run your tests. We will start by exploring the `qasm_simulator` backend, and then take a look at the unitary and state vector simulators.

# Technical requirements

The quantum programs that we discuss in this chapter can be found here: `https://github.com/PacktPublishing/Quantum-Computing-in-Practice-with-Qiskit-and-IBM-Quantum-Experience/tree/master/Chapter07`.

# Understanding the usage of quantum simulators

A **quantum computer simulator** is a software program that simulates the quantum mechanical behavior of a real quantum computer. Simulators are useful for testing your quantum circuits in a local environment before you run them on the IBM Quantum® backends in the cloud. You can also use cloud-based simulators to test larger quantum circuits that might not yet be possible to run on actual quantum computers or just take too long to run on your local simulator.

In this recipe, we will take a quick tour to compare the available Qiskit® simulators—both local on **Qiskit Aer** and in the cloud on **IBM Quantum®**.

## Getting ready

Make sure you have everything working from *Chapter 1, Preparing Your Environment*.

The sample code for this recipe can be found here: `https://github.com/PacktPublishing/Quantum-Computing-in-Practice-with-Qiskit-and-IBM-Quantum-Experience/blob/master/Chapter07/ch7_r1_aer.py`.

# How to do it...

Let's take a look at the code:

1.  As usual, we start by importing the classes and we need. We import both `Aer` and `IBMQ`, as we will work with simulators both locally and remotely. If needed, we also load our account and get our providers:

```
from qiskit import Aer, IBMQ
if not IBMQ.active_account():
    IBMQ.load_account()
provider = IBMQ.get_provider()
```

2.  Then, we use the `backends()` method to take a look at the available local Qiskit Aer backends:

```
backends=Aer.backends()
print("\nAer backends:\n\n",backends)
```

The preceding code should give the following result:

```
Aer backends:

[<QasmSimulator('qasm_simulator') from AerProvider()>,
<StatevectorSimulator('statevector_simulator') from AerProvider()>,
<UnitarySimulator('unitary_simulator') from AerProvider()>,
<PulseSimulator('pulse_simulator') from AerProvider()>]
```

Figure 7.1 – The local Aer backends; all simulators

3.  We can store the configuration details for these simulators in a `simulators` list for further processing. Use the `backend.configuration()` method to pull out this information and loop through the available backends, appending the data for each to the list:

```
simulators=[]
for sim in range(0,len(backends)):
    backend = Aer.get_backend(str(backends[sim]))
    simulators.append(backend.configuration())
```

4.  For completeness, we'll add the configuration details for the IBM Quantum® simulator by appending that information to the list:

```
ibmq_simulator=provider.backends(simulator=True)
simulators.append(provider.get_backend(str(
ibmq_simulator[0])). simulator[0])).configuration()
```

5.  Display the raw simulator configuration details. Let's cycle through the
    simulators list to print out and look at the available configuration details for our
    simulators:

```
# Display the raw simulator configuration details
print("\nSimulator configuration details:")
for sim in range(0,len(simulators)):
    print("\n")
    print(simulators[sim].backend_name)
    print(simulators[sim].to_dict())
```

The code should be similar to the following output for each simulator:

```
qasm_simulator
QasmBackendConfiguration(backend_name='qasm_simulator', backend_version='0.5.2',
basis_gates=['u1', 'u2', 'u3', 'cx', 'cz', 'id', 'x', 'y', 'z', 'h', 's', 'sdg', 't', 'tdg',
'swap', 'ccx', 'unitary', 'diagonal', 'initialize', 'cu1', 'cu2', 'cu3', 'cswap', 'mcx',
'mcy', 'mcz', 'mcu1', 'mcu2', 'mcu3', 'mcswap', 'multiplexer', 'kraus', 'roerror'],
conditional=True, coupling_map=None, description='A C++ simulator with realistic noise for
QASM Qobj files', gates=[GateConfig(u1, ['lam'], gate u1(lam) q { U(0,0,lam) q; }, True,
'Single-qubit gate [[1, 0], [0, exp(1j*lam)]]'), GateConfig(u2, ['phi', 'lam'], gate
u2(phi,lam) q { U(pi/2,phi,lam) q; }, True, 'Single-qubit gate [[1, -exp(1j*lam)],
[exp(1j*phi), exp(1j*(phi+lam))]]/sqrt(2)'), GateConfig(u3, ['theta', 'phi', 'lam'], gate
u3(theta,phi,lam) q { U(theta,phi,lam) q; }, True, 'Single-qubit gate with three rotation
angles'), GateConfig(cx, [], gate cx c,t { CX c,t; }, True, 'Two-qubit Controlled-NOT
gate'), GateConfig(cz, [], gate cz a,b { h b; cx a,b; h b; }, True, 'Two-qubit Controlled-Z
gate'), GateConfig(id, [], gate id a { U(0,0,0) a; }, True, 'Single-qubit identity gate'),
GateConfig(x, [], gate x a { U(pi,0,pi) a; }, True, 'Single-qubit Pauli-X gate'),
GateConfig(y, [], TODO, True, 'Single-qubit Pauli-Y gate'), GateConfig(z, [], TODO, True,
'Single-qubit Pauli-Z gate'), GateConfig(h, [], TODO, True, 'Single-qubit Hadamard gate'),
GateConfig(s, [], TODO, True, 'Single-qubit phase gate'), GateConfig(sdg, [], TODO, True,
'Single-qubit adjoint phase gate'), GateConfig(t, [], TODO, True, 'Single-qubit T gate'),
GateConfig(tdg, [], TODO, True, 'Single-qubit adjoint T gate'), GateConfig(swap, [], TODO,
True, 'Two-qubit SWAP gate'), GateConfig(ccx, [], TODO, True, 'Three-qubit Toffoli gate'),
GateConfig(cswap, [], TODO, True, 'Three-qubit Fredkin (controlled-SWAP) gate'),
GateConfig(unitary, ['matrix'], unitary(matrix) q1, q2,..., True, 'N-qubit unitary gate. The
parameter is the N-qubit matrix to apply.'), GateConfig(diagonal, ['diag_elements'], TODO,
True, 'N-qubit diagonal unitary gate. The parameters are the diagonal entries of the N-qubit
matrix to apply.'), GateConfig(initialize, ['vector'], initialize(vector) q1, q2,..., False,
'N-qubit state initialize. Resets qubits then sets statevector to the parameter vector.'),
GateConfig(cu1, ['lam'], TODO, True, 'Two-qubit Controlled-u1 gate'), GateConfig(cu2,
['phi', 'lam'], TODO, True, 'Two-qubit Controlled-u2 gate'), GateConfig(cu3, ['theta',
'phi', 'lam'], TODO, True, 'Two-qubit Controlled-u3 gate'), GateConfig(mcx, [], TODO, True,
'N-qubit multi-controlled-X gate'), GateConfig(mcy, [], TODO, True, 'N-qubit multi-
controlled-Y gate'), GateConfig(mcz, [], TODO, True, 'N-qubit multi-controlled-Z gate'),
GateConfig(mcu1, ['lam'], TODO, True, 'N-qubit multi-controlled-u1 gate'), GateConfig(mcu2,
['phi', 'lam'], TODO, True, 'N-qubit multi-controlled-u2 gate'), GateConfig(mcu3, ['theta',
'phi', 'lam'], TODO, True, 'N-qubit multi-controlled-u3 gate'), GateConfig(mcswap, [], TODO,
True, 'N-qubit multi-controlled-SWAP gate'), GateConfig(multiplexer, ['mat1', 'mat2',
'...'], TODO, True, 'N-qubit multi-plexer gate. The input parameters are the gates for each
value.'), GateConfig(kraus, ['mat1', 'mat2', '...'], TODO, True, 'N-qubit Kraus error
instruction. The input parameters are the Kraus matrices.'), GateConfig(roerror, ['matrix'],
TODO, False, 'N-bit classical readout error instruction. The input parameter is the readout
error probability matrix.')], local=True, max_shots=1000000, memory=True, n_qubits=30,
open_pulse=False, simulator=True, url='https://github.com/Qiskit/qiskit-aer')
```

Figure 7.2 – A heap of simulator configuration details

This raw printout will produce a slew of information to wade through. In the next
step, we will sort out and display a few common parameters for comparison.

6.  Compare the simulators.

So, there is an awful lot of information for each simulator. To make a comparison, let's grab a few parameters of interest and list them for each simulator. For our purposes, the following parameters might be interesting:

**Name**: The name we use to set the specific simulator as our backend when we run our circuits

**Number of qubits**: The number of qubits each simulator supports

**Max shots**: The maximum number of runs you can do for your circuit

**Description**: The IBM Quantum®-provided description of the simulator

If you look closely at the `ibmq_qasm_simulator` details, you will see that this non-local IBM Quantum® simulator doesn't have a description:

```
ibmq_qasm_simulator
QasmBackendConfiguration(allow_object_storage=True, allow_q_object=True,
backend_name='ibmq_qasm_simulator', backend_version='0.1.547', basis_gates=['u1', 'u2', 'u3', 'cx',
'cz', 'id', 'x', 'y', 'z', 'h', 's', 'sdg', 't', 'tdg', 'ccx', 'swap', 'unitary', 'initialize',
'kraus'], conditional=True, coupling_map=None, gates=[GateConfig(u1, ['lambda'], gate u1(lambda) q {
U(0,0,lambda) q; }), GateConfig(u2, ['phi', 'lambda'], gate u2(phi,lambda) q { U(pi/2,phi,lambda) q;
}), GateConfig(u3, ['theta', 'phi', 'lambda'], u3(theta,phi,lambda) q { U(theta,phi,lambda) q; }),
GateConfig(cx, [], gate cx q1,q2 { CX q1,q2; })], local=False, max_experiments=300, max_shots=8192,
memory=True, n_qubits=32, online_date=datetime.datetime(2019, 5, 2, 8, 15, tzinfo=tzutc()),
open_pulse=False, simulator=True)
```

Figure 7.3 – ibmq_qasm_simulator has no description

In the code, we add our own description for completeness by using an `if/elif` command for the `local` attribute for each simulator, adding our own description if `local==False`:

```
# Fish out criteria to compare
print("\n")
print("{0:25} {1:<10} {2:<10} {3:<10}".
    format("Name","#Qubits","Max shots.","Description"))
print("{0:25} {1:<10} {2:<10} {3:<10}".
    format("----","-------","--------","-----------"))
description=[]
for sim in range(0,len(simulators)):
    if simulators[sim].local==True:
        description.append(simulators[sim].description)
    elif simulators[sim].local==False:
        description.append("Non-local IBM Quantum
            simulator")
    print("{0:25} {1:<10} {2:<10} {3:<10}".
        format(simulators[sim].backend_name,
```

```
        simulators[sim].n_qubits,
        simulators[sim].max_shots, description[sim]))
```

The previous sample code will result in something similar to the following:

```
Name                     #Qubits    Max shots. Description
----                     -------    ---------- -----------
qasm_simulator           30         1000000    A C++ simulator with realistic noise for QASM Qobj files
statevector_simulator    30         1000000    A C++ statevector simulator for QASM Qobj files
unitary_simulator        15         1000000    A C++ unitary simulator for QASM Qobj files
pulse_simulator          20         1000000    A pulse-based Hamiltonian simulator for Pulse Qobj files
ibmq_qasm_simulator      32         8192       Non-local IBM Q simulator
```

Figure 7.4 – A list of selected simulator properties

From this list, we can get a high-level overview of what the simulators can do, and what the specific criteria for each are:

qasm_simulator: This simulator lets you run your quantum programs and returns results as if you were running on a perfect quantum computer, with no errors and no noise, but with the option to add errors and a noise profile to simulate a *NISQ backend*. This simulator is written in C++ and runs locally on your machine.

statevector_simulator: With this simulator, you can simulate the state vector for your qubits at any point in your circuit. This simulator is written in C++ and runs locally on your machine.

unitary_simulator: With the unitary simulator, you can compute the unitary matrix for your circuit. This simulator is implemented as a local Python simulator.

pulse_simulator: A pulse-based Hamiltonian simulator for Pulse Qobj files. With this simulator, you can test interacting with the backend qubits directly using pulse-based programming that bypasses the standard gates.

ibmq_qasm_simulator: This is the only non-local simulator in the group. It works much like the local qasm_simulator simulator but with higher performance.

We now know what simulators are available for us to work with, and we will explore them further in this chapter. The only simulator we will not touch is the pulse_simulator as using this simulator is beyond the scope of this book. If you are interested, do take a look at the *Get to the heart of real quantum hardware* link at the end of the recipe.

## There's more...

Take a look at the performance data for the two QASM simulators—**Number of qubits** and **Max shots**. They both let you play with around *30 qubits* and run many thousands of shots with each run. So, what is the difference?

One thing to keep in mind when running the simulators is that they are simulating quantum computers—the very computers that we expect to beat classical computers at complex problems going forward. This essentially means that simulating quantum computers on a classical computer like yours gets roughly twice as complicated with each added qubit.

For the online `ibmq_qasm_simulator` simulator, this doesn't necessarily pose a big problem as it is running on an IBM POWER9™ server, which is a fairly massive piece of hardware. You can throw seriously sized quantum programs, up to *32 qubits*, at it with no problems.

Your own hardware, on the other hand, is a different matter. The performance of the local `qasm_simulator` simulator will depend on the hardware you run it on. When you start to feel a lag and slowness on your local machine, it might be time for the online `ibmq_qasm_simulator` simulator.

## See also

- *An Open High-Performance Simulator for Quantum Circuits, IBM Research Blog,* May 1, 2018: `https://www.ibm.com/blogs/research/2018/05/quantum-circuits/`

- *Get to the heart of real quantum hardware, IBM Research Blog,* December 12, 2019: `https://www.ibm.com/blogs/research/2019/12/qiskit-openpulse/`

- *IBM Power systems*: `https://www.ibm.com/it-infrastructure/power`

# Comparing the Qiskit Aer simulator with an IBM quantum computer

In this recipe, we will create a long quantum circuit that *swaps* a $|1\rangle$ state between two qubits. You will see that the circuit provides perfect results on your local Qiskit Aer simulator but not quite so perfect results on an actual IBM Quantum® machine.

## Getting ready

The sample code for this recipe can be found here: `https://github.com/PacktPublishing/Quantum-Computing-in-Practice-with-Qiskit-and-IBM-Quantum-Experience/blob/master/Chapter07/ch7_r2_ootb.py`.

## How to do it...

Here's the code, stored in the ch7_r2_ootb.py file:

1. As always, start by importing the required classes and methods and load your account:

```
# Import Qiskit
from qiskit import QuantumCircuit
from qiskit import Aer, IBMQ, execute

# Import visualization tools
from qiskit.tools.visualization import plot_histogram
from qiskit.tools.monitor import job_monitor

# Load account
if not IBMQ.active_account():
    IBMQ.load_account()
provider = IBMQ.get_provider()
```

2. Select the number of SWAP gates to include:

```
# Enter number of SWAP gates to include with your circuit
# with (default 10)
user_input = input("Enter number of SWAP gates to use:")
try:
    n = int(user_input)
except ValueError:
    n=10
n_gates=n
```

3. We now build a quantum circuit with the selected number of SWAP gates in a row:

```
# Construct quantum circuit
circ = QuantumCircuit(2, 2)
circ.x(0)
while n >0:
    circ.swap(0,1)
    circ.barrier()
    n=n-1
```

```
circ.measure([0,1], [0,1])
print("Circuit with",n_gates,"SWAP gates.\n",circ)
```

4.  Run the circuit on the `qasm_simulator` and get the results:

```
# Select the QasmSimulator from the Aer provider
simulator = Aer.get_backend('qasm_simulator')

# Execute and get counts
result = execute(circ, simulator,
    shots=simulator.configuration().max_shots).result()
counts = result.get_counts(circ)
print("Simulated SWAP counts:",counts)
display(plot_histogram(counts, title='Simulated counts
    for '+str(n_gates)+' SWAP gates.'))
```

The result is displayed with a prompt to run the same circuit on an IBM Quantum®
backend. Take a break here and read on.

## How it works...

When you run this quantum circuit on a simulator, it simulates perfectly and we get a
perfect 100% result of the expected outcome:

```
Simulated SWAP counts: {'01': 10000}
```

If you follow along in the following circuit, you will see that we first use an X gate to set
qubit **q0** to |1⟩, and then we swap qubits **q0** and **q1** 10 times. What we expect to end up
with is **q0** in |1⟩ and **q1** in |0⟩, or, in two-qubit notation, |10⟩:

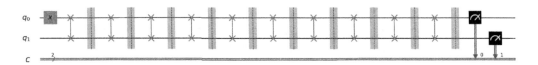

Figure 7.5 – A quantum circuit with 10 SWAP gates

> **Tip**
>
> Note the *barrier gates* here. These are to instruct the Qiskit® transpiler to not transpile across the barriers, and not simplify the circuit by just removing the consecutive SWAP gates as they negate each other. For a quick reminder, refer to the *Tossing a quantum coin* recipe in *Chapter 3, IBM Quantum Experience® – Quantum Drag and Drop*.

When running the program for 10 SWAP gates, you should get the following output:

```
Simulated SWAP counts: {'01': 100000}
```

This is seen numerically and in the following bar diagram:

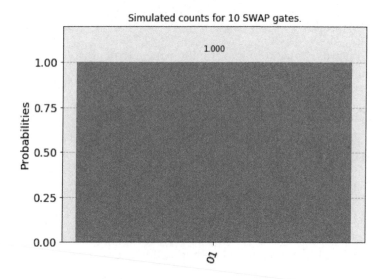

Figure 7.6 – The expected result after 10 SWAP gates on a perfect quantum computer: 01

This means that the program ran perfectly and that we swapped the initial $|1\rangle$ qubit back and forth 10 times to end up with the qubits back where they started, in $|1\rangle$. There were no errors.

In a future **universal error-correcting quantum computer**, you will be able to run long quantum circuits like this with perfectly consistent error-corrected logical qubits throughout your calculations. By default, a Qiskit Aer simulator emulates an error-free universal quantum computer.

However, when you run the same program on today's **NISQ** hardware, errors start to pile up as your quantum circuits grow in size and execution time. To check this out, you can now press *Enter* and run the circuit on an IBM Quantum® backend.

We now import the least-busy backend with five qubits, and run the same circuit on it:

```
# Import the least busy backend
from qiskit.providers.ibmq import least_busy
backend = least_busy(provider.backends(n_qubits=5,
    operational=True, simulator=False))
print("Least busy backend:",backend)

# Execute and get counts
job = execute(circ, backend, shots=backend.configuration().
    max_shots)
job_monitor(job)
nisq_result=job.result()
nisq_counts=nisq_result.get_counts(circ)
print("NISQ SWAP counts:",nisq_counts)
display(plot_histogram(nisq_counts, title='Counts for
    '+str(n_gates)+' SWAP gates on '+str(backend)))
```

The preceding code might give the following result:

```
Least busy backend: ibmq_vigo
Job Status: job has successfully run
NISQ SWAP counts: {'00': 1002, '10': 585, '11': 592, '01':
6013}
```

This is seen numerically and in the bar diagram that follows:

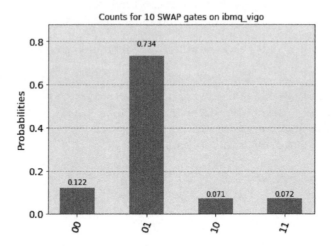

Figure 7.7 – After 10 SWAP gates, some errors have crept in; we get results other than the expected 01

As you can see, the crystal-clear result of the QASM simulator turned a little murky when run on one of the IBM Quantum® machines. You will most likely still get a prominent peak for the correct result (01), but also a lot of wrong results.

## There's more...

You might think that 10 SWAP gates would be a fairly small example of a quantum circuit and that we shouldn't see errors like these in a circuit that size. What you have to keep in mind, though, is that the relatively simple logical circuit that you build will get transpiled into a circuit that can be run using just the basis gates that are available to the backend.

Use the following `transpile` example to print the basis gates for the backend, and check the gate depth for the SWAP circuit before and after transpiling:

```
# Comparing the circuit with the transpiled circuit
from qiskit.compiler import transpile
trans_swap = transpile(circ, backend)
print(trans_swap)
print("Basis gates:",backend.configuration().basis_gates)
print("SWAP circuit depth:",circ.depth(),"gates")
print("Transpiled SWAP circuit depth:",
    trans_swap.depth(),"gates")
```

The preceding code should give the following result on an IBM Quantum® five-qubit machine such as `ibmq_vigo`:

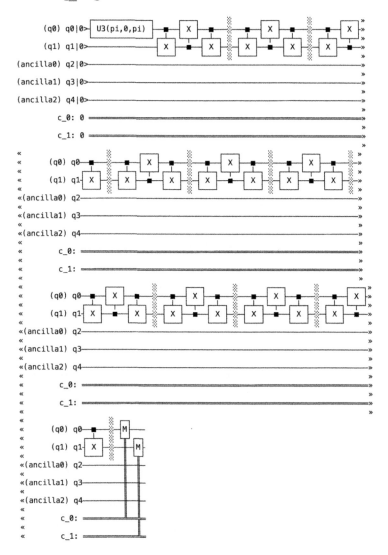

Figure 7.8 – What a transpiled 10 SWAP gate circuit looks like

The previous code sample should give an output similar to the following:

```
Basis gates: ['u1', 'u2', 'u3', 'cx', 'id']
SWAP circuit depth: 12 gates
Transpiled SWAP circuit depth: 32 gates
```

When you run on a real quantum computer, noise and gate errors are introduced for each gate. As you can see in the previous figure, a single SWAP gate, when transpiled, might turn into three successive CX gates, and adding 10 of these in a row results in 30 CX gates. This makes for some potential big errors. Note that the number of transpiled gates depends on the selected backend and might be larger than the 30 in this example.

## See also

*Quantum Computing in the NISQ era and beyond* by John Preskill from the Institute for Quantum Information and Matter and the Walter Burke Institute for Theoretical Physics, California Institute of Technology, Pasadena, CA, 91125, USA: `https://quantum-journal.org/papers/q-2018-08-06-79/`.

# Adding noise profiles of IBM Quantum® backends to local simulators

In this recipe, we find the noise data for the IBM Quantum® backends to build a noise profile that we can then add to our simulator when we run it. This will make the simulator behave like a *real NISQ backend*.

## Getting ready

The sample code for this recipe can be found here: `https://github.com/PacktPublishing/Quantum-Computing-in-Practice-with-Qiskit-and-IBM-Quantum-Experience/blob/master/Chapter07/ch7_r3_noise.py`.

## How to do it...

Let's look at the following code:

1.  Get a list of the available backends and select one to simulate.

    We will get the noise profile of one of the IBM Quantum® backends and use it with our simulators. First, we use the `select_backend()` function to list the backends and make the selection:

    ```
    def select_backend():
        # Get all available and operational backends.
        available_backends = provider.backends(filters=lambda
            b: not b.configuration().simulator and
            b.configuration().n_qubits > 1 and
            b.status().operational)
    ```

```
# Fish out criteria to compare
print("{0:20} {1:<10} {2:<10}".format("Name",
    "#Qubits","Pending jobs"))
print("{0:20} {1:<10} {2:<10}".format("----",
    "-------","-------------"))
for n in range(0, len(available_backends)):
    backend = provider.get_backend(str(
        available_backends[n]))
    print("{0:20} {1:<10}".format(backend.name(),
        backend.configuration().n_qubits),
        backend.status().pending_jobs)
select_backend=input("Select a backend (
    'exit' to end): ")
if select_backend!="exit":
    backend = provider.get_backend(select_backend)
else:
    backend=select_backend
return(backend)
```

The preceding code might result in the following listing:

| Name | #Qubits | Pending jobs |
| --- | --- | --- |
| ibmqx2 | 5 | 4 |
| ibmq_16_melbourne | 15 | 33 |
| ibmq_vigo | 5 | 23 |
| ibmq_ourense | 5 | 5 |
| ibmq_valencia | 5 | 13 |
| ibmq_santiago | 5 | 15 |

Figure 7.9 – List of available IBM Quantum® backends

As we will also run the quantum circuit on the backend, you should pick one with a reasonably short queue to avoid having to wait excessively for the results.

2. Get the noise profile. The noise model can be extracted from the backend by using the NoiseModel.from_backend(backend) method:

```
def build_noise_model(backend):
    # Construct the noise model from backend
    noise_model = NoiseModel.from_backend(backend)
    print(noise_model)
    return(noise_model)
```

The noise model will look different depending on the backend that you selected. A sample model is shown here:

```
NoiseModel:
  Basis gates: ['cx', 'id', 'u2', 'u3']
  Instructions with noise: ['id', 'u2', 'u3', 'measure', 'cx']
  Qubits with noise: [0, 1, 2, 3, 4]
  Specific qubit errors: [('id', [0]), ('id', [1]), ('id', [2]),
('id', [3]), ('id', [4]), ('u2', [0]), ('u2', [1]), ('u2', [2]),
('u2', [3]), ('u2', [4]), ('u3', [0]), ('u3', [1]), ('u3', [2]),
('u3', [3]), ('u3', [4]), ('cx', [0, 1]), ('cx', [1, 0]), ('cx', [1,
2]), ('cx', [1, 3]), ('cx', [2, 1]), ('cx', [3, 1]), ('cx', [3, 4]),
('cx', [4, 3]), ('measure', [0]), ('measure', [1]), ('measure', [2]),
('measure', [3]), ('measure', [4])]
```

Figure 7.10 – Noise model for an IBM Quantum® backend

We can now run the simulator with the noise model and other parameters to have the NISQ characteristics of the selected backend applied to the simulator calculations and make it behave like an actual physical backend and not a perfect simulator.

3.  Build a GHZ state circuit and run it on four different backends.

    The **GHZ state,** or **Greenberger–Horne–Zeilinger state,** is an entanglement state similar to the two-qubit Bell state that we have encountered before, but with three entangled qubits.

    We will run the circuit on the following simulators:

    **The local QASM simulator**, as a baseline

    **The local QASM simulator** with a noise model

    **The IBM Quantum QASM simulator** with a noise model

    **The IBM Quantum backend**, for comparison

    We will use the execute_circuit() function to run on the backends with all the variations.

    In Python, we start by getting the basis gates and a coupling map for the backend:

```
def execute_circuit(backend, noise_model):
    # Basis gates for the noise model
    basis_gates = noise_model.basis_gates
    # Coupling map
    coupling_map = backend.configuration().coupling_map
    print("Coupling map: ",coupling_map)
```

We then build a GHZ state quantum circuit, execute it on a simulator, and get the counts:

```
circ = QuantumCircuit(3, 3)
circ.h(0)
circ.cx(0, 1)
circ.cx(0, 2)
circ.measure([0,1,2], [0,1,2])
print(circ)
# Execute on QASM simulator and get counts
counts = execute(circ, Aer.get_backend(
    'qasm_simulator')).result().get_counts(circ)
display(plot_histogram(counts, title='Ideal counts
    for 3-qubit GHZ state on local qasm_simulator'))
```

Then, we use the noise model and coupling map to execute a noisy simulation on both the local and the IBM Quantum® QASM simulator and get the counts:

```
counts_noise = execute(circ, Aer.get_backend(
    'qasm_simulator'), noise_model=noise_model,
    coupling_map=coupling_map,
    basis_gates=basis_gates).result().get_
    counts(circ)
display(plot_histogram(counts_noise, title="Counts
    for 3-qubit GHZ state with noise model on local
    qasm simulator"))
# Execute noisy simulation on the ibmq_qasm_simulator
# and get counts
counts_noise_ibmq = execute(circ, provider.get_
    backend('ibmq_qasm_simulator'),
    noise_model=noise_model, coupling_map=coupling_
    map, basis_gates=basis_gates).result().get_
    counts(circ)
display(plot_histogram(counts_noise_ibmq,
    title="Counts for 3-qubit GHZ state with noise
    model on IBMQ qasm simulator"))
```

Finally, we execute the job on the IBM Quantum® backend and get the counts:

```
job = execute(circ, backend)
job_monitor(job)
counts_ibmq=job.result().get_counts()
title="Counts for 3-qubit GHZ state on IBMQ backend "
    + backend.name()
display(plot_histogram(counts_ibmq, title=title))
```

The final step is to display the collected results for all runs:

```
display(plot_histogram([counts, counts_noise,
    counts_noise_ibmq, counts_ibmq], bar_labels=True,
    legend=["Baseline","Noise on simulator",
    "Noise on IBMQ simulator", "IBM Q backend"],
    title="Comparison"))
```

As we walk through these four executions of the GHZ circuit, we will see how the initial perfect simulation, which provides an output of only |000⟩ or |111⟩ with ~50% chance, gets *contaminated* with errors; we get outputs in all possible states.

In the final output, we compare all the executions with the final execution on the selected backend. What you might see when running the program would look something like the following set of screenshots:

1.  First, we run on the simulator without noise and you get the following output:

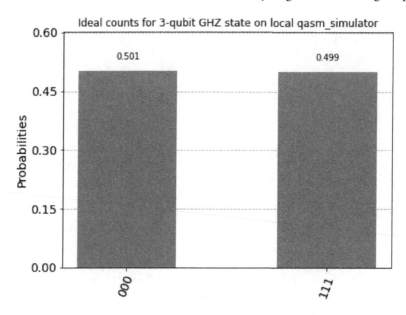

Figure 7.11 – First, ideal run on the local simulator

2.  Then, we add the noise model and run it again:

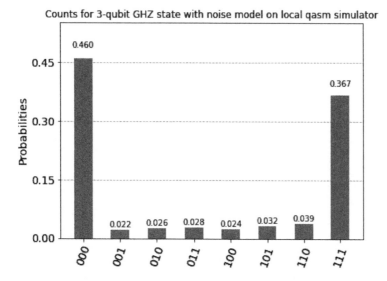

Figure 7.12 – Adding the noise model to the local simulator

As we can now see, we no longer get the nice, clean, and perfect quantum computer result but rather a result that is much closer to what you would get if you run the circuit on an actual IBM Quantum® backend.

3.  We test one more time by running with the noise model on the online IBM Quantum® QASM simulator:

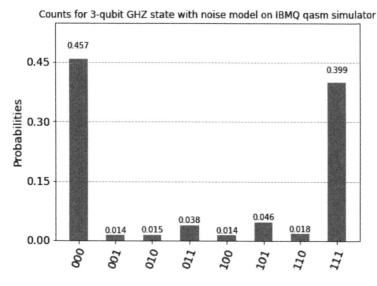

Figure 7.13 – Adding the noise model to the IBM Quantum® simulator

4. Finally, we run the circuit one final time, now on the backend that we selected at the beginning:

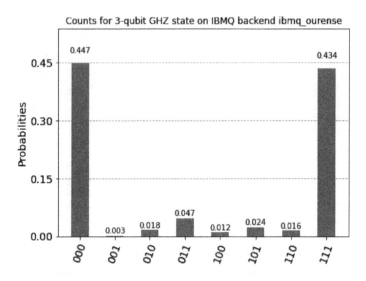

Figure 7.14 – Running the circuit on the IBM Quantum® backend

The result of this run should be similar to our simulated runs based on the noise model we derived from the actual IBM Quantum® backend.

We can now merge all the results into a single diagram for comparison:

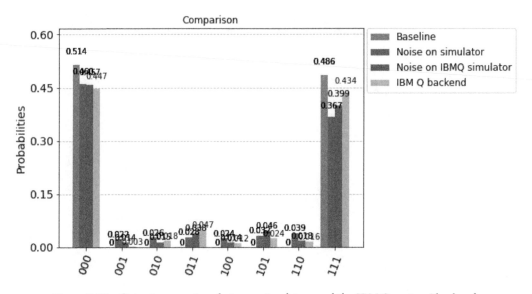

Figure 7.15 – Output comparison between simulators and the IBM Quantum® backend

In the final output, you can see that the simulators with the added noise model behave, at least statistically, like the IBM Quantum® backend on which they are modeled. As you can see, for the **Baseline** Aer simulation, we only get the expected |000⟩ and |111⟩ results for a GHZ state, but for all the other runs, we also get *noise* in the form of results such as |001⟩ and |010⟩.

## See also

*Qiskit Backend Specifications for OpenQASM and OpenPulse Experiments*, arXiv, IBM Research et.al., September 11, 2018: `https://arxiv.org/pdf/1809.03452.pdf`.

# Understanding your circuits by using the unitary simulator

As it turns out, any valid quantum circuit that consists only of gates can be translated into a unitary matrix that describes the expected outcome for each possible state vector input. As you have seen in *Chapter 2, Quantum Computing and Qubits with Python*, each quantum gate is in itself a **unitary matrix**, and the combination of the unitaries that make up the complete quantum circuit can in itself be described as a **unitary**.

Qiskit® lets you use the Qiskit Aer `unitary_simulator` simulator to return the unitary matrix that corresponds with your quantum circuit. You run the job just like you would for `qasm_simulator` jobs.

When running `unitary_simulator`, you only run the circuit once. We can then use the `get_unitary(qc)` method on the returned results to see the unitary as a matrix for a circuit, such as this one-qubit superposition circuit using a Hadamard gate:

Figure 7.16 – Quantum circuit with one Hadamard gate

The circuit corresponds to the following unitary:

```
[[ 0.707+0.j   0.707+0.j]
 [ 0.707+0.j  -0.707+0.j]]
```

In a cleaner printout, this would look as follows:

$$\frac{1}{\sqrt{2}} \begin{bmatrix} 1 & 1 \\ 1 & -1 \end{bmatrix}$$

You might recognize this as the *Hadamard gate* matrix, which is just what it is. Just like this, you can use the unitary simulator to return the unitary matrixes for any valid quantum circuit. That is what we will explore in this recipe.

We will create a few simple quantum circuits and run them through a unitary simulator to get the unitary matrix. We then compare the Qiskit® unitary with the theoretical unitary for the gate combination that is represented by the circuit.

Finally, we run the circuit on the qasm simulator and compare the result with a calculation of the input qubit state vectors, [1,0] (for one qubit) and [1,0,0,0] (for two qubits), which represent all qubits starting in the state |0⟩.

The script includes a set of functions that we define to control the creation of circuits and other calculations that need to be done.

For example, we use the circuits() function to create three basic quantum circuits and store them in a list for later use.

In the script, we are also using two functions that we create ourselves to process the unitary information: show_unitary() and calc_unitary().

The input and function calls are controlled by the main loop at the end of the script.

## Getting ready

The sample code for this recipe can be found here: https://github.com/PacktPublishing/Quantum-Computing-in-Practice-with-Qiskit-and-IBM-Quantum-Experience/blob/master/Chapter07/ch7_r4_unitary.py.

## How to do it...

1.  In your Python environment, run ch7_r4_unitary.py.

2.  When you first launch the script, you get an input menu:

```
Enter the number for the circuit to explore:
---------------------------------------------
0. Exit
1. One qubit superposition
2. Two qubit superposition
3. Two qubit entanglement
4. Import QASM from IBM Quantum Experience
```

Figure 7.17 – Input menu

Enter a number to select the circuit to run with. Options **1**–**3** are predefined in the script, while option **4** lets you input QASM code from IBM Quantum Experience® to test, much like we did in the *Moving between worlds* recipe in *Chapter 3, IBM Quantum Experience® – Quantum Drag and Drop*.

> **Important: No measurement instructions**
>
> If you include measurement instructions with your quantum circuit, you must strip these out before you submit it as input. If the code includes measurement circuits, the simulator will crash with an Aer error.

3.  After you select the circuit to explore, the program creates the circuits we need, and return them as a list:

```
def circuits():
    circuits=[]
    # Circuit 1 - one qubit in superposition
    circuit1 = QuantumCircuit(1,1)
    circuit1.h(0)
    # Circuit 2 - two qubits in superposition
    circuit2 = QuantumCircuit(2,2)
    circuit2.h([0,1])
    # Circuit 3 - two entangled qubits
    circuit3 = QuantumCircuit(2,2)
    circuit3.h([0])
    circuit3.cx(0,1)
    # Bundle the circuits in a list and return the list
    circuits=[circuit1,circuit2,circuit3]
    return(circuits)
```

4. We will now send the circuit that we selected to print the unitary.

In show_unitary(), we set the backend to unitary_simulator and run the circuit. The returned unitary is retrieved from the execution results and printed as a matrix:

```
# Calculate and display the unitary matrix
def show_unitary(circuit):
    global unit
    backend = Aer.get_backend('unitary_simulator')
    unit=execute(circuit, backend).result().
        get_unitary(qc)
    print("Unitary matrix for the circuit:\n-------------
    ------------------\n",unit)
```

5. Finally, the unitary is used to calculate the predicted outcome for the circuit and the circuit is run on qasm_simulator for comparison.

In the calc_unitary() function, we use the returned unitary as input together with the quantum circuit. We then create a state vector for the number of qubits specified by the circuit and use **NumPy** to calculate the dot product of the vector with the unitary to get the qubit parameters. For a reminder, refer to the *A quick introduction to quantum gates* recipe in *Chapter 2, Quantum Computing and Qubits with Python*.

We then calculate the probabilities of the various outcomes by squaring the parameters and finally multiplying by the number of shots to get probabilities for all outcomes.

Finally, we run the circuit on qasm_simulator to compare the calculated results with the simulated results:

```
def calc_unitary(circuit,unitary):
    # Set number of shots
    shots=1000
    # Calculate possible number of outcomes, 2^n qubits
    binary=int(pow(2,circuit.width()/2))
    # Set the binary key for correct binary conversion
    bin_key='0'+str(int(circuit.width()/2))+'b'
    # Create a qubit vector based on all qubits in the
    # ground state |0> and a results list for all
    # possible outcomes.
    vector=[1]
    outcomes=[format(0, bin_key)+":"]
    for q in range (1,binary):
```

```
        vector.append(0)
        outcomes.append(format(q, bin_key)+":")
qubits=np.array(vector)
# Calculate the dot product of the unitary matrix and
# the qubits set by the qubits parameter.
a_thru_d=np.dot(unitary,qubits)
# Print the probabilities (counts) of the calculated
# outcome.
calc_counts={}
for out in range (0,len(a_thru_d)):
    calc_counts[outcomes[out]]=(int(pow(abs(
        a_thru_d[out]),2)*shots))
print("\nCalculated counts:\n------------------\
    n",calc_counts)
# Automate creation of measurement gates from number
# of qubits
# Run the circuit on the backend
if circuit.width()==2:
    circuit.measure([0],[0])
else:
    circuit.measure([0,1],[0,1])
backend_count = Aer.get_backend('qasm_simulator')
counts=execute(circuit, backend_count,shots=shots).
    result().get_counts(qc)
# Print the counts of the measured outcome.
print("\nExecuted counts:\n----------------\
    n",counts,"\n")
```

All in all, if we run the script with input **1**, for *one-qubit superposition*, we will get a result that is similar to the following:

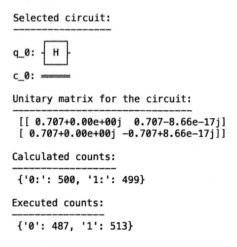

```
Selected circuit:
----------------------

q_0: ┤ H ├

c_0: ═════

Unitary matrix for the circuit:
----------------------------------
[[ 0.707+0.00e+00j   0.707-8.66e-17j]
 [ 0.707+0.00e+00j  -0.707+8.66e-17j]]

Calculated counts:
--------------------
 {'0:': 500, '1:': 499}

Executed counts:
------------------
 {'0': 487, '1': 513}
```

Figure 7.18 – One-qubit superposition output

6.  For the one-qubit superposition, we will create a simple quantum circuit with just a Hadamard gate. The unitary for this circuit is as follows:

$$\frac{1}{\sqrt{2}}\begin{bmatrix} 1 & 1 \\ 1 & -1 \end{bmatrix}$$

7.  The calculated outcomes correspond nicely with the returned counts from running the circuit on the QASM simulator.

8.  Now, test options **2** and **3** to see what the unitaries look like for slightly more complicated circuits. When you feel that you have a good grasp of what is going on, take a look at the next recipe to import any circuit as a QASM string.

# Running diagnostics with the state vector simulator

In this recipe, we will explore the state vector simulator and see how you can use it to run diagnostics on your circuits to see how your qubits are behaving. The state vector simulator is not a quantum computer simulator per se, but a tool that runs through your quantum circuit with one shot and returns the qubit state vector that results. As these are simulators, you can actually use them to do diagnostic tests of your circuits without disturbing them and breaking the quantum state.

You will notice that we have used the state vector simulator before, when displaying the qubits as **Bloch spheres**, but we did not go into any great detail at that point. Using Bloch sphere visualization works well with single or multiple qubit visualization when each qubit has a definite simple state that can be projected on a Bloch sphere.

There is a different output—actually, several—that we will touch on. Each of these lets you present the state of your qubits at a specific point in your circuit, before measuring.

So, here's what we will work with. The state vector simulator returns a state vector, much like the following examples:

- For a qubit in superposition: `[0.707+0.j  0.707+0.j]`

- For a Bell-state entangled qubit pair: `[0.707+0.j 0.    +0.j 0.    +0.j 0.707+0.j]`

Written out in standard matrix form, these correspond to the following:

- Qubit in superposition:

$$|\psi\rangle = \frac{1}{\sqrt{2}}\begin{bmatrix}1\\1\end{bmatrix}$$

- An entangled qubit pair:

$$|\psi\rangle = \frac{1}{\sqrt{2}}\begin{bmatrix}1\\0\\0\\1\end{bmatrix}$$

We can try displaying these using the `plot_bloch_multivector()` method. This visualization lets you observe how each individual qubit changes as the circuit progresses:

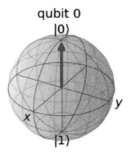

Figure 7.19 – Single qubit in state $|0\rangle$

This works fine as long as the qubits can be expressed individually. For entangled qubits, this visualization method no longer works:

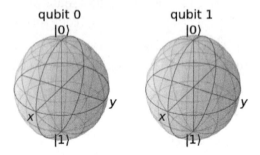

Figure 7.20 – Entangled qubit pair in state $\frac{1}{\sqrt{2}}(|00\rangle + |11\rangle)$

As you can see, Bloch spheres are not a good tool for entangled visualization, where the qubits cannot be described individually, but only as a combined entity. For more complex visualizations like these, we can use the `plot_state_qsphere()` method instead. The Q-sphere visualization is unique to Qiskit® and displays the quantum state as one or more vectors on a Q-sphere.

The Q-sphere displays a circle (for single-qubit states) or a sphere (for multiple-qubit states), with one or more vectors that represent the state. The relative size of the vector and tip shows the probability of measuring the indicated state; for a one-qubit Q-sphere, the north pole represents the ground state, $|0\rangle$, and the south pole the excited state, $|1\rangle$, and the color indicates the phase angle of the state:

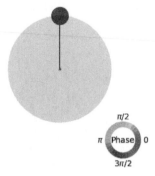

Figure 7.21 – Single qubit in state $|0\rangle$ with a 100% probability of measuring 0

For example, the one-qubit example indicates that the probability of measuring the state $|0\rangle$ is 1 (vector pointing up), and the phase angle is 0. You can use the Q-sphere to visualize the entangled qubit pair that we could not visualize with the Bloch sphere:

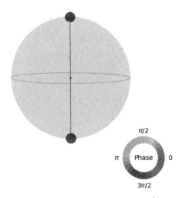

Figure 7.22 – Entangled qubit pair in state $\frac{1}{\sqrt{2}}(|00\rangle + |11\rangle)$, with
a 50% probability of measuring either 0 or 1

In the entangled qubit example, there are two possible outcomes with equal probability: $|00\rangle$ (vector pointing up) and $|11\rangle$ (vector pointing down), both with phase 0.

Note that for the two-qubit example, you also see an equator for the sphere. The reason for the equator is the two additional possible outcomes: $|01\rangle$ and $|10\rangle$ for a two-qubit system. In this case, the results occupy two opposite nodes along the equator: $|01\rangle$ on the left extreme and $|10\rangle$ on the right:

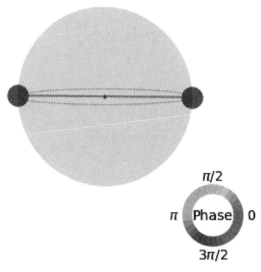

Figure 7.23 – Entangled qubit pair in state $\frac{1}{\sqrt{2}}(|01\rangle + |10\rangle)$, with an
equal 50% probability of measuring 01 and 10

As we will see, if you add more qubits, the Q-sphere will come equipped with additional latitude lines like these, each representing states with equal **Hamming** values, or the number of qubits in state |1⟩. For example, a three-qubit Q-sphere will have two latitude lines, each with three possible nodes.

Three qubits in individual superposition are of two types:

- Three-qubit superposition state vector: `[0.354+0.j  0.354+0.j  0.354+0.j` `0.354+0.j  0.354+0.j  0.354+0.j  0.354+0.j  0.354+0.j]`

- Three-qubit superposition in standard matrix form:

$$|\psi\rangle = \frac{1}{\sqrt{8}}\begin{bmatrix}1\\1\\1\\1\\1\\1\\1\\1\end{bmatrix}$$

The following outcomes will be displayed on the Q-sphere:

- **North pole**: |000⟩

- **First latitude line**: |001⟩, |010⟩, and |100⟩

- **Second latitude line**: |011⟩, |101⟩, and |110⟩

- **South pole**: |111⟩:

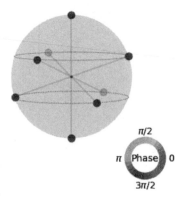

Figure 7.24 – Example of a three-qubit Q-sphere with nodes for equal probability ($\frac{1}{8}$, or 12.5%) of all the outcomes

Alright, with that under our belt, let's dive straight in.

# Getting ready

The sample code for this recipe can be found here: `https://github.com/ PacktPublishing/Quantum-Computing-in-Practice-with-Qiskit-and- IBM-Quantum-Experience/blob/master/Chapter07/ch7_r5_state_ vector.py`.

# How to do it...

For this recipe, we will set up a quantum circuit with either simple superpositions on all qubits, or with entanglement between all the qubits. As we build the circuit, we will do a state vector measurement after each gate, storing the results in a list. We will then print the returned state vectors and plot them on Bloch spheres and Q-spheres to illustrate how the qubit moves around as the circuit is executed:

1. Set the number of qubits.

   In this first step, we set the number of qubits, and then select to build a superposition circuit or a circuit with entanglement by using s or e as input:

   ```
   Ch 7: Running "diagnostics" with the state vector simulator
   ------------------------------------------------------------


   Number of qubits:
   3

   Superposition 's or entanglement 'e'?
   (To add a phase angle, use 'sp or 'ep'.)
   ep
   3 qubit quantum circuit:
   ------------------------
   ```

   Figure 7.25 – Selecting the number of qubits and the type of circuit

   We then immediately create the circuit and call the s_vec() function to display the state vector. The s_vec() function takes a circuit as input, runs the state vector simulator on the circuit, and displays the result as a Bloch sphere and a Q-sphere. It also displays the state vector for the circuit:

   ```
   def s_vec(circuit):
       backend = Aer.get_backend('statevector_simulator')
       print(circuit.num_qubits, "qubit quantum
           circuit:\n------------------------")
       print(circuit)
       psi=execute(circuit, backend).result().
           get_statevector(circuit)
       print("State vector for the",circuit.num_qubits,
           "qubit circuit:\n\n",psi)
   ```

```
print("\nState vector as Bloch sphere:")
display(plot_bloch_multivector(psi))
print("\nState vector as Q sphere:")
display(plot_state_qsphere(psi))
measure(circuit)
input("Press enter to continue...\n")
```

2.  The state vector simulator can be selected by using the following command:

```
backend = Aer.get_backend('statevector_simulator')
```

3.  With that simulator chosen, when you execute a quantum circuit, the simulator runs through the circuit one time, one shot, and returns the calculated state vector of your qubits. The outcome for a two-qubit circuit should look like this:

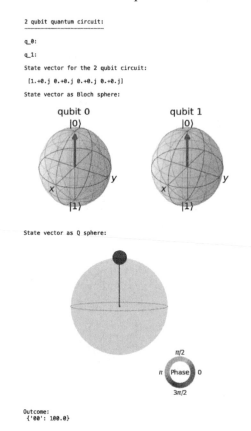

Figure 7.26 – Two-qubit circuit as Bloch spheres and a Q-sphere

The outcome is calculated in the `measure()` function by running the circuit with 10,000 shots on the Aer `qasm_simulator` simulator. For clarity, we are using 10,000 shots to get a good, even spread, and then converting the outcome into percentages for easier interpretation:

```
def measure(circuit):
    measure_circuit=QuantumCircuit(circuit.width())
    measure_circuit+=circuit
    measure_circuit.measure_all()
    #print(measure_circuit)
    backend_count = Aer.get_backend('qasm_simulator')
    counts=execute(measure_circuit,
        backend_count,shots=10000).result().
    get_counts(measure_circuit)
    # Print the counts of the measured outcome.
    print("\nOutcome:\n",{k: v / total for total in
        (sum(counts.values()),) for k, v in
        counts.items()},"\n")
```

As you can see, with an empty two-qubit circuit, we expect the measurement result 00 with 100% certainty, which we can see from the state vector:

$$|\psi\rangle = \begin{bmatrix} 1 \\ 0 \\ 0 \\ 0 \end{bmatrix}$$

You can also see both qubits pointing to $|0\rangle$, and the Q-sphere vector pointing to $|00\rangle$.

4.  Next, hit **Return** to add a first Hadamard gate to one of the qubits and run the display function again:

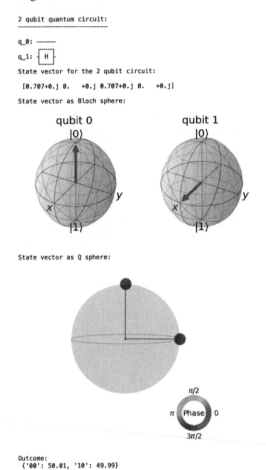

Figure 7.27 – Two qubits, with one in superposition, as Bloch spheres and a Q-sphere

Now we see the effect on the state vector when the second qubit is set in superposition with the Bloch vector pointing to the $|+\rangle$ state. Looking at the Q-sphere, we now see two possible outcomes, each with equal probability: $|00\rangle$ and $|10\rangle$.

5.  Finally, press **Return** again to add the second Hadamard, and display it again:

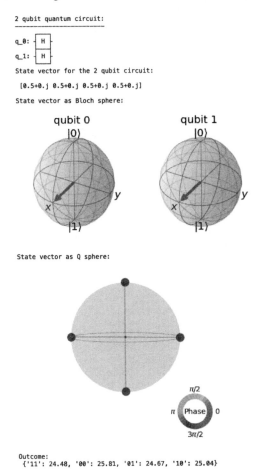

```
2 qubit quantum circuit:
-----------------------------

q_0: ─┤ H ├
q_1: ─┤ H ├

State vector for the 2 qubit circuit:

  [0.5+0.j 0.5+0.j 0.5+0.j 0.5+0.j]

State vector as Bloch sphere:
```

```
State vector as Q sphere:
```

```
Outcome:
  {'11': 24.48, '00': 25.81, '01': 24.67, '10': 25.04}
```

Figure 7.28 – Two qubits in superposition as Bloch spheres and a Q-sphere

We have now walked ourselves through our superposition step by step.

In the final step, you can see that the two-qubit Bloch vectors are both in the $|+\rangle$ state for a $|++\rangle$ superposition. The state vector is now as follows:

This is reflected in the final outcome, where the following states all have the same 25%, probability, as displayed by the Q-sphere: $|00\rangle, |01\rangle, |10\rangle,$ and $|11\rangle$.

6.  You can now run the circuit again with two qubits, but select **e** for entanglement to see how the qubits behave step by step.

7. Finally, try running the program with sp or ep as input, to include a phase angle to your superposition or entanglement circuit by adding a T-gate to the final qubit. As you will recall from *Chapter 6, Understanding the Qiskit® Gate Library*, this will introduce a π/4 phase to that qubit, which will be reflected in the Q-sphere output:

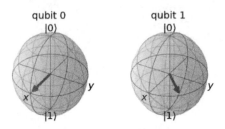

Figure 7.29 – A π/**4** phase added to qubit 1

Again, you can see the expected measurement results of |00⟩, |01⟩, |10⟩, and |11⟩ with 25% certainty, with the added twist that the |11⟩ and |10⟩ states have the phase π/4:

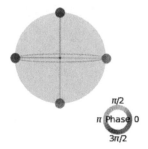

Figure 7.30 – The |10⟩ and |11⟩ results now have a π/4 phase

Note how there is no change to the counts output; adding a phase to a qubit does not change the probability of the outcomes. The phase, however, can be very useful for other, more complex quantum algorithms, as we will see in *Chapter 9, Grover's Search Algorithm*.

# There's more...

At this point, you might have a feeling of déjà vu; you have seen this before, and you are right. Flip back to the *Building quantum scores with Circuit Composer* recipe in *Chapter 3, IBM Quantum Experience® – Quantum Drag and Drop*, and take a look at the **Inspect** feature that we discussed there. What we have discussed in this recipe is the corresponding way to inspect your circuits in Qiskit®.

This has been a whirlwind tour of the simulators that are included with Qiskit®. We have touched on the most basic examples of how to use them when coding your quantum programs but have just barely scratched the surface of all of the features that are available to you. Go explore, take them for a spin, and see how they can be used as tools when developing your real quantum algorithms.

# 8

# Cleaning Up Your Quantum Act with Ignis

We have explored running our quantum programs on idealized Qiskit Aer simulators and gotten our hands dirty with the actual IBM Quantum machines. We understand that real qubits are noisy and that we cannot expect quantum computers to solve actual real-world problems of any significant magnitude (yet). On the path to this future application lies fighting and mitigating noise and errors, and on that path lies Qiskit Ignis.

Qiskit® includes a lot of automation, such as the optimization of the assigned qubits according to connectivity and performance; but this automation is, to an extent, limited by the physical layout of a quantum chip, which controls how the qubits can communicate with each other. By studying the qubit performance and specifying which actual physical qubits you want to use with your quantum programs, you can optimize your circuits for optimal entanglement and decoherence, to name a few examples.

In this chapter, we will explore how running your programs on different sets of qubits on the same backend might cause you to end up with different results. We will also use the Qiskit Ignis methods to do readout correction on our simpler algorithms on simulated and existing hardware.

Finally, we will take a look at quantum error correction using the Shor code, seeing how you can create a single logical qubit by using several physical qubits for quantum error correction.

In this chapter, we will cover the following recipes:

- Exploring your qubits to understand T1, T2, errors, and gates
- Comparing the qubits on a chip
- Estimating the number of gates you have time for
- Correcting the expected with readout correction
- Mitigating the unexpected with quantum error correction

## Technical requirements

The quantum programs that we'll discuss in this chapter can be found here: `https://github.com/PacktPublishing/Quantum-Computing-in-Practice-with-Qiskit-and-IBM-Quantum-Experience/tree/master/Chapter08`.

# Exploring your qubits to understand T1, T2, errors, and gates

Let's start off with a quick overview of some things that can go wrong when you send your perfectly working and simulator-verified quantum program to an actual, physical quantum computer. As we have seen, as soon as we step away from our perfect simulated qubits and start using physical qubits that work quantum-mechanically, we also have to contend with another physical feature of reality: noise.

In a quantum computer, the noise differs between backends, between qubits on a backend, between different types of gates, and between the readouts of each qubit. Building and programming quantum computers really is a complex task.

## Getting ready

The file required for this recipe can be downloaded from here: `https://github.com/PacktPublishing/Quantum-Computing-in-Practice-with-Qiskit-and-IBM-Quantum-Experience/blob/master/Chapter08/ch8_r1_gates_data.py`.

This recipe builds on the work we did in *Chapter 5, Touring the IBM Quantum® Hardware with Qiskit® Tools*, but this time we are specifically looking at the qubit properties that hint at the many ways that things can go wrong.

We will be using the `backend.properties()` Qiskit® method to pull out the following properties for qubits:

- `t1()`: The T1 or relaxation time for the given qubit

- `t2()`: The T2 or dephasing time for the given qubit

- `readout_error()`: The risk of misreading the qubit during measurement

- `gate_length()`: The duration of the gate in units of seconds

- `gate_error()`: The gate error estimate

## The sample code

1.  First, we import the class that we need and load our account:

```
from qiskit import IBMQ
print("Getting providers...")
if not IBMQ.active_account():
    IBMQ.load_account()
provider = IBMQ.get_provider()
```

2.  We use `select_backend()` here to load and display the data for the available backends, and then prompt to select one:

```
def select_backend():
    # Get all available and operational backends.
    print("Getting backends...")
    available_backends = provider.backends(filters=lambda
        b: not b.configuration().simulator and
        b.configuration().n_qubits > 0 and
        b.status().operational)
    # Fish out criteria to compare
    print("{0:20} {1:<10}".format("Name","#Qubits"))
    print("{0:20} {1:<10}".format("----","-------"))
    for n in range(0, len(available_backends)):
        backend = provider.get_backend(str(
            available_backends[n]))
        print("{0:20} {1:<10}".format(
        backend.name(),backend.configuration().n_qubits))
    select_backend=input("Select a backend ('exit' to
        end): ")
```

```
        if select_backend!="exit":
            backend = provider.get_backend(select_backend)
        else:
            backend=select_backend
        return(backend) F
```

3.  The `display_information(backend)` function retrieves the backend
    information such as the number of qubits and the qubit coupling map, and then
    uses that to cycle through the backend's qubits to retrieve the T1, T1, readout error,
    and gate information. The function comprises two parts.

    First, we gather the qubit information:

```
def display_information(backend):
    basis_gates=backend.configuration().basis_gates
    n_qubits=backend.configuration().n_qubits
    if n_qubits>1:
        coupling_map=backend.configuration().coupling_map
    else:
        coupling_map=[]
    micro=10**6
```

    Then, we print out the basic qubit information and the qubit-specific information
    for each gate:

```
    for qubit in range(n_qubits):
        print("\nQubit:",qubit)
        print("T1:",int(backend.properties().
            t1(qubit)*micro),"\u03BCs")
        print("T2:",int(backend.properties().
            t2(qubit)*micro),"\u03BCs")
        print("Readout error:",round(backend.
            properties().readout_error(qubit)*100,2),"%")
        for bg in basis_gates:
            if bg!="cx":
                if backend.properties().
                    gate_length(bg,[qubit])!=0:
                    print(bg,round(
                        backend.properties().gate_
                        length(bg,[0])*micro,2),"\
                        u03BCs", "Err:",round(backend.
                        properties().gate_error(bg,
                        [qubit])*100,2),"%")
                else:
                    print(bg,round(
```

```
                              backend.properties().gate_
                              length(bg,[0])*micro,2),"\
                              u03BCs",  "Err:",round(backend.
                              properties().gate_
                              error(bg,[qubit])*100,2),"%")
            if n_qubits>0:
                for cm in coupling_map:
                    if qubit in cm:
                        print("cx",cm,round(
                              backend.properties().gate_
                              length("cx",cm)*micro,2),"\
                              u03BCs",  "Err:",round(backend.
                              properties().gate_
                              error("cx",cm)*100,2),"%")
```

4.  The main function calls the `select_backend()` and `display_information(backend)` functions to help you see all the qubit information for a selected backend:

```
def main():
    backend=select_backend()
    display_information(backend)


if __name__ == '__main__':
    main()
```

# How to do it...

To explore the qubit properties of a specific backend, follow these steps:

1.  In your Python environment, run `ch8_r1_gates_data.py`.

    The script loads Qiskit® and grabs and displays a list of the available backends as shown here:

    ```
    Ch 8: Qubit properties
    ----------------------
    Getting providers...
    Getting backends...
    Name                #Qubits
    ----                -------
    ibmqx2               5
    ibmq_16_melbourne    15
    ibmq_vigo            5
    ibmq_ourense         5
    ibmq_valencia        5
    ibmq_armonk          1
    ibmq_athens          5
    ibmq_santiago        5

    Select a backend ('exit' to end): ibmq_vigo
    ```

    Figure 8.1 – Select a backend to investigate

2.    When prompted, enter the name of the IBM Quantum® backend that you want to take a look at:

We now pull in `backend.properties()` for the selected backend, and from these, sift through and display the following parameters: qubit readout error, T1 and T2 decoherence times, gate length, and error for all the basis gates for the backend.

```
Qubit: 0                              Qubit: 0
T1: 93 µs                            T1: 93 µs
T2: 16 µs                            T2: 16 µs
Readout error: 1.83 %                Readout error: 1.83 %
id 0.04 µs Err: 0.05 %               id 0.04 µs Err: 0.05 %
u1 0.0 µs Err: 0 %                   u1 0.0 µs Err: 0 %
u2 0.04 µs Err: 0.05 %               u2 0.04 µs Err: 0.05 %
u3 0.07 µs Err: 0.11 %               u3 0.07 µs Err: 0.11 %
cx [0, 1] 0.52 µs Err: 1.17 %        cx [0, 1] 0.52 µs Err: 1.17 %
cx [1, 0] 0.55 µs Err: 1.17 %        cx [1, 0] 0.55 µs Err: 1.17 %

Qubit: 1                              Qubit: 1
T1: 118 µs                           T1: 118 µs
T2: 146 µs                           T2: 146 µs
Readout error: 1.78 %                Readout error: 1.78 %
id 0.04 µs Err: 0.05 %               id 0.04 µs Err: 0.05 %
u1 0.0 µs Err: 0 %                   u1 0.0 µs Err: 0 %
u2 0.04 µs Err: 0.05 %               u2 0.04 µs Err: 0.05 %
u3 0.07 µs Err: 0.09 %               u3 0.07 µs Err: 0.09 %
cx [0, 1] 0.52 µs Err: 1.17 %        cx [0, 1] 0.52 µs Err: 1.17 %
cx [1, 0] 0.55 µs Err: 1.17 %        cx [1, 0] 0.55 µs Err: 1.17 %
cx [1, 2] 0.23 µs Err: 0.79 %        cx [1, 2] 0.23 µs Err: 0.79 %
cx [1, 3] 0.5 µs Err: 1.1 %          cx [1, 3] 0.5 µs Err: 1.1 %
cx [2, 1] 0.26 µs Err: 0.79 %        cx [2, 1] 0.26 µs Err: 0.79 %
cx [3, 1] 0.46 µs Err: 1.1 %         cx [3, 1] 0.46 µs Err: 1.1 %

Qubit: 2                              Qubit: 2
T1: 84 µs                            T1: 84 µs
T2: 92 µs                            T2: 92 µs
Readout error: 1.67 %                Readout error: 1.67 %
id 0.04 µs Err: 0.05 %               id 0.04 µs Err: 0.05 %
u1 0.0 µs Err: 0 %                   u1 0.0 µs Err: 0 %
u2 0.04 µs Err: 0.05 %               u2 0.04 µs Err: 0.05 %
u3 0.07 µs Err: 0.1 %                u3 0.07 µs Err: 0.1 %
cx [1, 2] 0.23 µs Err: 0.79 %        cx [1, 2] 0.23 µs Err: 0.79 %
cx [2, 1] 0.26 µs Err: 0.79 %        cx [2, 1] 0.26 µs Err: 0.79 %

Qubit: 3                              Qubit: 3
T1: 110 µs                           T1: 110 µs
T2: 104 µs                           T2: 104 µs
Readout error: 2.7 %                 Readout error: 2.7 %
id 0.04 µs Err: 0.05 %               id 0.04 µs Err: 0.05 %
u1 0.0 µs Err: 0 %                   u1 0.0 µs Err: 0 %
u2 0.04 µs Err: 0.05 %               u2 0.04 µs Err: 0.05 %
u3 0.07 µs Err: 0.1 %                u3 0.07 µs Err: 0.1 %
cx [1, 3] 0.5 µs Err: 1.1 %          cx [1, 3] 0.5 µs Err: 1.1 %
cx [3, 1] 0.46 µs Err: 1.1 %         cx [3, 1] 0.46 µs Err: 1.1 %
cx [3, 4] 0.27 µs Err: 0.91 %        cx [3, 4] 0.27 µs Err: 0.91 %
cx [4, 3] 0.31 µs Err: 0.91 %        cx [4, 3] 0.31 µs Err: 0.91 %

Qubit: 4                              Qubit: 4
T1: 103 µs                           T1: 103 µs
T2: 48 µs                            T2: 48 µs
Readout error: 2.01 %                Readout error: 2.01 %
id 0.04 µs Err: 0.08 %               id 0.04 µs Err: 0.08 %
u1 0.0 µs Err: 0 %                   u1 0.0 µs Err: 0 %
u2 0.04 µs Err: 0.08 %               u2 0.04 µs Err: 0.08 %
u3 0.07 µs Err: 0.16 %               u3 0.07 µs Err: 0.16 %
cx [3, 4] 0.27 µs Err: 0.91 %        cx [3, 4] 0.27 µs Err: 0.91 %
cx [4, 3] 0.31 µs Err: 0.91 %        cx [4, 3] 0.31 µs Err: 0.91 %
```

Figure 8.2 – Qubit data for the ibmq_vigo 5-qubit backend

# How it works...

That is a fair bit of data, but it only represents a small piece of the data that can be collected for a specific backend. For a refresher, see the *Exploring a selected backend using Qiskit®* recipe in *Chapter 5, Touring the IBM Quantum® Hardware with Qiskit® Tools.*

The first pieces of data that we will touch on are the **T1** and **T2** times and the **readout error**:

```
Qubit: 0
T1: 93 µs
T2: 16 µs
```

Figure 8.3 – Data for qubit 0

This first set of data represents the physical reasons that you might not get the results that you expect when you run your quantum code on the backend:

- **T1, or relaxation time**: The T1 value, displayed as µ in *Figure 8.3,* is a statistical value of how long it takes for the qubit to spontaneously relax from the "excited" state $|1\rangle$ to the ground state $|0\rangle$. In essence, T1 is an estimate of the time that you have at your disposal to perform high-quality actions on the qubit.

- **T2, or dephasing time:** Similar to T1, the T2 value, displayed as *ms* in *Figure 8.3,* is a measure of how phase information is lost for a qubit. An example of phase change is when the state $|+\rangle$ spontaneously changes to $|-\rangle$. Again, if the running time for your circuit starts to approach the T2 time, the quality of your readout data will suffer.

Now for the rest of the data that we pulled in:

```
Readout error: 1.83 %
id 0.04 µs Err: 0.05 %
u1 0.0 µs Err: 0 %
u2 0.04 µs Err: 0.05 %
u3 0.07 µs Err: 0.11 %
cx [0, 1] 0.52 µs Err: 1.17 %
cx [1, 0] 0.55 µs Err: 1.17 %
```

Figure 8.4 – Data for qubit 0

`readout_error`, `gate_length`, and `gate_error` represent the quality of the gates that you can run on each qubit.

- `readout_error`: The readout error rate, displayed as a percentage in *Figure 8.4*, is simply the probability that you will get the incorrect value when reading the qubit. For example, a qubit in state $|0\rangle$ will be read as $|1\rangle$ and vice versa. This really has nothing to do with any other qubit manipulations but is simply the error rate for the final readout of the collapsed qubit. It is possible to get a statistical picture of each qubit and mitigate these readout errors. We will do that in the *Correct the expected with readout correction* recipe.

- `gate_length`: The gate length, displayed as μ in *Figure 8.4*, represents the time it takes to make the adjustment to the qubit that corresponds to the gate. If you look at the data returned, you see that the gate length for a U3 gate might be in the order of a twentieth of a microsecond or so, whereas the T1/T2 times might be much longer than that. This, however, doesn't mean that you can just add hundreds or thousands of these gates within that time span and expect the results to be great. This is where gate errors come in.

- `gate_error`: The gate error, displayed as a percentage in *Figure 8.4*, is a statistical value for how accurate the gate is at executing the expected results. As you can see, the errors range from 0.05% to a few percent. For short circuits of just a few gates, we can run the circuit many times and statistically derive the correct values even with gate errors popping up. For longer circuits, of hundreds or thousands of gates, even these small gate errors start to make an impact. In *Chapter 9, Grover's Search Algorithm*, you will build quantum circuits with hundreds of gates.

Remember from the *What are the IBM Quantum® machines?* recipe in *Chapter 5, Touring the IBM Quantum® Hardware with Qiskit®*, that the gates are not physical things like the bundles of transistors that make up the gates in classical computing. Instead, quantum gate logic constitutes a series of microwave pulses that are sent down to and interact with the cryogenically chilled qubits. The quality of gates thus hinges on quite a few things: the physical properties of the **Josephson junction** and resonator circuit that constitute the physical qubit, the accuracy of the carrier wave and gate-coded wave package, the microwave resonators, the cryostats, and much more.

# There's more

You can also get to the backend qubit data from IBM Quantum Experience®.

Let's take a look:

1. Log in to IBM Quantum Experience® at https://quantum-computing.ibm.com.

2. On the **Welcome** page, on the right side, you'll see a list of the available backends:

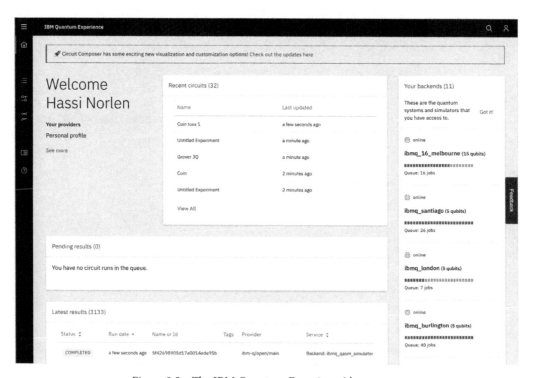

Figure 8.5 – The IBM Quantum Experience® home page

3. Click on the backend that you are interested in, for example, `ibmq_vigo`, to see the chip layout and additional information:

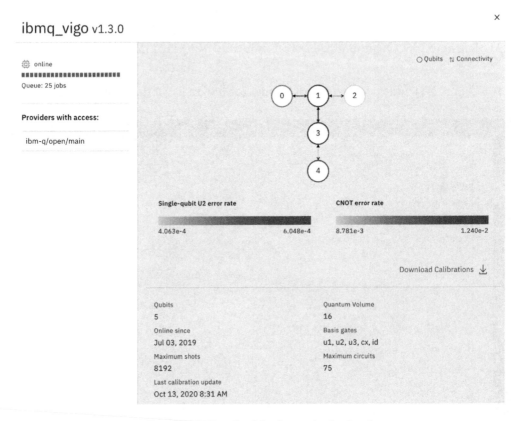

Figure 8.6 – Details of the ibmq_vigo backend

4. Click **Download Calibrations** for a CSV file with the qubit information. The downloaded calibration data looks as shown in the following screenshot:

Figure 8.7 – Downloaded calibration data from IBM Quantum Experience®

You can now bring the data into your favorite spreadsheet software for further processing as needed.

# Comparing the qubits on a chip

In the previous recipe, we looked at some of the pieces of information that you can glean about the IBM Quantum® hardware, illustrating the nature of today's NISQ machines. In this recipe, we will show a real comparison between the different qubits of a selected IBM backend.

We will run the same Bell state quantum program on three different setups: an ideal quantum computer (qasm_simulator), the best qubit pair, and the worst qubit pair on a 5-qubit, least busy IBM Quantum® machine.

We will print and plot the end result to compare the ideal result ($|00\rangle$ and $|11\rangle$ at 50%) with the real results (a probabilistic mix of $|00\rangle$, $|01\rangle$, $|10\rangle$, and $|11\rangle$) to illustrate how today's quantum computers still have a little way to go.

## Getting ready

The file required in the following recipe can be downloaded from here: `https://github.com/PacktPublishing/Quantum-Computing-in-Practice-with-Qiskit-and-IBM-Quantum-Experience/blob/master/Chapter08/ch8_r2_compare_qubits.py`

### The sample code

1.  First, we import the classes and methods that we need and load our account. In this recipe, we combine a lot of important concepts from earlier in the book, such as simulators and noise models:

```
from qiskit import IBMQ, Aer, QuantumCircuit,
ClassicalRegister, QuantumRegister, execute
from qiskit.tools.monitor import job_monitor
from qiskit.visualization import plot_histogram,
plot_error_map
from IPython.core.display import display
print("Getting provider...")
if not IBMQ.active_account():
    IBMQ.load_account()
provider = IBMQ.get_provider()
```

2.  The `select_backend()` function lets you select an available backend. You can also have the system pick the least busy one:

```
def select_backend():
    # Get all available and operational backends.
    available_backends = provider.backends(filters=lambda
```

```
        b: not b.configuration().simulator and
        b.configuration().n_qubits > 1 and
        b.status().operational)
    # Fish out criteria to compare
    print("{0:20} {1:<10} {2:<10}".
        format("Name","#Qubits","Pending jobs"))
    print("{0:20} {1:<10} {2:<10}".format("----",
        "-------","------------"))
    for n in range(0, len(available_backends)):
        backend = provider.get_backend(str(
            available_backends[n]))
        print("{0:20} {1:<10}".format(backend.
            name(),backend.configuration().
            n_qubits),backend.status().pending_jobs)
    select_backend=input("Select a backend ('LB' for
        least busy): ")
    if select_backend not in ["LB","lb"]:
        backend = provider.get_backend(str(
            select_backend))
    else:
        from qiskit.providers.ibmq import least_busy
        backend = least_busy(provider.backends(
            filters=lambda b: not b.configuration().
            simulator and b.configuration().n_qubits > 1
            and b.status().operational))
    print("Selected backend:",backend.status().
        backend_name)
    return(backend)
```

3. Pull out the best and worst CX gate performance information, then cycle through
   the CX gate couplings to find the best and worst performing connection, before
   returning this information as a `cx_best_worst` list for later usage. We can now
   take a look at the best and worst performing CX gate information that we stored. To
   verify that we have collected the correct information, we can display the error map
   for the backend, and check that the CX connectors really do represent the best
   and worst:

```
def get_gate_info(backend):
    # Pull out the gates information.
    gates=backend.properties().gates
    #Cycle through the CX gate couplings to find the best
    # and worst
    cx_best_worst = [[[0,0],1],[[0,0],0]]
```

```
    for n in range (0, len(gates)):
        if gates[n].gate ==  "cx":
            print(gates[n].name, ":", gates[n].
                parameters[0].name,"=",
                gates[n].parameters[0].value)
            if cx_best_worst[0][1]>gates[n].
                parameters[0].value:
                cx_best_worst[0][1]=gates[n].
                    parameters[0].value
                cx_best_worst[0][0]=gates[n].qubits
            if cx_best_worst[1][1]<gates[n].
                parameters[0].value:
                cx_best_worst[1][1]=gates[n].
                    parameters[0].value
                cx_best_worst[1][0]=gates[n].qubits
    print("Best cx gate:", cx_best_worst[0][0], ",",
        round(cx_best_worst[0][1]*100,3),"%")
    print("Worst cx gate:", cx_best_worst[1][0], ",",
        round(cx_best_worst[1][1]*100,3),"%")

    return(cx_best_worst)
```

4. Create two quantum circuits sized for the selected backend. With the qubit information gathered, we can create a quantum program that specifies CX gates for the best and worst qubit pairs. Here is where we use that qubits variable we pulled earlier. First, we build two circuits (qc_best and qc_worst) that have the correct number of qubits depending on the selected backend. That information is gathered using the backend.configuration().n_qubits method. We use the cx_best_worst list that we created earlier to place the H and CX gates on the correct qubits and then print the circuits:

```
def create_circuits(backend, cx_best_worst):
    print("Building circuits...")
    q1 = QuantumRegister(backend.configuration().
        n_qubits)
    c1 = ClassicalRegister(backend.configuration().
        n_qubits)
    qc_best = QuantumCircuit(q1, c1)
    qc_worst = QuantumCircuit(q1, c1)

    #Best circuit
    qc_best.h(q1[cx_best_worst[0][0][0]])
    qc_best.cx(q1[cx_best_worst[0][0][0]], q1[cx_best_
```

```
        worst[0][0][1]])
    qc_best.measure(q1[cx_best_worst[0][0][0]], c1[0])
    qc_best.measure(q1[cx_best_worst[0][0][1]], c1[1])
    print("Best CX:")
    display(qc_best.draw('mpl'))

    #Worst circuit
    qc_worst.h(q1[cx_best_worst[1][0][0]])
    qc_worst.cx(q1[cx_best_worst[1][0][0]], q1[cx_best_
        worst[1][0][1]])
    qc_worst.measure(q1[cx_best_worst[1][0][0]], c1[0])
    qc_worst.measure(q1[cx_best_worst[1][0][1]], c1[1])

    print("Worst CX:")
    display(qc_worst.draw('mpl'))

    return(qc_best,qc_worst)
```

5.  Run the best and worst circuits on the backend. With all pieces assembled, we can now run the best circuit, followed by the worst. Of course, we also want a benchmark job on the perfect `qasm_simulator` using the same number of qubits as when we ran on the actual backend. Create and run a benchmark circuit on a local simulator. Print the results for the best, worst, and baseline qubit pair and plot the results in a diagram. We can also use the Qiskit® histogram feature to display the results in diagram form for clarity.

6.  We start by displaying the best and worst CX-pair circuits, and running these on the selected backend:

```
def compare_cx(backend,qc_best,qc_worst):
    print("Comparing CX pairs...")
    print("Best CX 2:")
    display(qc_best.draw('mpl'))
    job_best = execute(qc_best, backend, shots=8192)
    job_monitor(job_best)
    print("Worst CX 2:")
    display(qc_worst.draw('mpl'))
    job_worst = execute(qc_worst, backend, shots=8192)
    job_monitor(job_worst)
```

7.  Then we build a generic CX circuit (Bell circuit), and run this one on the local `qasm_simulator` to get a baseline result:

```
q = QuantumRegister(backend.configuration().n_qubits)
c = ClassicalRegister(backend.configuration().
    n_qubits)
qc = QuantumCircuit(q, c)
qc.h(q[0])
qc.cx(q[0], q[1])
qc.measure(q[0], c[0])
qc.measure(q[1], c[1])
backend_sim = Aer.get_backend('qasm_simulator')
job_sim = execute(qc, backend_sim)
```

8.  Finally, we collect the best, worst, and baseline job results. We then print them and display them together in a diagram for comparison:

```
best_result = job_best.result()
counts_best  = best_result.get_counts(qc_best)
print("Best qubit pair:")
print(counts_best)
worst_result = job_worst.result()
counts_worst  = worst_result.get_counts(qc_worst)
print("Worst qubit pair:")
print(counts_worst)
sim_result = job_sim.result()
counts_sim  = sim_result.get_counts(qc)
print("Simulated baseline:")
print(counts_sim)
display(plot_histogram([counts_best, counts_worst,
                        counts_sim],
                        title = "Best and worst qubit
                        pair for: " + backend.name(),
                        legend = ["Best qubit
                        pair","Worst qubit
                        pair","Simulated baseline"],
                        sort = 'desc',
                        figsize = (15,12),
                        color = ['green',
                        'red','blue'],
                        bar_labels = True))
```

9. And finally, the `main` function pulls it all together:

```
def main():
    backend=select_backend()
    cx_best_worst=get_gate_info(backend)
    qc_best, qc_worst=create_circuits(backend,
        cx_best_worst)
    compare_cx(backend,qc_best,qc_worst)

if __name__ == '__main__':
    main()
```

## How to do it...

The IBM Quantum® backends are actual physical semiconductor circuits, each with slightly different behavior. In addition, the qubits are physically connected to make it possible to directly entangle them the way that you specify in your quantum programs. This type of qubit communication can only take place directly as specified by the coupling map that we looked at in the *Visualizing the backends* recipe in *Chapter 5, Touring the IBM Quantum® Hardware with Qiskit®*.

In this recipe, we extract the error rate for 2-qubit communication from our selected backend. We then pick the best and the worst qubit pairs and run the same quantum program on each pair to see how the outcome of the program differs.

Let's see how it is done:

1. In your Python environment, run `ch8_r3_time.py`. The script loads Qiskit® and grabs and displays a list of the available backends:

```
Getting provider...
Name                      #Qubits      Pending jobs
____                      _____      _____
ibmqx2                    5            19
ibmq_16_melbourne         15           9
ibmq_vigo                 5            24
ibmq_ourense              5            5
ibmq_valencia             5            3
ibmq_athens               5            4
ibmq_santiago             5            3

Select a backend ('LB' for least busy): ibmq_santiago
```

Figure 8.8 – First, we select a backend to test on, such as ibmq_santiago

Enter the name of a backend that you want to test on or enter LB to have the system pick the least busy system for you.

2.  The best and worst CX gate performance information is displayed as a list and as an error map:

```
Select a backend ('LB' for least busy): ibmq_santiago
Selected backend: ibmq_santiago
cx0_1 : gate_error = 0.007239607077796195
cx1_0 : gate_error = 0.007239607077796195
cx1_2 : gate_error = 0.0068267609051510525
cx2_1 : gate_error = 0.0068267609051510525
cx2_3 : gate_error = 0.008142773411309812
cx3_2 : gate_error = 0.008142773411309812
cx3_4 : gate_error = 0.00867161203710265
cx4_3 : gate_error = 0.00867161203710265
Best cx gate: [1, 2] , 0.683 %
Worst cx gate: [3, 4] , 0.867 %
```

Figure 8.9 – The various CX gate errors for the qubit combinations of ibmq_santiago

To verify that we have collected the correct information, we display the error map for the backend.

Take a look at the CNOT error rate legend in *Figure 8.10* and verify that the CX connectors that we have selected really are the best [1,2] and worst [3,4]:

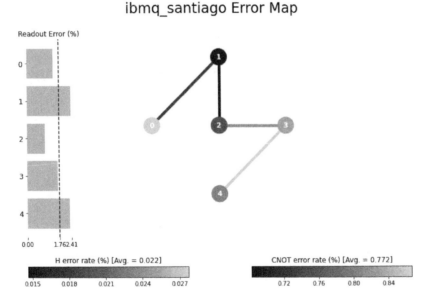

Figure 8.10 – Error map showing the best [1,2] and worst [3,4] CX connectors for ibmq_santiago

3. Two quantum circuits sized for the selected backend are created and displayed. These circuits represent the best and the worst CX connections for the backend.

The best Bell circuit for the backend is shown in the next figure:

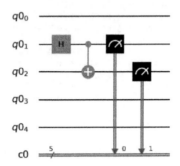

Figure 8.11 – A Bell-state circuit for the best performing CX gate

The worst Bell circuit for the backend is shown in the following figure:

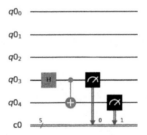

Figure 8.12 – A Bell-state circuit for the worst-performing CX gate

If you, like me, are curious about what the transpiled circuit that we will run on the backend actually looks like, you can test-transpile the circuits by adding a test transpilation right after you create the circuits in `create_circuits()`; something like this:

```
. . .
trans_qc_best = transpile(qc_best, backend)
print("Transpiled qc_best circuit:")
display(trans_qc_best.draw())
. . .
```

The result of the preceding code will be something like this:

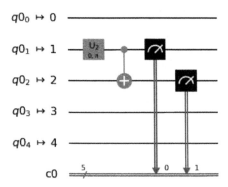

Figure 8.13 – A transpiled Bell-state circuit for the best performing CX gate

As you can see, when we follow the qubit coupling map, our transpiled CX circuit looks exactly like the original circuit.

4.  We now run the best and worst circuits on the backend together with a baseline execution of the same circuit on the Aer simulator:

```
Job Status: job has successfully run
Best qubit pair:
{'00000': 4107, '00001': 130, '00010': 95, '00011': 3860}
Worst qubit pair:
{'00000': 4343, '00001': 154, '00010': 231, '00011': 3464}
Simulated baseline:
{'00000': 491, '00011': 533}
```

Figure 8.14 – The results of the best, worst, and benchmark CX gate pairs

5.    And finally, we plot the results in a diagram for comparison:

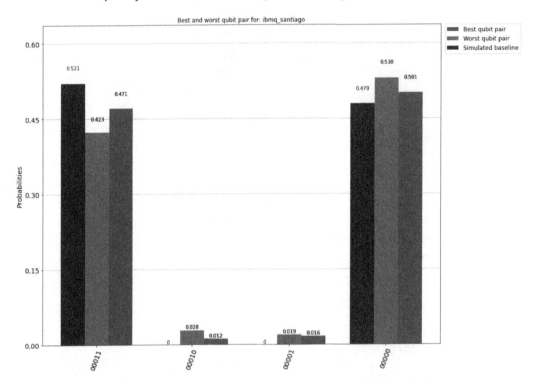

Figure 8.15 – The benchmark, best, and worst results on the 5-qubit ibmq_santiago backend

You now have a visual view, as well as numerical evidence that the qubits and gates on a chip differ in performance.

Take a look at the results here. We expect the simulated baseline (blue bars) to return perfect results for $|00\rangle$ and $|11\rangle$ only at the expected 50/50 spread. Note how there are no blue $|01\rangle$ and $|10\rangle$ results for the simulator.

On a real machine, the results are affected by qubit errors, as can be seen in the red (worst) and green (best) bars, with the IBM backends to return noisy results for all combinations $|00\rangle$, $|01\rangle$, $|10\rangle$, and $|11\rangle$, with the best qubit pair slightly less noisy than the worst pair.

## There's more...

Keep in mind that the results that you see are not just based on the CNOT coupling error, but also on qubit errors and read and write errors for your qubits. To completely understand the results of runs like these, you need to consider error mitigation.

## See also

- *Qiskit Backend Specifications for OpenQASM and OpenPulse Experiments:* `https://arxiv.org/pdf/1809.03452.pdf`.

# Estimating the number of gates you have time for

In addition to the gate errors that we have explored in the first two recipes, the end result of your recipes depends on another physical aspect of the qubits that we run on: the T1 and T2 times. We first discussed these in the *Explore your qubits to understand T1, T2, and errors* recipe:

- **T1**, or **relaxation time**: The T1 value is a statistical value of how long it takes for the qubit to spontaneously relax from the "excited" state $|1\rangle$ to the ground state $|0\rangle$. In essence, T1 is the upper limit, in microseconds, that you have at your disposal to perform high-quality actions on the qubit.

- **T2**, or **dephasing time**: Similar to T1, the T2 value is a statistical measure of how phase information is lost for a qubit. An example of phase change is when the state $|+\rangle$ spontaneously changes to $|-\rangle$. Again, if the running time for your circuit starts to approach the T2 time, the quality of your readout data will suffer.

With this data, we can make a rough estimate of how the size of our programs might affect the end result. Not only do we have to take into account the error rates for the individual gates but we have to also understand how the T1/T2 times limit the number of gates that can actually be run. How many gates can we squeeze into our programs before they just return garbage? Let's take a look.

## Getting ready

The file required in the following recipe can be downloaded from here: `https://github.com/PacktPublishing/Quantum-Computing-in-Practice-with-Qiskit-and-IBM-Quantum-Experience/blob/master/Chapter08/ch8_r3_time.py`.

## The sample code

1.  First, we import the class that we need and load our account. In this recipe, we combine a lot of important concepts from earlier in the book, such as simulators and noise models:

```
from qiskit import Aer, IBMQ, QuantumCircuit, execute
from qiskit.providers.aer.noise import NoiseModel
from qiskit.tools.visualization import plot_histogram
from qiskit.tools.monitor import job_monitor
from IPython.core.display import display
print("Getting providers...")
if not IBMQ.active_account():
    IBMQ.load_account()
provider = IBMQ.get_provider()
```

2.  The select_backend() function lets you select an available backend:

```
def select_backend():
    # Get all available and operational backends.
    print("Getting backends...")
    available_backends = provider.backends(filters=lambda
        b: not b.configuration().simulator and
        b.configuration().n_qubits > 0 and
        b.status().operational)
    # Fish out criteria to compare
    print("{0:20} {1:<10} {2:<10}".
        format("Name","#Qubits","Pending jobs"))
    print("{0:20} {1:<10} {2:<10}".format("----",
        "-------","-------------"))
    for n in range(0, len(available_backends)):
        backend = provider.get_backend(str(
            available_backends[n]))
        print("{0:20} {1:<10}".format(backend.
            name(),backend.configuration().
            n_qubits),backend.status().pending_jobs)
    select_backend=input("Select a backend:\n")
    backend = provider.get_backend(select_backend)
    return(backend)
```

3.  When passed an IBM Quantum® backend name, the `display_information(backend,n_id,ttype)` function pulls the T1, T2, readout error, and length of an `id` gate for qubit 0 of that backend:

```
def display_information(backend,n_id,ttype):
    micro=10**6
    qubit=0
    T1=int(backend.properties().t1(qubit)*micro)
    T2=int(backend.properties().t2(qubit)*micro)
    id_len=backend.properties().
        gate_length("id",[0])*micro
    if ttype=="T1":
        T=T1
    else:
        T=T2
    print("\nBackend data:")
    print("\nBackend online since:",backend.
        configuration().online_date.strftime('%Y-%m-%d'))
    print("Qubit:",qubit)
    print("T1:",T1,"\u03BCs")
    print("T2:",T2,"\u03BCs")
    print("Readout error:",round(backend.properties().
        readout_error(qubit)*100,2),"%")
    print("Qubit",qubit,"Id length:",round(id_len,3),
        "\u03BCs")
    print(ttype,"-id =", round(T-n_id*id_len,2),
        "\u03BCs",int((100*n_id*id_len)/T),"%")
    return(T)
```

4.  The `build_circuit(ttype,n_id)` function takes a number and builds a basic circuit that includes that amount of Id gates. It starts the circuit with an X gate to place the qubit in the |1⟩, or excited state. The purpose of the circuit is to wait for a period of time and then measure the qubit, and the Id gate is perfect for the job; it doesn't perform any qubit manipulation, but still takes a certain amount of time to execute. If we have waited long enough, the qubit will spontaneously relax down to the ground state, or |0⟩. This will require more or less gates depending on the T1 value for the qubit.

    Depending on the value of the `ttype` parameter, we will build one of the following:

    T1: Set up a simple circuit that puts the qubit in state |1⟩, then add a number of Id gates to make time pass, and finally perform the measurement of the outcome at different circuit lengths.

T2: Similarly, set up a simple circuit that puts the qubit in state |1⟩, then in superposition |+⟩ with phase π. Then add a number of Id gates to make time pass, and finally apply another H gate and measure. If the qubit is still in |+⟩, it will now measure as |1⟩, but if it has spontaneously changed phase, approaching |−⟩, it will read as |0⟩ with a certain probability:

```
def build_circuit(ttype,n_id):
    qc = QuantumCircuit(1,1)
    qc.x(0)
    if ttype in ["T2","t2"]:
        qc.h(0)
    for n in range(int(n_id)):
        qc.id(0)
        qc.barrier(0)
    if ttype in ["T2","t2"]:
        qc.h(0)
    qc.measure(0,0)
    return(qc)
```

5.  If we run the circuit on a simulator, we use the `build_noisemodel(backend)` function to build a noise model for the selected backend. We then use the noise model in `execute_circuit()` to simulate running the circuit on the actual backend:

```
def build_noise_model(backend):
    print("Building noise model...")
    # Construct the noise model from backend
    noise_model = NoiseModel.from_backend(backend)
    return(noise_model)
```

6.  With the `execute_circuit(backend, circuit,noise_model, n_id)` function, we run the circuit on a simulated version of the selected backend by using the noise model we created in `build_noisemodel()`:

```
def execute_circuit(backend, circuit,noise_model, n_id):
    # Basis gates for the noise model
    basis_gates = noise_model.basis_gates
    # Coupling map
    coupling_map = backend.configuration().coupling_map
    # Execute noisy simulation on QASM simulator and get
    # counts
    noisy_counts = execute(circuit,
        Aer.get_backend('qasm_simulator'),
        noise_model=noise_model, coupling_map=coupling_
```

```
        map, basis_gates=basis_gates).result().get_
        counts(circuit)
    return(noisy_counts)
```

7.  The `main` function can be broken up into a set of processes, starting with the input and information section:

```
def main():
    # Set the time type
    ttype="T1"
    # Select the backend to simulate or run on
    backend=select_backend()
    back_sim=input("Enter Q to run on the selected
        backend, S to run on the simulated backend:\n")
    if back_sim in ["Q","q"]:
        sim=False
    else:
        sim=True
        noise_model=build_noise_model(backend)
    n_id=int(input("Number of id gates:\n"))
    t=display_information(backend,n_id,ttype)
    qc=build_circuit(ttype,n_id)
    # Print sample circuit
    print("\nSample 5-Id gate",ttype,"circuit:")
    display(build_circuit(ttype,5).draw('mpl'))
```

With all input, noise model, and initial circuit creation taken care of, we can now run the circuit on a pure simulator and then on the selected backend, either simulated or on IBM Quantum®. We store our results in an `entry` dictionary, and the lengths of the executed circuits in a `legend` array, then use them to present the results:

```
    job = execute(qc, backend=Aer.get_backend(
        'qasm_simulator'), shots=8192)
    results = job.result()
    sim_counts = results.get_counts()
    print("\nRunning:")
    print("Results for simulator:",sim_counts)
    # Run the circuit
    entry={'sim':sim_counts}
    legend=['sim']
    length=n_id
    while length!=0:
        qc=build_circuit(ttype,length)
```

```
        if sim:
            noisy_counts=execute_circuit(backend,qc,
                noise_model,length)
        else:
            job = execute(qc, backend=backend,
                shots=8192)
            job_monitor(job)
            results = job.result()
            noisy_counts = results.get_counts()
        print("Results for",length,"Id gates:",
            noisy_counts)
        entry.update({str(length):noisy_counts})
        legend.append(str(length))
        length=int(length/4)
```

8.  Finally, we merge the results from the results dictionary into a `results_array` array, matching the lengths from the `legend` array, then display all the results in a combined diagram:

```
results_array=[]
for i in legend:
    results_array.append(entry[i])
# Display the final results
title="ID-circuits on "+str(backend)+" with
    "+ttype+"= "+str(t)+" \u03BCs"
if sim:
    title+=" (Simulated)"
title+=" \nOnline since: "+str(backend.
    configuration().online_date.strftime('%Y-%m-%d'))
display(plot_histogram(results_array, legend=legend,
    title=title))
```

# How to do it...

To explore how a qubit relaxes from the excited $|1\rangle$ state to the ground state $|0\rangle$, follow these steps:

1. In your Python environment, run `ch8_r3_time.py`.

   The script loads Qiskit® and grabs and displays a list of the available backends. Enter the name of a backend that you want to test on, then enter S to run on a noise-simulated version of the backend. Finally, enter the number of Id gates that you want to include in your circuit, for example, `1024`:

   ```
   Ch 8: How many gates do I have time for
   ------------------------------------------------
   Getting providers...
   Getting backends...
   Name                 #Qubits      Pending jobs
   ------               -------      ------------
   ibmqx2               5            5
   ibmq_16_melbourne    15           12
   ibmq_vigo            5            7
   ibmq_ourense         5            3
   ibmq_valencia        5            2
   ibmq_armonk          1            10
   ibmq_athens          5            3
   ibmq_santiago        5            22

   Select a backend:
   ibmq_valencia

   Enter Q to run on the selected backend, S to run on the simulated backend:
   S
   Building noise model...

   Number of id gates:
   1024|
   ```

   Figure 8.16 – Select a backend, whether to run on the actual backend, and enter a number of Id gates

2. Various pieces of data for the first qubit of the selected backend are displayed. We are particularly interested in the T1 value and the Id gate length. From these, we can estimate how long our circuit will take to run, and the percentage of the T1 time that will be consumed. We are not particularly concerned about gate errors; the Id gate does not do any qubit manipulation but is really only a delay gate:

   ```
   Backend data:

   Backend online since: 2019-07-03
   Qubit: 0
   T1: 157 µs
   T2: 67 µs
   Readout error: 3.65 %
   Qubit 0 Id length: 0.036 µs
   T1 -id = 120.59 µs 23 %
   ```

   Figure 8.17 – The backend data

3.  We also display a representative sample circuit with five Id gates. Your actual circuit will be much, much bigger, but with the same architecture; a long string of barriers and Id gates:

`Sample 5-Id gate T1 circuit:`

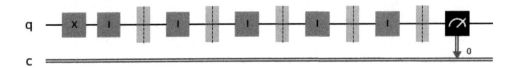

Figure 8.18 – Sample Id-circuit

4.  The circuit now runs, first on the build in the Qiskit Aer `qasm_simulator` for a clean result, then on the simulated or actual backend. It starts with a circuit with the selected number of Id gates, and then runs successively shorter circuits until it reaches a circuit with just one Id gate:

```
Running:
Results for simulator: {'1': 8192}
Results for 1024 Id gates: {'0': 313, '1': 711}
Results for 256 Id gates: {'0': 128, '1': 896}
Results for 64 Id gates: {'0': 67, '1': 957}
Results for 16 Id gates: {'0': 44, '1': 980}
Results for 4 Id gates: {'0': 54, '1': 970}
Results for 1 Id gates: {'0': 52, '1': 972}
```

Figure 8.19 – Raw T1 results on the simulated ibmq_valencia backend

5.  Finally, it collects and displays the results of all the runs in one diagram:

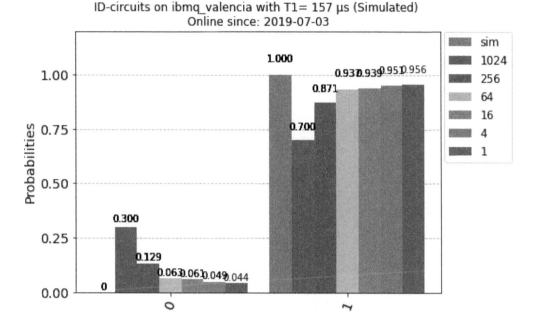

Figure 8.20 – T1 results on the simulated ibmq_valencia backend

Alright, so what do these results mean? Let's take a look…

As you can see, the probability of getting the result $|1\rangle$ gets lower and lower as the number of gates increases. At 1,024 gates, we are down to roughly 70%, which is pretty close to just noise. Try doubling the number of gates to 2,048 and see if the curve lands you somewhere close to 50% or so. So, where do you need to be to have a stab at actually getting good results from your circuits? Take a look at *Figure 8.20* again – this time, at the 1 Id gate circuit end. The probability of getting the result $|1\rangle$ hovers around 93-95%, and a bit of the uncertainty here comes from the readout error, which in our case was around 3.5%. This hints at a max circuit length of around 64 Id gates before things start to go wrong.

Also remember that this measurement only takes into account the T1 relaxation time, and only really measures the performance of the qubit at various circuit lengths, only using Id gates, which are not really useful for building actual quantum circuits.

For actual, useful circuits, we also need to take into account other factors such as gate errors, transpiling architecture, and more. This means that you cannot just extrapolate the circuit count you deem OK quality-wise from this experiment and set that as your gate limit for a backend. Take a look back at the *Comparing the Qiskit Aer simulator with an IBM quantum computer* recipe in *Chapter 7, Simulating Quantum Computers with Aer*, for a rudimentary example of what gate errors can do in long circuits.

## There's more

After this first run-through, you can test a couple of other scenarios, as discussed next.

### Comparing backends

Try running identical circuits on different backends to see how the results differ. IBM Quantum® is hard at work—developing better and better qubits and control circuitry and you can see how progressively newer backends generally have longer T1/T2 times, and better performing qubits. You can estimate how old a backend is by looking at the **online since** dates in *Figure 8.21*.

Here, for example, are the results of the 1,024 Id gate circuit on the `ibmqx2` backend, which came online in January 2017. Compare these to the `ibmq_valencia` results that we just obtained. That backend has been online since July 2019:

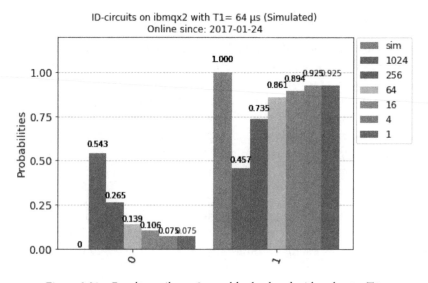

Figure 8.21 – Results on ibmqx2, an older backend with a shorter T1

By comparing the data in *Figure 8.20* (`ibmq_valencia`) with the data in *Figure 8.21* (`ibmqx2`), you can see that the T1 time is more than twice as long for the newer `ibmq_valencia` backend and that the probability of getting the correct result after 1,024 Id gates is much higher (70% versus 46%).

## Running on an IBM Quantum® backend

Now, test running the same test on the actual backend by running the sample script `ch8_r3_time.py` again and entering `Q` when prompted.

> **Pick a suitable backend**
>
> As we will be running about half a dozen individual jobs or so, the complete run might take some time depending on the number of users that are running jobs on the backend. Before you pick a backend to run on, check the **pending jobs** number for the backend.

When running on the actual backend, the job monitor provides information about your place in the queue. For the backend `ibmq_valencia`, this might give the following result:

```
Running:
Results for simulator: {'1': 8192}
Job Status: job has successfully run
Results for 1024 Id gates: {'0': 2312, '1': 5880}
Job Status: job has successfully run
Results for 256 Id gates: {'0': 825, '1': 7367}
Job Status: job has successfully run
Results for 64 Id gates: {'0': 497, '1': 7695}
Job Status: job has successfully run
Results for 16 Id gates: {'0': 389, '1': 7803}
Job Status: job has successfully run
Results for 4 Id gates: {'0': 333, '1': 7859}
Job Status: job has successfully run
Results for 1 Id gates: {'0': 344, '1': 7848}
```

Figure 8.22 – Raw T1 results on the ibmq_valencia backend

Plotted side by side, you get a visual comparison:

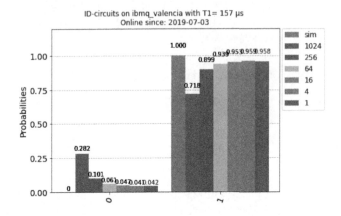

Figure 8.23 – T1 results on the ibmq_valencia backend

See how the qubit relaxes from $|1\rangle$ to $|0\rangle$ as the number of Id gates increases, and thus the *wait* time gets longer. Note how the actual backend results match the simulated results pretty well.

## Testing T2 dephasing

You can also test the T2 value – how your qubit dephases – by changing the type parameter from `"T1"` to `"T2"` in the sample code:

```
# Main
def main():
    # Set the time type
    ttype="T2"
```

How is the sample circuit different in this case? As the T2 time measures dephasing, we must first set up our qubit to actually have phase information. We start off our circuit with an X gate, putting our qubit in the $|1\rangle$ state. We then add an H gate, which brings the qubit to the $|-\rangle$ state, which is the same as the $|+\rangle$ state phase-shifted by $\pi$ radians:

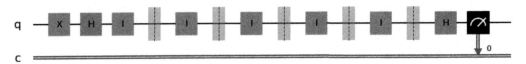

Figure 8.24 – The T2 circuit includes H gates to place our qubit in the $|-\rangle$ state, with a $\pi$ phase

We then let time pass, giving the qubit the opportunity to dephase a bit from the initial $\pi$ phase, before adding another H gate to bring us back to the computational basis so that we can measure the qubit:

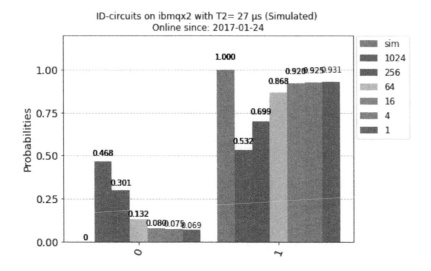

Figure 8.25 – T2 results on the ibmqx2 backend

By looking at *Figure 8.25* and *Figure 8.21*, you can now get a complete picture of the T1 and T2 impact on your qubit. Try running with even more Id gates to see how the behavior changes.

## See also

For a much more detailed description of T1 and T2 and how to measure it, take a look at *Learn Quantum Computing with Python and IBM Quantum Experience, Chapter 11, Mitigating Quantum Errors Using Ignis*, by Robert Loredo, Packt, 2020.

# Correcting for the expected with readout correction

Now that we have some knowledge about what might go wrong when we use our qubits for quantum calculations, is there anything that we can do about it? There are essentially two approaches here, at least for the small quantum backends that we have at our disposal.

First, we can make sure that the quantum programs that we run have a fighting chance of completing before the qubits get lost due to decoherence, the T1 and T2 times that we explored. This means that we make the programs short.

Second, we can take a good look at various readout errors and see if we can mitigate those. If you remember in *Chapter 7, Simulating Quantum Computers with Aer*, we could pull in actual backend qubit data to `qasm_simulator` and have it behave like an NISQ backend. We can do the same in reverse, analyze the measurement errors for a backend, and use that data to create a mitigation map to counteract erroneous measurements.

## Getting ready

The sample code for this recipe can be found here: `https://github.com/ PacktPublishing/Quantum-Computing-in-Practice-with-Qiskit-and- IBM-Quantum-Experience/blob/master/Chapter08/ch8_r4_ignis.py`.

### The sample code

To handle the creation and running of the readout correction, we build a number of functions in the `ch8_r4_ignis.py` script:

1.  First, we import the classes and methods that we need. You can import Qiskit® and load the account by running the following code:

    ```
    from qiskit import Aer, IBMQ, QuantumRegister, execute
    from qiskit import QuantumCircuit
    from qiskit.tools.visualization import plot_histogram
    from qiskit.tools.monitor import job_monitor
    from IPython.core.display import display
    print("Getting providers...")
    if not IBMQ.active_account():
        IBMQ.load_account()
    provider = IBMQ.get_provider()
    ```

2.  Using `select_backend()`, we load and display the data for the available backends, and then prompt to select one:

    ```
    def select_backend():
        # Get all available and operational backends.
        available_backends = provider.backends(filters=lambda
            b: not b.configuration().simulator and
            b.configuration().n_qubits > 1 and
            b.status().operational)
        # Fish out criteria to compare
        print("{0:20} {1:<10} {2:<10}".
            format("Name","#Qubits","Pending jobs"))
        print("{0:20} {1:<10} {2:<10}".format("----",
            "-------","------------"))
    ```

```
    for n in range(0, len(available_backends)):
        backend = provider.get_backend(str(
            available_backends[n]))
        print("{0:20} {1:<10}".format(backend.
            name(),backend.configuration().
            n_qubits),backend.status().pending_jobs)
    select_backend=input("Select a backend ('exit' to
        end): ")
    if select_backend!="exit":
        backend = provider.get_backend(select_backend)
    else:
        backend=select_backend
    return(backend)
```

3. Using `create_circuit()`, we create a basic GHZ-state circuit for which we know the expected outcomes – $|000\rangle$ and $|111\rangle$:

```
def create_circuit():
    #Create the circuit
    circuit = QuantumCircuit(3)
    circuit.h(0)
    circuit.cx(0,1)
    circuit.cx(0,2)
    circuit.measure_all()
    print("Our circuit:")
    display(circuit.draw('mpl'))
    return(circuit)
```

4. `simulator_results(circuit)` runs the provided circuit on the local Qiskit Aer simulator:

```
def simulator_results(circuit):
    # Run the circuit on the local simulator
    job = execute(circuit, backend=Aer.get_backend(
        'qasm_simulator'), shots=8192)
    job_monitor(job)
    results = job.result()
    sim_counts = results.get_counts()
    print("Simulator results:\n",sim_counts)
    return(sim_counts)
```

5. `noisy_results(circuit,backend)` runs the provided circuit on the provided backend:

```
def noisy_results(circuit,backend):
    # Select backend and run the circuit
    job = execute(circuit, backend=backend, shots=8192)
    job_monitor(job)
    results = job.result()
    noisy_counts = results.get_counts()
    print(backend,"results:\n",noisy_counts)
    return(noisy_counts,results)
```

6. This `mitigated_results(backend,circuit,results)` function is the main function we build to run error mitigation on the provided results, based on backend measurement error data:

```
def mitigated_results(circuit,backend,results):
    # Import the required methods
    from qiskit.providers.aer.noise import NoiseModel
    from qiskit.ignis.mitigation.measurement import
        (complete_meas_cal,CompleteMeasFitter)
    # Get noise model for backend
    noise_model = NoiseModel.from_backend(backend)
    # Create the measurement fitter
    qr = QuantumRegister(circuit.num_qubits)
    meas_calibs, state_labels = complete_meas_cal(qr=qr,
        circlabel='mcal')
    job = execute(meas_calibs, backend=Aer.get_
        backend('qasm_simulator'), shots=8192,
        noise_model=noise_model)
    cal_results = job.result()
    meas_fitter = CompleteMeasFitter(cal_results,
        state_labels, circlabel='mcal')
    # Plot the calibration matrix
    print("Calibration matrix")
    meas_fitter.plot_calibration()
    # Get the filter object
    meas_filter = meas_fitter.filter
    # Results with mitigation
    mitigated_results = meas_filter.apply(results)
    mitigated_counts = mitigated_results.get_counts(0)
    print("Mitigated",backend,"results:\n",
        mitigated_counts)
    return(mitigated_counts)
```

7.  And finally, the `main()` function helps in wrapping up the function flow and final data presentation:

```
def main():
    backend=select_backend()
    circ=create_circuit()
    sim_counts=simulator_results(circ)
    noisy_counts,results=noisy_results(circ,backend)
    # Analyze and error correct the measurements
    mitigated_counts=mitigated_results(circ,backend,
        results)
    # Show all results as a comparison
    print("Final results:")
    display(plot_histogram([sim_counts, noisy_counts,
        mitigated_counts], legend=['sim','noisy',
        'mitigated']))
```

# How to do it...

1.  In your local Qiskit® environment, run the `ch8_r4_ignis.py` sample, then select one of the available backends to test on:

```
Ch 8: Correct for the expected
----------------------------------
Getting providers...
Name                  #Qubits    Pending jobs
----                  -------    ------------

ibmqx2                5          4
ibmq_16_melbourne     15         12
ibmq_vigo             5          3
ibmq_ourense          5          5
ibmq_valencia         5          20
ibmq_athens           5          5
ibmq_santiago         5          2

Select a backend ('exit' to end): ibmqx2
```

Figure 8.26 – Select an available backend

2.  We'll now build the GHZ-state circuit that we will be testing with. We know that the expected outcomes are $|000\rangle$ and $|111\rangle$, and can use that information to validate how well our circuit runs on the selected backend, and how well we can error correct:

Our circuit:

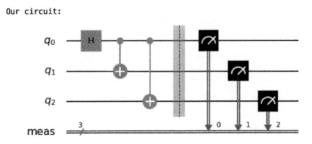

Figure 8.27 – The GHZ-state circuit that we will test with

3.  The script now runs the circuit on a local simulator and on the selected backend:

```
Job Status: job has successfully run
Simulator results:
 {'000': 4101, '111': 4091}
Job Status: job has successfully run
ibmqx2 results:
 {'000': 3477, '001': 240, '010': 180, '011': 131, '100': 69, '101': 213, '110': 246,
'111': 3636}
```

Figure 8.28 – Results on the local qasm_simulator and on the ibmqx2 backend

4.  Now that we have the results of the circuit when run on the backend, we can pull in
    the actual qubit and gate data from the backend and build a noise model.

    The model includes statistics on the measurement behavior for the backend's qubits:

Calibration matrix

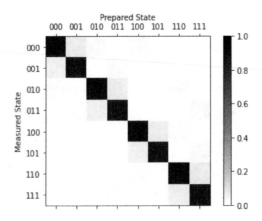

Figure 8.29 – Calibration matrix with the expected results and the statistical measurement errors

In *Figure 8.29*, you can see the expected results in the diagonal, and the statistical measurement errors as gray shading away from the diagonal. The darker the shading, the higher the probability of getting that result.

We can use this data to rerun the circuit on the local simulator, with the measurement calibration data as input. We can then run the original results through a measurement filter and get the mitigated results as follows:

```
Mitigated ibmqx2 results:
 {'000': 3796.9401456056394, '001': 43.78835359865318, '010': 111.03029097839597, '011'
1.5865949701636701, '101': 114.59024711838815, '111': 4124.064367728765}
```

Figure 8.30 – The mitigated results for ibmq_16_melbourne

5.  Finally, we can plot the simulator results, the original backend results, and the mitigated results for comparison:

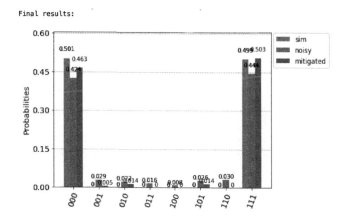

Figure 8.31 – A comparison of results for simulator, backend, and mitigated backend

From the final chart, you can see that the expected results for a GHZ-state circuit, $|000\rangle$ and $|111\rangle$ with roughly a 50/50 chance, is not what we get on the backend. There are a large number of noisy bars between the expected results. With the error mitigation, we shrink these bars and bring the results closer to the expected.

# Mitigating the unexpected with quantum error correction

As we saw in the previous recipe, it is good to understand how your measurements behave, to statistically be able to correct incorrect readouts. But in the end, a measurement is just a measurement, and a measurement of a qubit will result in either 0 or 1. If the state of the qubit that you measure turns out to be $|1\rangle$ instead of the expected $|0\rangle$, it doesn't matter that you statistically corrected for measurement mistakes; your qubit is off by 100%.

There are a lot of things that can perturb our qubits, from gate errors to just plain physics that causes the qubit to decohere and dephase (remember the T1 and T2 times). In the classical computing world, we can periodically check in on our bits, and apply error correction coding to make sure that they behave. Digital error correction is one of the reasons that digital communication works and that you can play digital media, CDs, DVDs, and Blu-ray disks and actually hear or see what you expect.

One way of performing classical error correction is to duplicate one bit that you want to transfer into three bits, and at the end compare the bit with its duplicated brethren. If they are different, then at least one of the bits has been *errored*. Very simply put, you can then take a majority vote and flip the offending bit, and thus get the original back.

For qubits, it is not so simple. For one, you cannot make copies of qubits like you can for classical bits. Instead, we have to make use of **superposition** and **entanglement**.

We discussed superposition at length in the *Comparing a bit and a qubit* recipe of *Chapter 2, Quantum Computing and Qubits with Python*, and entanglement in the *Quantum-cheating in a coin toss? – Introducing the Bell State* recipe of *Chapter 4, Starting at the Ground Level with Terra*. Feel free to go back for a refresher.

Let's use these tools to explore further... Read on!

## Getting ready

The sample code for this recipe can be found here: `https://github.com/PacktPublishing/Quantum-Computing-in-Practice-with-Qiskit-and-IBM-Quantum-Experience/blob/master/Chapter08/ch8_r5_shor.py`.

# The sample code

To handle the creation and running of the Shor code algorithm, we will build a number of functions in the `ch8_r5_shor.py` script:

1.  First, we import the methods that we need and set the backend:

    ```
    from qiskit import QuantumCircuit, execute, Aer
    from qiskit.visualization import plot_bloch_multivector,
    plot_state_qsphere
    # Supporting methods
    from math import pi
    from random import random
    from IPython.core.display import display
    # Set the Aer simulator backend
    backend = Aer.get_backend('qasm_simulator')
    ```

2.  The `get_psi(qc)` function is an old friend that we are reusing to return the state vector of the circuit, to display Bloch spheres and Q-spheres:

    ```
    def get_psi(qc):
        global psi
        backend = Aer.get_backend('statevector_simulator')
        result = execute(qc, backend).result()
        psi = result.get_statevector(qc)
        return(psi)
    ```

3.  Instead of expecting the first qubit errors to occur naturally, we use the `add_error(error, circuit,ry_error, rz_error)` function to create four different types of errors – **Bit flip**, **Bit flip + phase flip**, **Theta + phi shift**, and **Random**:

    ```
    def add_error(error, circuit,ry_error, rz_error):
        circuit.barrier([x for x in range(circuit.num_
            qubits)])
        if error=="1": #Bit flip error
            circuit.x(0)
        elif error=="2": #Bit flip plus phase flip error
            circuit.x(0)
            circuit.z(0)
        else: #Theta plus phi shift and Random
            circuit.ry(ry_error,0)
            circuit.rz(rz_error,0)
    ```

```
circuit.barrier([x for x in range(circuit.num_
    qubits)])
return(circuit)
```

4.  The not_corrected(error, ry_error, rz_error) function creates
    a simple 1-qubit circuit and introduces the error that we select in the main process,
    then displays the results as a Bloch sphere and a Q-sphere. We also run the circuit
    on the Qiskit Aer qasm_simulator to see the results of our contaminated qubit:

```
def not_corrected(error, ry_error, rz_error):
    # Non-corrected code
    qco = QuantumCircuit(1,1)
    print("\nOriginal qubit, in state |0>")
    display(plot_bloch_multivector(get_psi(qco)))
    display(plot_state_qsphere(get_psi(qco)))
    # Add error
    add_error(error,qco, ry_error, rz_error)
    print("\nQubit with error...")
    display(plot_bloch_multivector(get_psi(qco)))
    display(plot_state_qsphere(get_psi(qco)))
    qco.measure(0,0)
    display(qco.draw('mpl'))
    job = execute(qco, backend, shots=1000)
    counts = job.result().get_counts()
    print("\nResult of qubit error:")
    print("----------------------")
    print(counts)
```

5.  Now it is time to add the quantum correction code that Peter Shor developed. We
    are building the same circuit as before, but with 8 **ancilla** qubits, which we use to
    process the qubit information. Our creation will be a combination of a 3-qubit
    phase flip code, and 3-qubit bit flip codes. This displays the qubit state (actually
    the state of all 9 qubits, but we are mainly interested in the state of the first qubit,
    the least significant bit in the ket-notation: $|{\ldots}0\rangle$). It also displays the final result of
    measuring the qubit after quantum error correction.

The function contains several sections:

**The first half of the phase-flip correction**: Here, we create the quantum circuit and put together the start of the phase-flip correction part of the circuit:

```
def shor_corrected(error, ry_error, rz_error):
    # A combination of a three qubit phase flip code, and
    # 3 bit flip codes
    qc = QuantumCircuit(9,1)
    print("\nOriginal LSB qubit, in state |...0⟩")
    display(plot_state_qsphere(get_psi(qc)))
    # Start of phase flip code
    qc.cx(0,3)
    qc.cx(0,6)
    qc.h(0)
    qc.h(3)
    qc.h(6)
    qc.barrier([x for x in range(qc.num_qubits)])
```

**The first half of the bit-flip correction**: Each of the 3 qubits used for the phase-flip correction must now be protected against phase-flip. We have now engaged all 9 qubits to help us:

```
    qc.cx(0,1)
    qc.cx(3,4)
    qc.cx(6,7)
    qc.cx(0,2)
    qc.cx(3,5)
    qc.cx(6,8)
```

**Introduce errors to the first qubit**: At this stage in the circuit creation, we now add some errors to the first qubit by using the add_error() function. This simulates real-world perturbance of the qubit:

```
    add_error(error,qc, ry_error, rz_error)
    print("Qubit with error... LSB can be in |...0⟩ and in
        |...1⟩, with various phase.")
    display(plot_state_qsphere(get_psi(qc)))
    display(qc.draw('mpl'))
```

**The end of the bit-flip correction**: After the errors have been introduced, we now start collecting our qubits again, starting with wrapping up the bit-flip correction and adjusting each of the phase-shift qubits if needed:

```
qc.cx(0,1)
qc.cx(3,4)
qc.cx(6,7)
qc.cx(0,2)
qc.cx(3,5)
qc.cx(6,8)
qc.ccx(1,2,0)
qc.ccx(4,5,3)
qc.ccx(8,7,6)
```

**The end of the phase-flip correction**: And similar to the bit flip wrapping up, we now close the phase-flip correction, applying any necessary correction to the first qubit:

```
qc.h(0)
qc.h(3)
qc.h(6)
qc.cx(0,3)
qc.cx(0,6)
qc.ccx(6,3,0)
```

**Measure and print**: We can now measure the qubit and print the result:

```
qc.barrier([x for x in range(qc.num_qubits)])
qc.measure(0,0)
print("Error corrected qubit... LSB in |...0)
    with phase 0.")
display(plot_state_qsphere(get_psi(qc)))
display(qc.draw('mpl'))
job = execute(qc, backend, shots=1000)
counts = job.result().get_counts()
print("\nResult of qubit error after
    Shor code correction:")
print("-------------------------------------------
    ----")
print(counts)
```

6.  The program prompts for a numeric input to select the error to introduce, and then runs the `not_corrected()` and `shor_corrected()` functions:

```
def main():
    error="1"
    ry_error=0
    rz_error=0
    while error!="0":
        error=input("Select an error:\n1. Bit flip\n2.
            Bit flip plus phase flip\n3. Theta plus phi
            shift\n4. Random\n")
        if error=="3":
            ry_error=float(input("Enter theta:\n"))
            rz_error=float(input("Enter phi:\n"))
        if error=="4":
            ry_error=pi*random()
            rz_error=2*pi*random()
        not_corrected(error, ry_error, rz_error)
        input("Press enter for error correction...")
        shor_corrected(error, ry_error, rz_error)
```

The code we have built here can now be run, simulating the quantum error correction of any phase and the bit perturbation of the qubit.

## How to do it...

Let's take the Shor code for a spin:

1.  In your Python environment, run `ch8_r5_shor.py`.
2.  When prompted, enter the error type for a bit flip: 1.

3.   The error-free qubit is displayed:

```
Select an error:
1. Bit flip
2. Bit flip plus phase flip
3. Delta plus phi shift
4. Random
1

Original qubit, in state |0>
```

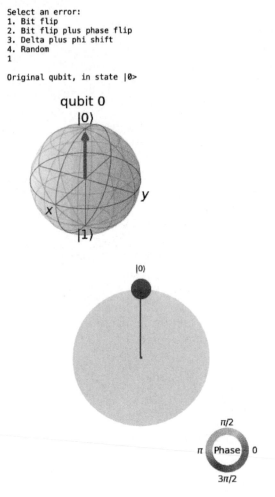

Figure 8.32 – The qubit with no error, in state $|0\rangle$

4.  Then, the selected error is added, and the results are displayed. The qubit has now flipped from $|0\rangle$ to $|1\rangle$:

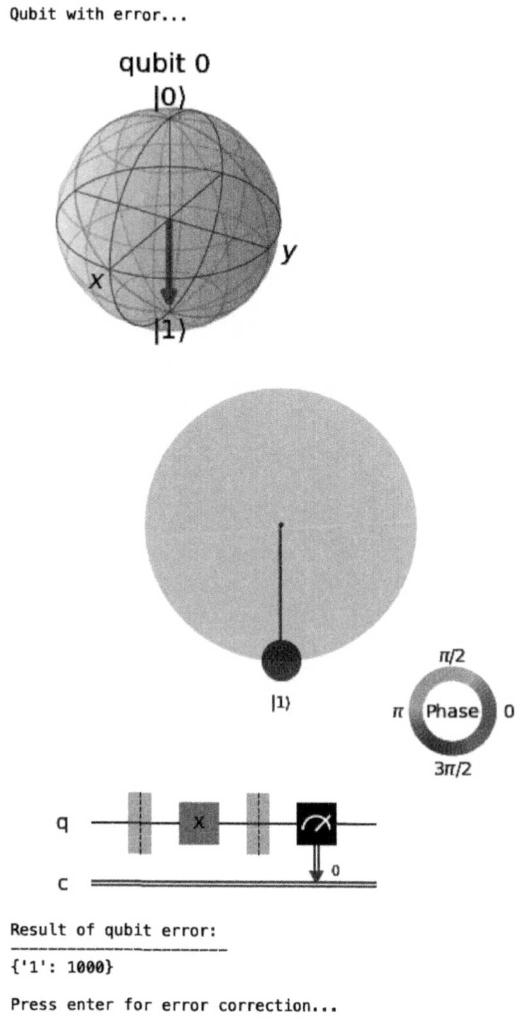

Figure 8.33 – The qubit with the selected bit-flip error, turning the qubit from $|0\rangle$ to $|1\rangle$

5.  Now, press *Enter* to create a new circuit and display the undisturbed qubit with its 8 ancilla qubits. The Q-sphere displays the possible outcomes of this new unperturbed circuit, all 9 qubits in $|0\rangle$:

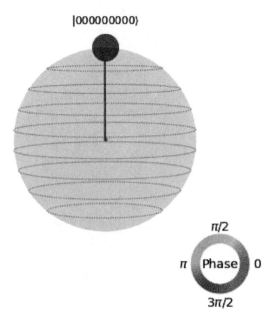

Figure 8.34 – Undisturbed qubit with 8 ancilla qubits

6. We now start the Shor code creation and add the simulated error. The Q-sphere now shows a number of possible outcomes as qubits 0, 3, and 6 are now in a superposition, giving a probabilistic outcome for those qubits, and for their entangled counterparts. Notice that qubit 0 can now appear as both $|\dots0\rangle$ and $|\dots1\rangle$:

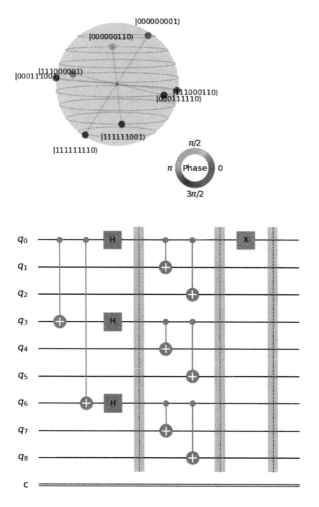

Figure 8.35 – Qubit with added bit-flip error, turning the qubit from $|\mathbf{0}\rangle$ to $|\mathbf{1}\rangle$

7.   Finally, we complete the Shor code, display the expected outcomes for the circuit, and then run it on the Aer `qasm_simulator`:

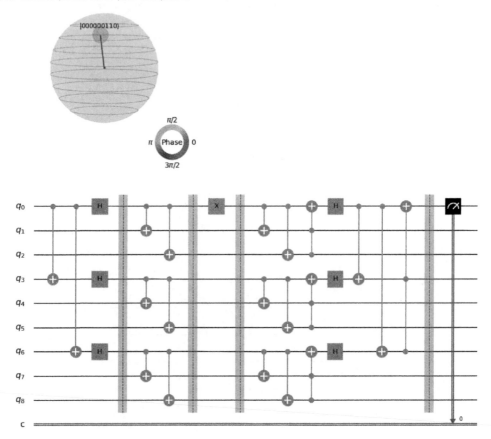

Figure 8.36 – Result of the error-corrected qubit, back at $|0\rangle$ again

Take a look at the Q-sphere and the results count. The state vector has safely put our qubit back at $|0\rangle$ again; note how the least-significant bit that represents the first qubit is now $|\dots 0\rangle$. The result also points to our qubit being safely error-corrected, with a 100% chance of 0.

# How it works...

Here's a short explanation of how qubit error correction works. We first create what is called a **syndrome** by entangling our qubit with two other ancilla qubits. The entangled qubits now walk through life as one entity, indistinguishable from each other with one exception: errors to the qubits are not entangled, but unique to each qubit.

Before using our qubit for anything, we first disentangle it from the other 2 qubits; it is now a standalone qubit again. Now it is time to use the **syndrome** to correct any errors.

To do this, we set up a Toffoli (**CCX**) gate from our two syndrome qubits to our qubit of interest. If the syndrome qubits differ from our original qubit, that is, our qubit has been disturbed, the CCX flips the qubit right again.

That's it. Simple, eh? Well, let's take a closer look.

There are two methods we can use, for two different qubit errors:

- **Bit-flip correction**: Correcting flipped qubits, from $|1\rangle$ to $|0\rangle$ and vice versa
- **Phase-flip**: Correcting flipped phases, from $|+\rangle$ to $|-\rangle$ and vice versa

## Bit-flip correction

In the bit correction method, we set up a GHZ-state entangled circuit, using the first qubit as the controller for a CXX gate (or two CX gates in this case), where two additional ancilla qubits are used as the error correction syndrome only and are not used in the final measurement:

1. If the first qubit is $|..1\rangle$, we now have the following state:

   $|111\rangle$

   If it is $|..0\rangle$, we now have $|000\rangle$ – nothing new there.

2. After setting up the initial qubit and its ancillas, we let the world act on the first qubit, potentially introducing bit-flip errors, sending our $|..1\rangle$, for example, to $|..0\rangle$.

   In the diagram that follows, this is represented by the two barriers between the two sets of CX gates.

3. Our 3 qubits might now be in the following two states:

   $|110\rangle$ or $|001\rangle$

4.  We then run a second GHZ-entanglement to disentangle the first qubit, and end up with the following states:

    $|110\rangle$, nothing changes as the first qubit is now $|..0\rangle$, and $|111\rangle$ if the first qubit is $|..1\rangle$.

5.  At this point, we add a supremely clever piece of coding by adding a Toffoli gate, with the two syndrome qubits as controllers, and the first qubit as the controlled qubit. What happens?

    $|110\rangle$ turns into $|111\rangle$, and $|111\rangle$ into $|110\rangle$, and like magic, our first qubit has returned to its original state of $|..1\rangle$ or $|..0\rangle$:

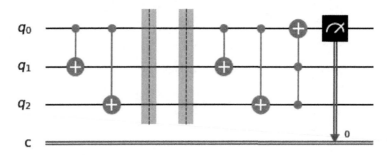

Figure 8.37 – The bit-flip quantum correction circuit

## Phase-flip correction

But a qubit also differs from a classical bit by one critical aspect: in addition to 0 and 1, a qubit can also have a phase value, and thus also phase errors. Can we error correct for that? Turns out that we can, with basically the same method, with yet another clever twist:

1.  Like before, we start out with our 3 qubits, and our GHZ-state:

    $|111\rangle$ and $|000\rangle$

2.  The next step is to transform our measurement basis state into a state where we can work with phase information, by adding a Hadamard gate to each qubit. We now have the following two states instead:

    $|---\rangle$ and $|+++\rangle$

3.  Again, we let nature act on the first qubit, potentially ending up with a phase-shifted first qubit, like this:

    $|--+\rangle$ and $|++-\rangle$

    In the diagram that follows, the error occurs between the two barriers between the H gates.

4.  Like in the bit-flip example, we now apply the Hadamard gate and the GHZ-creating CXX gates again, and now end up with the following:

    $|110\rangle$ and $|001\rangle$ after H

    $|110\rangle$ and $|111\rangle$ after CXX

5.  And finally, the Toffoli (CCX) gate turns the qubit trio into the following:

    $|111\rangle$ and $110\rangle$

    Again, our first qubit has returned to its original state of $|\cdot\cdot1\rangle$ and $|\cdot\cdot0\rangle$:

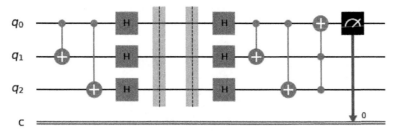

Figure 8.38 – The phase-flip quantum correction circuit

## Shor code

That is all great; we can tackle bit-flip errors as well as phase-flip errors. But what if both types of errors occur? After all, qubits are physical entities, and who really knows how they will behave? It turns out that we can do that as well. Peter Shor, of Shor's algorithm fame (see *Chapter 10, Getting to Know Algorithms with Aqua*) invented the Shor code, which is a combination of the phase-flip and bit-flip methods using 9 qubits in total. The first qubit is the one we want to do quantum error correction on, and the eight following are the ancillas, only used for working the correction magic:

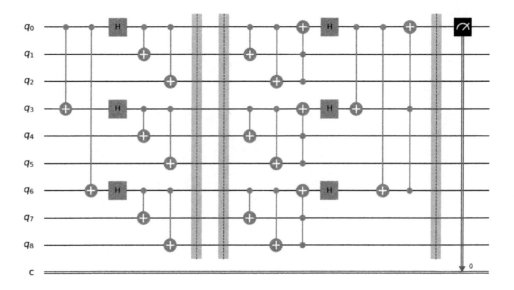

Figure 8.39 – The Shor code circuit

Here's a quick description, but do take a look at *Figure 8.39*:

1.  Set up the first half of the phase-flip circuit using qubits 0, 3, and 6.

2.  Set up the first half of three bit-flip circuits for qubits 0, 3, and 6.

3.  Leave some room for nature and the error to happen to qubit 0. The two barriers between the triplicate CX gate sets below.

4.  Set up the second half of three bit-flip circuits for qubits 0, 3, and 6, effectively correcting any bit flips on these 3 qubits.

5.  Set up the second half of the phase-flip circuit for qubits 0, 3, and 6, correcting any phase shifts for these three qubits.

6.  Measure qubit 0.

Now the math turns somewhat complicated, with Ket-representations for 9 qubits looking like this, for example: $|011000101\rangle$. Not to mention what unitary matrices for 9-qubit circuits look like.

## There's more

The first example that we ran, a simple bit-flip error, didn't really make use of the full power of the Shor code. Try some of the other options to simulate any type of conceivable error that might occur, from the simple to the very complex.

The following options are available:

- **Bit flip**: This error flips the bit upside-down, from $|0\rangle$ to $|1\rangle$.

- **Bit flip plus phase flip**: A combined bit and phase flip.

- **Theta plus phi shift**: Create your own error by entering the theta $\theta$ and phi $\varphi$ angles to point your state vector at any point on the Bloch sphere. If you need a reminder about what these two angles represent, take a quick look at the *Visualizing a qubit in Python* recipe in *Chapter 2, Quantum Computing and Qubits with Python*.

- **Random**: A random error.

## See also

- *Quantum Error Correction for Beginners*, Simon J. Devitt, William J. Munro, and Kae Nemoto, June 24, 2013, https://arxiv.org/pdf/0905.2794.pdf

- *Quantum Computation and Quantum Information* by Isaac L. Chuang; Michael A. Nielsen, Cambridge University Press, 2010, Chapter 10.2 Shor code

# 9
# Grover's Search Algorithm

In this chapter, we will take a look at a fairly well-known quantum algorithm: **Grover's search algorithm**. We will learn how to code it by building our own circuits for the following variations: a 2-qubit version, a 3-qubit version, and a 4- and more qubit version, to see how the complexity of the circuit grows with the number of qubits.

We will run our algorithm both on a local simulator and on an IBM Quantum® backend and will see how the algorithm works pretty well on the relatively short circuit that is required for a 2-qubit Grover, but not as well on the much larger circuits that are required for more qubits. The number of gates in your circuit gets successively larger, and the various errors that we explored in *Chapter 8, Cleaning Up Your Quantum Act with Ignis*, start to dominate.

In this chapter, we will cover the following recipes:

- Exploring quantum phase kickback
- A quick interlude on classical search
- Building Grover's search algorithm
- Searching with a 3-qubit Grover

- Adding more qubits to the Grover search
- Using the Grover circuit in your own code

# Technical requirements

The quantum programs that we will discuss in this chapter can be found here: `https://github.com/PacktPublishing/Quantum-Computing-in-Practice-with-Qiskit-and-IBM-Quantum-Experience/tree/master/Chapter09`.

Much like we did in *Chapter 6, Understanding the Qiskit® Gate Library*, we will create one main Python file to contain the more complex functions that we will use: `ch9_grover_functions.py`.

Among other functions, this program includes a set of core functions that are used to build the Grover algorithm:

- `create_oracle()`: This function builds a 2-5-qubit Oracle for the correct solution.
- `create_amplifier()`: This function builds the phase amplification part of your Grover circuit.
- `create_grover()`: This function puts the pieces together and returns a functioning Grover circuit that you can run on a simulator or on a real quantum computer.

We will discuss these further in the *Building the Grover search algorithm* recipe. Suffice to say that these main functions are all that is required to build the Grover algorithm, and the rest of the components in the program are there to assist in visualizing the process.

The other functions that are included in the `ch9_grover_functions.py` file are as follows:

- `print_psi()`: This function prints out a nicely formatted statevector for your circuits.
- `get_psi()`: This function returns the statevector for your circuit, and also displays it as a Q-sphere, Bloch sphere, or plain vector.

- `print_unitary()`: This function prints out the unitary matrix for your circuit. For this chapter, where we expect no imaginary components of the unitary; we simplify things a bit and only print out the real values and use the BasicAer `unitary_simulator` to create the unitary.

- `display_circuit()`: This function displays the circuit, and optionally a Q-sphere view of the circuit statevector and the unitary matrix of the circuit.

Finally, we have a set of functions that we use to run our circuits on simulators, quantum computers, and transpilers:

- `run_grover()`: Included for completeness, a function that runs your Grover circuit on a simulator or on an IBM Quantum® backend.

- `mitigated_results()`: Revisiting the previous chapter, *Chapter 8, Cleaning Up Your Quantum Act with Ignis*, we use this function to run error mitigation on our 2-qubit Grover. As we will see, running error mitigation on the 3- and 4+-qubit circuits will not produce any better results.

- `transpile_circuit()`: To provide insight, we bring back the transpile functionality that we used in the *What your quantum circuit really looks like* recipe of *Chapter 6, Understanding the Qiskit® Gate Library*.

But before we dive into the algorithm, we will start by taking a look at one of the building blocks for many quantum algorithms (Grover included)—so-called **phase kickback**.

# Exploring quantum phase kickback

In this first recipe, we will take a closer look at a staple component of many quantum algorithms, quantum phase kickback, which is used to let one or more qubits pick up the phase angle of a second qubit without changing that second qubit. In the *Building the Grover algorithm* recipe, we will use phase kickback to identify the correct solution for our search and to amplify the probability of measuring that solution.

This recipe will require a little bit of math to explain some pretty unintuitive aspects of the process and results, but we'll walk through it. It is a really good starting point for the mind-blowing aspects of quantum algorithms.

# Getting ready

The sample code for this recipe can be found here: `https://github.com/PacktPublishing/Quantum-Computing-in-Practice-with-Qiskit-and-IBM-Quantum-Experience/blob/master/Chapter09/ch9_r1_kickback.py`.

The recipe in itself is pretty simple and consists of a set of steps that will walk you through the phase kickback process, first on one, then two qubits.

With each step, we will use the `display_circuit()` function from `ch9_grover_functions.py` to display what happens to the qubits, so let's start by taking a look at that function:

```
def display_circuit(circuit,psi,unitary):
    disp=True
    if disp:
        display(circuit.draw(output="mpl"))
        if psi:
            get_psi(circuit,"Q")
        if unitary:
            print_unitary(circuit)
```

The `display_circuit()` function is the main visualization function of the collection and takes a quantum `circuit` and two logical arguments as input. If `psi=True`, we will call the `get_psi()` function, which displays the circuit as a Q-sphere and calls the `print_psi()` function to print a nice version of the resulting circuit statevector. If `unitary=True`, then it calls the `print_unitary()` function to display the unitary matrix of the circuit.

In this recipe, we set `unitary=False` and focus on the statevector visualization.

# How to do it...

Let's explore how to add phases to qubits:

1. We start by importing the required classes and methods and the `display_circuit()` function, which will let us display what we are doing:

```
from qiskit import QuantumCircuit
from ch9_grover_functions import display_circuit
```

2. Now, let's create a single qubit initialized to state $|0\rangle$:

```
qc1 = QuantumCircuit(1)
display_circuit(qc1,True,False)
```

The `display_circuit()` function shows us the Q-sphere visualization of our qubit initialized to state $|0\rangle$:

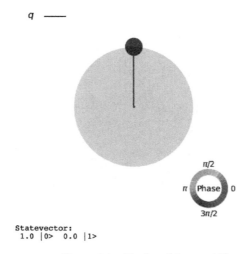

Let's start with initalizing a single qubit to |0>...

Statevector:
 1.0 |0>   0.0 |1>

Figure 9.1 – Single qubit set to $|\mathbf{0}\rangle$

Let's take a look at the underlying math, as we discussed in *Chapter 2, Quantum Computing and Qubits with Python*. What we have done here is create a statevector that can be displayed like this:

$$|\psi\rangle = \alpha\,|0\rangle + \beta\,|1\rangle$$

Or described in the form of the angles θ and φ:

$$|\psi\rangle = \cos\frac{\theta}{2}|0\rangle + e^{i\phi}\sin\frac{\theta}{2}|1\rangle$$

For our qubit, initiated to $|0\rangle$, $\theta = 0$ and with $\sin(0) = 0$ and $\cos(0) = 1$, the statevector resolves to the following:

$$|\psi\rangle = |0\rangle$$

3.  Set the qubit in superposition:

```
qc1.h(0)
display_circuit(qc1,True,False)
```

With the qubit in superposition, the Q-sphere shows that there is an equal probability of getting $|0\rangle$ and $|1\rangle$:

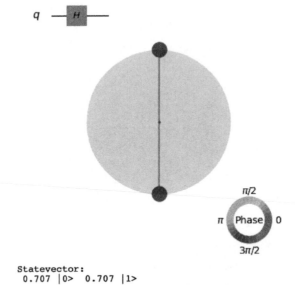

Statevector:
0.707 |0>  0.707 |1>

Figure 9.2 – Single qubit in superposition

For a qubit in superposition, with $\theta = \pi/2$, which is what we will work with here, the formula from the previous step translates into the following:

$$|\psi\rangle = \frac{1}{\sqrt{2}}|0\rangle + \frac{e^{i\phi}}{\sqrt{2}}|1\rangle$$

This means that we describe the relative phase of the qubit by the angle $\phi$. If $\phi = \pi$, then $e^{i\pi} = -1$ and the phase of the qubit is the opposite of the phase when $\phi$ is 0 or $2\pi$, in which case, $e^{i\pi} = 1$. As you can see from the equation, the phase angle only affects the $|1\rangle$ part of the qubit. This will be important in the next step.

4.  Now, let's add a phase to the second qubit using the Z gate.

    From here on, I will not show the `display_circuit(qc1,True,False)` code; just assume it is included after each step to show the progress:

    ```
    qc1.z(0)
    ```

    Remember that the Q-sphere represents the end states of the qubit, the size of the vector tip represents the relative probability of measuring the corresponding outcome, and the color represents the relative phase of the outcome.

    When you measure the qubit, the phase has no impact, only the probabilities. Here you can see that state $|0\rangle$ with phase angle 0 has a 50% probability of giving the result 0, and state $|1\rangle$ with phase angle $\pi$ also a 50% chance of giving the result 1:

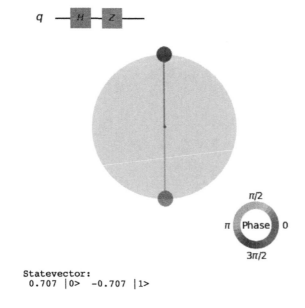

Statevector:
0.707 |0>  -0.707 |1>

Figure 9.3 – A single qubit in superposition with phase angle $\pi$

In this recipe, we will be using the Z *gate*, which is also called the **phase gate**, to add the phase $\pi$ to the $|1\rangle$ state:

$$Z = \begin{bmatrix} 1 & 0 \\ 0 & -1 \end{bmatrix}$$

Expressed with the preceding statevector nomenclature, this transformation looks like this:

Qubit in superposition with phase 0 (or with phase $2\pi$):

$$|\psi\rangle = \frac{1}{\sqrt{2}}(|0\rangle + |1\rangle)$$

Qubit in superposition with phase $\pi$ (after passing through a Z gate):

$$|\psi\rangle = \frac{1}{\sqrt{2}}(|0\rangle - |1\rangle)$$

Notice how the + sign in front of $|1\rangle$ changes to -, signifying the state flip.

5.  Now let's go through the same steps for 2 qubits, adding the phase $\pi$ to each:

```
qc = QuantumCircuit(2)
qc.h([0,1])
qc.z(1)
qc.z(0)
```

Skipping the intermediate steps, the end result of the preceding code when printed using the two psi functions is the following:

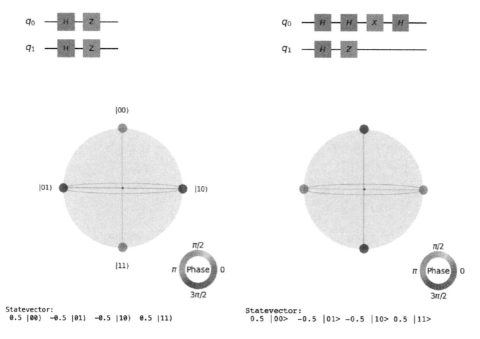

Statevector:
0.5 |00)  -0.5 |01)  -0.5 |10)  0.5 |11)

Statevector:
0.5 |00>  -0.5 |01> -0.5 |10> 0.5 |11>

Figure 9.4 – Two qubits in superposition, both with phase angle $\pi$

For two qubits in superposition, what feels somewhat intuitive for the preceding single-qubit example gets a little muddled, so let's do it step by step.

Like in the 1-qubit example, each qubit can be described like this:

$$|\psi_0\rangle = \alpha_0 |0\rangle + \beta_0 |1\rangle \text{ and } |\psi_1\rangle = \alpha_1 |0\rangle + \beta_1 |1\rangle$$

Setting the qubits up in a superposition, they can be written out like this:

$$|\psi\rangle = \alpha_0\alpha_1 |00\rangle + \alpha_1\beta_0 |01\rangle + \beta_1\alpha_0 |10\rangle + \beta_0\beta_1 |11\rangle$$

In our simplified superpositioned view, this resolves into the following expression:

$$|\psi_0\rangle = \frac{1}{\sqrt{2}}(|0\rangle + e^{i\phi_0}|1\rangle) \text{ and } |\psi_1\rangle = \frac{1}{\sqrt{2}}(|0\rangle + e^{i\phi_1}|1\rangle)$$

$$|\psi\rangle = \frac{1}{2}\left(|00\rangle + e^{i\phi_0} |01\rangle + e^{i\phi_1} |10\rangle + e^{i(\phi_0 + \phi_1)} |11\rangle\right)$$

And for two qubits, the phase shift transformation is done as in the following steps: First, two qubits in superposition with 0 (or indeed $2\pi$) phase angle $(e^{i0} = 1)$:

$$|\psi\rangle = \frac{1}{2}\,(|00\rangle + |01\rangle + |10\rangle + |11\rangle)$$

Then, 2 qubits in superposition with the second $(|\psi_1\rangle)$ having phase angle $\pi$ $(e^{i\pi} = -1)$:

$$|\psi\rangle = \frac{1}{2}\,(|00\rangle + |01\rangle - |10\rangle - |11\rangle)$$

Finally, 2 qubits in superposition with both having phase angle $\pi$ $(e^{i\pi} = -1, e^{i2\pi} = 1)$:

$$|\psi\rangle = \frac{1}{2}\,(|00\rangle - |01\rangle - |10\rangle + |11\rangle)$$

This last example represents the final outcome of the preceding sample code. The Q-sphere has four equally probable outcomes, with two of them **tagged** with the phase $\pi$, namely $|01\rangle$ and $|10\rangle$.

This makes sense if you remember that only the $|1\rangle$ state includes the phase parameter, and that if both qubits have the phase $\pi$, the exponential sum for the combination is $2\pi$, which results in no phase for $|11\rangle$. Remember this result. It will appear in the next step.

6.  Entangle a qubit with a phase angle.

    So far, this is math, and as you saw in the first recipe, this is what Qiskit® will build for you. You can change the phase of one qubit without touching the other. The real interesting part comes when you entangle the qubits using a CX gate, from qubit 0 to qubit 1:

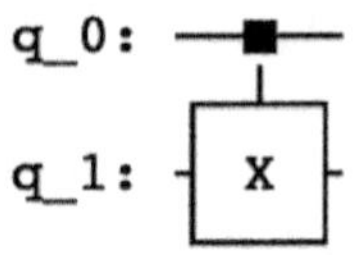

Figure 9.5 – CX (Controlled-NOT) gate from 0 to 1

The unitary matrix version of that gate is as follows:

$$CX = \begin{bmatrix} 1 & 0 & 0 & 0 \\ 0 & 0 & 0 & 1 \\ 0 & 0 & 1 & 0 \\ 0 & 1 & 0 & 0 \end{bmatrix}$$

For two qubits, each in superposition, the outcome is not that exciting; you end up with what you started with:

$$\begin{bmatrix} 1 & 0 & 0 & 0 \\ 0 & 0 & 0 & 1 \\ 0 & 0 & 1 & 0 \\ 0 & 1 & 0 & 0 \end{bmatrix} \frac{1}{2} \begin{bmatrix} 1 \\ 1 \\ 1 \\ 1 \end{bmatrix} = \frac{1}{2} \begin{bmatrix} 1 \\ 1 \\ 1 \\ 1 \end{bmatrix}$$

But now add a phase shift of $\pi$ to the controlled qubit 1,
$|\psi\rangle = \frac{1}{2} (|00\rangle + |01\rangle - |10\rangle - |11\rangle)$ from the preceding and do the calculation again:

$$\begin{bmatrix} 1 & 0 & 0 & 0 \\ 0 & 0 & 0 & 1 \\ 0 & 0 & 1 & 0 \\ 0 & 1 & 0 & 0 \end{bmatrix} \frac{1}{2} \begin{bmatrix} 1 \\ 1 \\ -1 \\ -1 \end{bmatrix} = \frac{1}{2} \begin{bmatrix} 1 \\ -1 \\ -1 \\ 1 \end{bmatrix}$$

7.  This is how it is done in the sample code:

```
qc = QuantumCircuit(2)
qc.h([0,1])
qc.z(1)
qc.cx(0,1)
```

Again, we are skipping the intermediate steps and focusing on the end result. Do step through them and compare them to the preceding calculations:

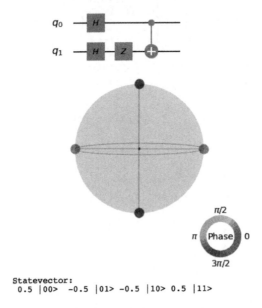

Statevector:
0.5 |00>   -0.5 |01> -0.5 |10> 0.5 |11>

Figure 9.6 – Two entangled qubits with the same π phase, using phase kickback

Take a look at that result. It is pretty astounding!

Let me explain: we started out with two qubits in superposition, one of them with a phase angle π. Then we entangled the qubits, using the qubit with no phase angle as the controlling qubit, and the qubit with a phase angle being the controlled qubit. What we ended up with is the following:

$$|\psi\rangle = \frac{1}{2} \left( |00\rangle - |01\rangle - |10\rangle + |11\rangle \right)$$

Two qubits in superposition, both having phase angle π, just like the example that we manually built before.

This is called phase kickback and is a common trick used in quantum algorithms. In the remaining recipes of this chapter, we will look at the Grover algorithm, which uses phase kickback to tag a correct solution of a problem with a phase to set it apart from incorrect solutions.

For 2-qubit Grover, we will use the CX gate (controlled-NOT) to achieve this, for 3-qubit Grover, the CCX (controlled-controlled NOT), and finally for 4 qubits, the CCCX gate (controlled-controlled-controlled-NOT).

# A quick interlude on classical search

Before we hit the Grover algorithm, let's just take a quick peek at a standard, classical linear search algorithm. For a classical algorithm that searches an unordered database, the average number of times you have to look for a given entry is of the order of $\frac{N}{2}$ where $N$ is the number of items in the database. For example, if your unordered database has four items, you will generally have to look an average of two times to find your item.

## Getting ready

The sample code for this recipe can be found here: `https://github.com/PacktPublishing/Quantum-Computing-in-Practice-with-Qiskit-and-IBM-Quantum-Experience/blob/master/Chapter09/ch9_r2_classic_search.py`.

## How to do it...

Let's search for a specific two-bit entry in a small database with four items:

1.  First, we need to enter the two-bit string that we are searching for, and then the number of searches to try to get some statistics:

    ```
    Searching in a scrambled database with 4 entries:
     ('00', '01', '10', '11')
    Enter a two bit string for the two qubit state to search
    for, such as '10' ('Exit' to stop):
    10
    Number of searches to test:
    20
    ```

    The two-bit format here will be reused in the Grover recipes of this chapter and will then symbolize the statevector of two qubits, for example, $|10\rangle$. We will also use 3- and 4-bit entries for the corresponding number of qubits.

2.  The script now scrambles the initial database and runs the search function:

    ```
    for m in range(searches):
        database=random.sample(values,len(values))
        result=simple_search(database, oracle)
        average.append(result+1)
        search.append(m+1)
    ```

The `simple_search()` function takes a database list as input, and then walks through it until it finds the entry that we are searching for. The position of the item is returned, and is shunted as the number of searches in the `search` variable:

```
def simple_search(database, oracle):
    for position, post in enumerate(database):
        if post == oracle:
            return position
```

3.  And finally, the collected statistics are displayed using the `plot_results()` function:

```
def plot_results(average,search,values):
    import matplotlib.pyplot as plt
    from statistics import mean
    print("Average searches to find:", mean(average))
    # Plot the search data
    plt.bar(search, average, align='center', alpha=0.5)
    plt.ylabel('Searches')
    plt.title(str(mean(average))+' average searches\nto
        find one item among '+str(len(values)))
    plt.axhline(mean(average))
    plt.show()
```

The preceding code should create something similar to this:

```
Enter a two bit string for the two qubit state to search for, such as '10' ('Exit' to stop):
10

Number of searches to test:
20
Average searches to find: 2.1
```

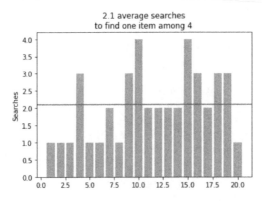

Figure 9.7 – Typical outcome of a classical linear search among four unsorted items

This small search example illustrates one classical algorithm that can be used to find a single item in a database. In this example, we have statistically shown that finding a single entry in an unordered database of four items takes in the order of *two searches* to achieve, which matches the prediction of *N/2 searches*.

If you add random items to the database, then you can convince yourself that this is true for databases of 8 and 16 items as well, which corresponds to 3- and 4-bit search strings.

In *The Grover search algorithm* recipe, we will see how we can use the Grover quantum algorithm to find the item in the order of $\sqrt{N}$ searches. That is a quadratic speedup. Not much difference in a four-item database, but if your database contains hundreds of thousands or even millions of items, it makes a difference.

# Building Grover's search algorithm

Let's take our first bite into Grover's search algorithm, one of the more straightforward quantum algorithms for solving an actual problem using quantum computing, namely finding information in an indexed but unsorted database. As we discussed in *A quick interlude on classical search*, Grover is expected to be quadratically faster than its classical counterpart.

In Qiskit Terra, we can create an implementation of Grover that uses a phase-kickback oracle combined with another neat trick: **phase amplification**. Phase amplification increases the amplitude of the correct phase-shifted answer and thereby increases the probability of that outcome when you measure your circuit.

First, we create a so-called **oracle function**, which is designed to take as input a set of qubits in initial superposition and switch the phase of the correct answer by π, while leaving the phase of the incorrect answers alone. The oracle circuit is what is called a **black box**, which is coded to identify an answer from a set of inputs.

In our example, we explicitly code the oracle to identify a specific answer, which feels like cheating. If we already know the answer, what is the point of running the Grover algorithm to find it? In our simple example, this is true, but an oracle black box might be any type of function in a hybrid classical/quantum computing program.

You can see it this way: an oracle can identify the correct answer if that answer exists in the input that you feed it; it cannot calculate the correct answer.

The oracle unitary matrix is essentially an identity matrix, with a single negative entry that represents the solution and will switch the phase for the corresponding state. This unitary matrix can be realized using standard gates in a quantum circuit.

In this recipe, we will build the Grover circuit for two qubits. For each step, we will display what we are doing using the Q-sphere and the statevector of the circuit. For the two vital components—the oracle and the amplifier—we also display the unitary matrixes that they represent.

# Getting ready

The sample code for this recipe can be found here: `https://github.com/PacktPublishing/Quantum-Computing-in-Practice-with-Qiskit-and-IBM-Quantum-Experience/blob/master/Chapter09/ch9_r3_grover_main.py`.

The script, in turn, uses three steps to create the Grover circuit. Let's go over them one by one, with our initial example for a two-qubit Grover circuit in the next subsections. The basic features of the circuit that we are implementing here are the same as you add more qubits.

The sample code for building the Oracle, the amplifier circuit, and the final Grover circuit can be found here: `https://github.com/PacktPublishing/Quantum-Computing-in-Practice-with-Qiskit-and-IBM-Quantum-Experience/blob/master/Chapter09/ch9_grover_functions.py`.

### Creating the oracle circuit

The first component that we need is the oracle. One simple way of building an oracle to tag a correct answer with a phase shift is to use a phase kickback circuit like the one we built in the *Exploring quantum phase kickback* recipe.

As an example, let's set up a phase kickback oracle circuit that kicks back the phase for a specific outcome, such as $|10\rangle$. This means that the possible statevector $|10\rangle$ will be phase-shifted $\pi$ relative to all the other possible statevectors, in this case, $|00\rangle$, $|01\rangle$, and $|11\rangle$.

This is what the oracle circuit looks like when printed out from Qiskit®:

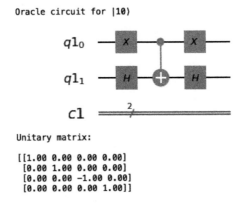

Unitary matrix:

```
[[1.00 0.00 0.00 0.00]
 [0.00 1.00 0.00 0.00]
 [0.00 0.00 -1.00 0.00]
 [0.00 0.00 0.00 1.00]]
```

Figure 9.8 – A phase kickback oracle circuit and corresponding unitary matrix for the correct result $|10\rangle$

How does this work? Let's walk through what each part of the circuit does:

1.  On the first controlling qubit, we add an X gate to make sure that $|...0\rangle$ on that qubit gets flipped to $|...1\rangle$, so that it triggers the CX gate.

2.  On the second qubit, we first add an H gate.

    What does this one do? In this case, we want to add a phase to the second qubit, so that we can then use the CX gate to kick back to the first qubit. Here, if the second qubit is an incorrect $|0...\rangle$, applying the H gate gives us a superposition $|+\cdots\rangle$ with phase 0. There is nothing to kick back, and the solution is not tagged. However, if the second qubit is a correct $|1...\rangle$, the H gate gives us $|-\cdots\rangle$, which has a phase of $\pi$, which is then promptly tagged to the solution by the CX gate.

3.  Finally, after the CX gate, we then add another X gate to flip the first qubit back to its initial state, and another H gate for the second qubit to do the same.

What we have achieved is tagging the statevector for the oracle answer $|10\rangle$ with a phase shift of $\pi$. Only that combination will get the phase shift; no other combination will.

Perhaps this is easier to see in the displayed unitary matrix, where all solutions except for the correct one are represented by a 1 in the diagonal, whereas the correct solution ($|01\rangle$) is represented by -1, which results in a phase shift in the resulting statevector.

And this is how we do it in our Python sample:

```
def create_oracle(oracle_type,size):
    from qiskit import QuantumCircuit, ClassicalRegister,
        QuantumRegister
    global qr, cr
    qr = QuantumRegister(size)
    cr = ClassicalRegister(size)
    oracleCircuit=QuantumCircuit(qr,cr)
    oracle_type_rev=oracle_type[::-1]
    for n in range(size-1,-1,-1):
        if oracle_type_rev[n] =="0":
            oracleCircuit.x(qr[n])
    oracleCircuit.h(qr[size-1])
    if size==2:
        oracleCircuit.cx(qr[size-2],qr[size-1]);
    if size==3:
        oracleCircuit.ccx(qr[size-3],qr[size-2],qr[size-1])
    if size==4:
        oracleCircuit.mcx([qr[size-4],qr[size-3],
            qr[size-2]],qr[size-1])
    if size>=5:
        oracleCircuit.mcx([qr[size-5],qr[size-4],
            qr[size-3],qr[size-2]],qr[size-1])
    oracleCircuit.h(qr[size-1])
    for n in range(size-1,-1,-1):
        if oracle_type_rev[n] =="0":
            oracleCircuit.x(qr[n])
    return(oracleCircuit)
```

Let's step through it:

1.  The input to the `create_oracle()` function is an oracle type and a size, where the type is a string that specifies the qubit combination we are looking for, for example, 10 for the $|10\rangle$ combination.

2.  Next, we step through the oracle type in reverse, adding an X gate for each 0 in the string to flip it to a 1, as per the preceding discussion.

    Notice here that the input to the oracle for a two-bit string is the reverse of how Qiskit® labels its qubits, so we need to reverse it into `oracle_input_rev` before processing it.

3.  We then add an H gate to the last qubit.

4.  Now for the real meat. Depending on the size of the circuit we are building, we add a superposition gate to take care of the phase kickback:

    For two qubits, a CX gate is added by the program.

    For three qubits, a CCX gate is added; we'll see more on that in *Searching with a 3-qubit Grover* recipe.

    For 4 and 5 qubits, an MCX (multi-control NOT) gate is added; we'll see more about that one in the *Adding more qubits to the Grover search* recipe.

5.  And finally, we perform the H gate and X gate steps in reverse to balance out the oracle circuit.

We now have an oracle circuit that will tag the oracle type that we passed it.

## Creating the amplifier circuit

The amplifier circuit is built the same way no matter how many qubits we use for the oracle. It takes the input statevector and amplifies the probability of the correct solution by reflecting the phase-changed probability across the average probability of all solutions.

Here is what that circuit looks like for a 2-qubit circuit:

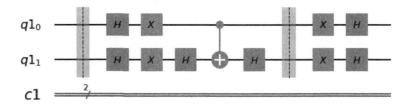

```
Unitary matrix:

[[ 0.50 -0.50 -0.50 -0.50]
 [-0.50  0.50 -0.50 -0.50]
 [-0.50 -0.50  0.50 -0.50]
 [-0.50 -0.50 -0.50  0.50]]
```

Figure 9.9 – A two-qubit amplifier circuit and its corresponding unitary matrix

Again, perhaps this is easier to see if you look at the amplifier unitary matrix. If you do the matrix multiplication for the phase-shifted solution, you will see that the probability for the phase-shifted solution is amplified, whereas the probability for the no-phase shifted ones is not. It turns out that in the special case of a two-qubit Grover circuit, the probability of getting the correct solution is actually 100%; you will find the correct solution among four possible ones in just one search. That is pretty amazing!

In the following matrix multiplication, we will multiply the amplifier matrix with the phase-tagged superposition vector to get a solution vector with just one possible result, $|10\rangle$, at 100% probability:

$$0.5 \begin{bmatrix} 0.5 & -0.5 & -0.5 & -0.5 \\ -0.5 & 0.5 & -0.5 & -0.5 \\ -0.5 & -0.5 & 0.5 & -0.5 \\ -0.5 & -0.5 & -0.5 & 0.5 \end{bmatrix} \begin{bmatrix} 1 \\ 1 \\ -1 \\ 1 \end{bmatrix} = \begin{bmatrix} 0 \\ 0 \\ -1 \\ 0 \end{bmatrix}$$

In our Python sample, this is how it is done:

```
def create_amplifier(size):
    from qiskit import QuantumCircuit
    # Let's create the amplifier circuit for two qubits.
    amplifierCircuit=QuantumCircuit(qr,cr)
    amplifierCircuit.barrier(qr)
    amplifierCircuit.h(qr)
    amplifierCircuit.x(qr)
    amplifierCircuit.h(qr[size-1])
    if size==2:
        amplifierCircuit.cx(qr[size-2],qr[size-1]);
    if size==3:
        amplifierCircuit.ccx(qr[size-3],qr[size-2],qr[size-1])
    if size==4:
        amplifierCircuit.mcx([qr[size-4],qr[size-3],
            qr[size-2]],qr[size-1])
    if size>=5:
        amplifierCircuit.mcx([qr[size-5],qr[size-4],
            qr[size-3],qr[size-2]],qr[size-1])
    amplifierCircuit.h(qr[size-1])
    amplifierCircuit.barrier(qr)
    amplifierCircuit.x(qr)
    amplifierCircuit.h(qr)
    return(amplifierCircuit)
```

The function `create_amplifier()` only takes size as input. The amplifier works the same no matter what the oracle is. As you can see, it is somewhat similar to the oracle circuit; it too builds a balanced circuit:

1. It starts with H gates on all qubits.

2. The second step is to add X gates on all qubits.

3. And again, depending on the size of the circuit, it adds a CX, CCX, or MCX gate for the phase kickback in the middle.

4. And just like for the oracle circuit, we now reverse the initial X and H gates, to balance out the circuit.

We now have our oracle and our amplifier; all we need to do is put them together.

## Creating the Grover circuit

The Grover circuit puts the pieces together, adds H gates at the beginning, to set up a superposition, and adds measurement gates at the end to let you run the circuit.

The create_grover() function takes the oracle circuit and the amplifier circuit as input. It also takes a Boolean showsteps parameter. With this one set to **True**, the script will create the Grover circuit in a graphically verbose way, displaying each step of the creation process with a view of the circuit, a Q-sphere representation of the statevector with probabilities and phase angles, and finally a prettified statevector for clarity. To see what this looks like, take a look at the *How to do it* section that follows. Change the showsteps parameter to **False** to just run the Grover circuit with no extra visualizations.

The Python code looks like this:

```python
def create_grover(oracleCircuit,amplifierCircuit,showstep):
    from qiskit import QuantumCircuit
    from math import sqrt, pow, pi
    groverCircuit = QuantumCircuit(qr,cr)
    # Initiate the Grover with Hadamards
    if showstep: display_circuit(groverCircuit,True,False)
    groverCircuit.h(qr)
    groverCircuit.barrier(qr)
    if showstep: display_circuit(groverCircuit,True,False)
    # Add the oracle and the inversion
    for n in range(int(pi/4*(sqrt(pow(2,
            oracleCircuit.num_qubits))))):
        groverCircuit+=oracleCircuit
        if showstep: display_circuit(groverCircuit,True,False)
        groverCircuit+=amplifierCircuit
        if showstep: display_circuit(groverCircuit,True,False)
    # Add measurements
    groverCircuit.measure(qr,cr)
    return(groverCircuit)
```

Here are the steps for the code we just saw:

1.  We create a quantum circuit with the global quantum and classical registers that we set when we created the oracle.

2.  Next, we add H gates on all the qubits and add a barrier instruction to keep our circuit intact on transpiling. There are a lot of duplicate gates that follow each other here, and we need to retain all of them for the circuit to work.

3.  Now comes the critical step where we add the oracle and amplifier circuits.

    To get a well-formed outcome from the Grover circuit, we need to perform the correct number of searches as we discussed in *A quick interlude on classical search*. In the quantum Grover algorithm, this is represented by running the oracle and amplifier circuits once for each search.

    For a database of size N=$2^q$, the optimal number of searches or repetitions is set by the following formula: n= $\pi\frac{\sqrt{N}}{4}$. In this case, $q$ is the number of qubits in our circuit.

    If you do the math, you see that for a 2-qubit Grover circuit, it is enough with 1 search only (n=1.57). For 3- and 4-qubit circuits, we add 2 and 3 repetitions respectively by just physically adding the oracle and amplifier circuits.

    For an insight into why we use $\pi\frac{\sqrt{N}}{4}$ repetitions, see the *What happens if we run Grover's algorithm for too long?* section of the *Lecture 22, Tues April 11: Grover* article that is listed in the *See also* section.

4.  Finally, we add the measurement instructions to the circuit, which is now ready to run.

These are the three functions that we need to build the Grover circuit. But if you want to, sit down and play around with building a set of oracles and testing them on simulators or real IBM Quantum® quantum computers; see what error mitigation does to the results and see what your Grover code actually looks like, and how big it becomes after it is transpiled for an IBM Quantum® backend.

## How to do it...

To create a two-qubit Grover circuit, follow these steps:

1.  In your Python environment, run `ch9_r3_grover_main.py`.

2.  When prompted, enter the Oracle answer you want to find in the form of a two-digit string consisting of only 1 and 0, for example, *10*.

3.  The program now uses the `create_oracle()` function from the `ch9_grover_functions.py` script to build a two-qubit oracle circuit, using the oracle type that you entered, and then displays what you created:

```
...
if size==2:
        amplifierCircuit.cx(qr[size-2],qr[size-1]);
...
```

The two-qubit oracle for $|10\rangle$ is displayed:

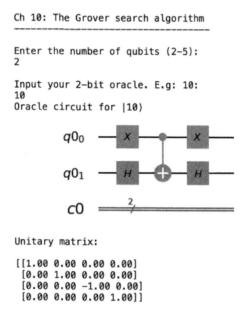

```
Ch 10: The Grover search algorithm
------------------------------------------

Enter the number of qubits (2-5):
2

Input your 2-bit oracle. E.g: 10:
10
Oracle circuit for |10)
```

```
Unitary matrix:

[[1.00 0.00 0.00 0.00]
 [0.00 1.00 0.00 0.00]
 [0.00 0.00 -1.00 0.00]
 [0.00 0.00 0.00 1.00]]
```

Figure 9.10 – Oracle circuit for $|10\rangle$, coded for **10 q01 = 0 and q00 = 0**

We are building a circuit with a CX gate to handle the phase kickback from the second qubit to the first qubit.

4.  Now build the amplifier circuit for two qubits.

    The next step is to create the amplifier circuit by using the `create_amplifier()` function. This also uses a CX gate for the phase kickback. The only input the function needs is the number of qubits.

This is where we make a couple of circuit manipulations on all the qubits at the same time, using the quantum register as input. For example, by using the following code, we add a Hadamard gate to all qubits in the qr two-qubit quantum register, that is, both of them: amplifierCircuit.h(qr).

The amplifier circuit and its corresponding unitary matrix look the same for all two-qubit Grover circuits:

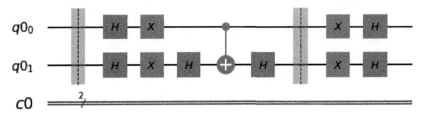

Unitary matrix:

```
[[0.50 -0.50 -0.50 -0.50]
 [-0.50 0.50 -0.50 -0.50]
 [-0.50 -0.50 0.50 -0.50]
 [-0.50 -0.50 -0.50 0.50]]
```

Figure 9.11 – Two-qubit amplifier circuit

Go back to the *Creating the amplifier circuit* section for a matrix multiplication refresher, if needed:

$$0.5 \begin{bmatrix} 0.5 & -0.5 & -0.5 & -0.5 \\ -0.5 & 0.5 & -0.5 & -0.5 \\ -0.5 & -0.5 & 0.5 & -0.5 \\ -0.5 & -0.5 & -0.5 & 0.5 \end{bmatrix} \begin{bmatrix} 1 \\ 1 \\ -1 \\ 1 \end{bmatrix} = \begin{bmatrix} 0 \\ 0 \\ -1 \\ 0 \end{bmatrix}$$

As you can see, the phase shifter state 10 has been amplified to -1. When we calculate the outcome probabilities by squaring the outcome state parameter as we did in the *Chapter 2, Quantum Computing and Qubits with Python*, in the *Comparing a bit and a qubit* section, we get the following probable outcome. Result 10 = 100%, and all other outcomes = 0%. The probability of getting the amplified correct answer is 100%.

5.  Create the Grover circuit step by step:

    In the next step, the program creates the Grover quantum circuit that encloses our oracle and amplifier and adds measurement gates. Again, we use the `create_grover()` function for this.

    With the verbose circuit creation display, we get the following output in a quick flow. Let's take a look at the circuits one at a time.

    Create a blank two-qubit circuit:

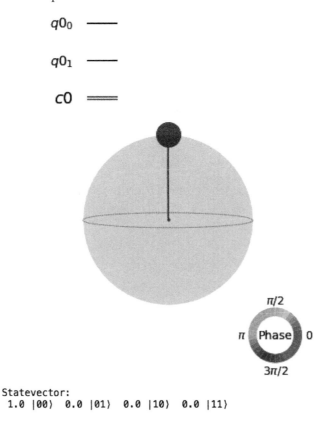

```
Statevector:
  1.0 |00)   0.0 |01)   0.0 |10)   0.0 |11)
```

Figure 9.12 – A blank circuit with 100% probability of getting the result |00⟩

Set the two qubits in superposition:

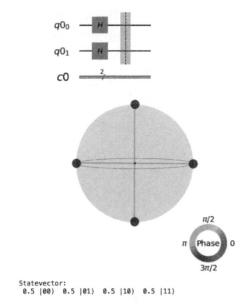

Statevector:
0.5 |00)   0.5 |01)   0.5 |10)   0.5 |11)

Figure 9.13 – A circuit with two qubits in superposition. There is an equal probability of 25% of getting each result: $|00\rangle$, $|01\rangle$, $|10\rangle$, and $|11\rangle$

Add the oracle circuit:

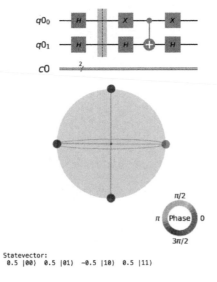

Statevector:
0.5 |00)   0.5 |01)   −0.5 |10)   0.5 |11)

Figure 9.14 – Adding the oracle circuit for $|10\rangle$. There is still an equal probability of 25% of getting each result: $|00\rangle$, $|01\rangle$, $|10\rangle$, and $|11\rangle$, but $|10\rangle$ is now phase-shifted $\pi$

Add the amplifier circuit:

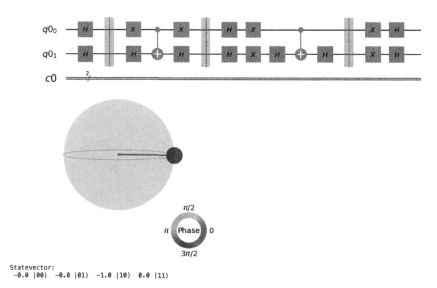

Statevector:
-0.0 |00⟩  -0.0 |01⟩  -1.0 |10⟩  0.0 |11⟩

Figure 9.15 – Adding the amplifier circuit, which amplifies the probability of the phase-shifted outcome. Now there is a 100% probability of getting |**10**⟩

Add the measurement components to finalize the circuit. The final circuit will look something like this:

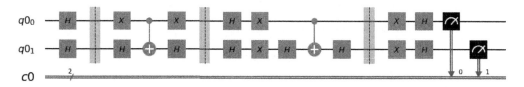

Figure 9.16 – Three-qubit Grover circuit with one repetition of the oracle for |**10**⟩ and an amplifier

As you can see, the first step of the Grover circuit is to set all the qubits in an even superposition by using the H gate. Then, the oracle and the amplifier circuits. Finally, we finish by adding measurement components for all the qubits so we can read out the end result.

6.  Now, let's run the circuit and see what result we get:

```
Sending job to: qasm_simulator
Job Status: job has successfully run
Grover search outcome for |10) oracle
```

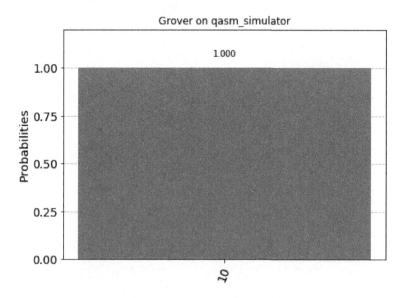

Figure 9.17 – Two-qubit Grover search outcome for $|\mathbf{10}\rangle$ oracle on the Aer simulator

7.  Enter Y to run the Grover circuit on the least busy 5-qubit IBM Q backend:

```
Getting least busy backend...
Sending job to: ibmqx2
Job Status: job has successfully run
Grover search outcome for |10) oracle
```

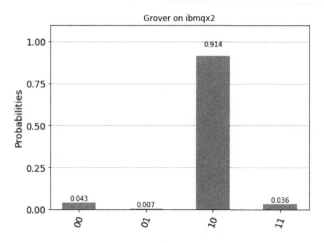

Figure 9.18 – Two-qubit Grover search outcome for $|\mathbf{10}\rangle$ oracle on an IBM Q backend

So, what is going on here? How come we are not getting the super-precise outcome that the oracle and amplifier circuits promised? With the simulator, we had a 100% chance of getting the correct result. Now we are down to ~91%. Can we use error mitigation to do better? For a two-qubit Grover circuit, it turns out we can.

8. Run the two-qubit Grover error mitigated for the behavior of the actual quantum computer.

Here we add in the mitigated run function that we tested in *Chapter 8, Cleaning Up Our Act with Ignis*, which is encoded as the `mitigated_results(backend,circuit,results)` function:

```
def mitigated_results(backend,circuit,results,
        results_sim):
    # Import the required classes
    from qiskit.providers.aer.noise import NoiseModel
    from qiskit.ignis.mitigation.measurement import
        (complete_meas_cal,CompleteMeasFitter)
    # Get noise model for backend
    noise_model = NoiseModel.from_backend(backend)
    # Create the measurement fitter
    qr = QuantumRegister(circuit.num_qubits)
    meas_calibs, state_labels = complete_meas_cal(
        qr=qr, circlabel='mcal')
    job = execute(meas_calibs,
        backend=Aer.get_backend('qasm_simulator'),
        shots=8192, noise_model=noise_model)
    cal_results = job.result()
    meas_fitter = CompleteMeasFitter(cal_results,
        state_labels, circlabel='mcal')
    print(meas_fitter.cal_matrix)
    # Get the filter object
    meas_filter = meas_fitter.filter
    # Results with mitigation
    mitigated_results = meas_filter.apply(results)
    mitigated_counts = mitigated_results.get_counts(0)
    return(mitigated_counts)
```

The mitigated results are displayed:

```
[[0.98 0.04 0.03 0.00]
 [0.01 0.96 0.00 0.03]
 [0.01 0.00 0.96 0.03]
 [0.00 0.01 0.01 0.94]]
```

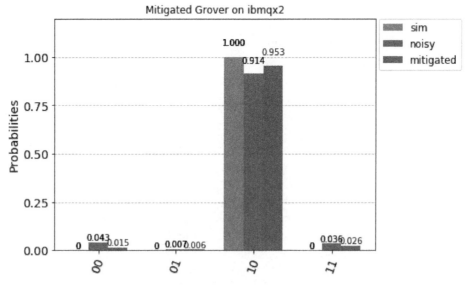

Figure 9.19 – Error-mitigated results of a two-qubit Grover search outcome for $|10\rangle$ oracle on an IBM Quantum® backend

Yes, that is better; we now see a ~95% chance of getting the correct result! The error mitigation of this circuit improved our results somewhat and reduced the probability of incorrect solutions. The error mitigation works as the circuit that we have built is relatively small.

9.  See the final transpiled circuit.

    The final step in our two-qubit Grover exploration is to take a look at the transpiled circuit that we ran on the quantum computer. For this, we reuse the `transpile_circuit(circuit,backend)` function that we introduced in the *What your quantum circuit really looks like* recipe of *Chapter 6, Understanding the Qiskit® Gate Library*:

    ```
    def transpile_circuit(circuit,backend):
        from qiskit.compiler import transpile
        trans_circ = transpile(circuit, backend)
        display(trans_circ.draw(output="mpl"))
        print("Circuit data\n\nDepth: ",trans_circ.depth(),"\
    nWidth: ",trans_circ.width(),"\nSize: ",trans_circ.
    size())
    ```

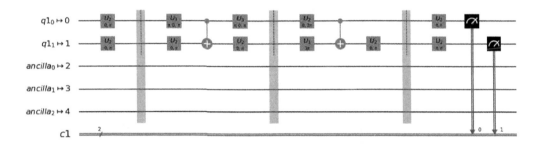

Figure 9.20 – Final backend executable quantum circuit for the two-qubit Grover circuit

And here are some statistics about our Grover circuit:

```
Depth:   9
Width:   7
Size:    15
```

Our Grover circuit has a total depth, from left to right, of 9 gate manipulations; there are a total of 15 individual gates.

For the two-qubit Grover, it turns out that we can use 100% backend basis gates, so our transpiled circuit is about the same size as our coded circuit. This will change for the three, four, and more qubit Grover circuits where we will be using the non-basis gates CCX and MCX. See the *Searching with a three qubit Grover* and *Adding more qubits to the Grover search* recipes to take a look.

# There's more...

A quick final note on the two-qubit Grover that we start out with. The two-qubit circuit we have built is just one of many different ways of approaching the Grover algorithm. I have intentionally chosen this approach to keep down the number of qubits that we use, and in doing so we are seeing the second qubit serve two purposes: it is part of the oracle, and it is also part of the phase kickback component.

Another way of building the circuit is to use an ancilla qubit strictly for the phase kickback. This keeps the oracle qubits free, but adds one qubit, and slightly more complexity to the circuit; we now have to use a CCX gate to do the phase kickback, not a CX gate.

An example of a Grover circuit coded for $|10\rangle$ and built with an ancilla qubit is here: https://github.com/PacktPublishing/Quantum-Computing-in-Practice-with-Qiskit-and-IBM-Quantum-Experience/blob/master/Chapter09/ch9_grover_ancilla.py.

Here's how that Python sample is built:

1.  We start by importing the required classes:

    ```
    from qiskit import QuantumCircuit, Aer, execute
    from IPython.core.display import display
    from qiskit.tools.visualization import plot_histogram
    ```

2.  Create a three-qubit circuit with two classical bits.

    We will use the third, ancilla qubit as the phase kickback controller:

    ```
    qc=QuantumCircuit(3,2)
    qc.h([0,1])
    qc.x(2)
    ```

3.  Add the code for the oracle:

    ```
    qc.barrier([0,1,2])
    qc.x(0)
    qc.barrier([0,1,2])
    ```

4.  Now we add the phase kickback using the ancilla qubit:

    ```
    qc.h(2)
    qc.ccx(0,1,2)
    qc.h(2)
    ```

5.  We complete the coding of the oracle:

```
qc.barrier([0,1,2])
qc.x(0)
qc.barrier([0,1,2])
```

6.  Before we are done, we need to build the amplifier:

```
qc.h([0,1])
qc.x([0,1])
qc.h(1)
qc.cx(0,1)
qc.h(1)
qc.barrier([0,1,2])
qc.x([0,1])
qc.h([0,1])
```

7.  Add the measurements of the two first qubits.

    As the ancilla qubit is just a tool we use inside the circuit, we do not need to measure it:

```
qc.measure([0,1],[0,1])
```

8.  Finally, we display the circuit, execute it on a simulator, and show the results:

```
display(qc.draw('mpl'))
backend = Aer.get_backend('qasm_simulator')
job = execute(qc, backend, shots=1)
result = job.result()
counts = result.get_counts(qc)
display(plot_histogram(counts))
```

The $|10\rangle$ oracle circuit looks like this:

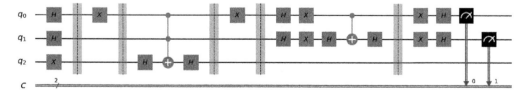

Figure 9.21 – A $|10\rangle$ oracle Grover circuit using three qubits with an ancilla qubit

Note that to expand the oracle with additional qubits, the only thing you have to do is add new qubits at the top and expand the CCX and CX gates to accommodate for the additional phase kickback requirements.

## See also

For a good read on understanding the Grover algorithm, take a look at *Lecture 22, Tues April 11: Grover* from the lecture series by Scott Aaronson, David J. Bruton Centennial Professor of Computer Science at The University of Texas at Austin: `https://www.scottaaronson.com/qclec/22.pdf`.

# Searching with a three qubit Grover

The 3-qubit Grover algorithm is very similar to the two qubit implementation that we explored in the previous recipe. The main difference is in how we build the oracle circuit for three instead of two qubits, building a phase kickback that adds the phase to two qubits instead of one.

To do this, we have to use a controlled-NOT gate that uses two qubits as input to flip the third to entangle the qubits and mark the correct answer with a $\pi$ phase. That gate is the Toffoli (CCX) gate instead of the CX gate.

In the following example, the two qubit input Toffoli gate (CCX) with 2 controlling qubits and 1 controlled qubit serves as the phase kickback that shifts the phase of the state by $\pi\,(-1)$ if the value of the three qubits matches the correct answer:

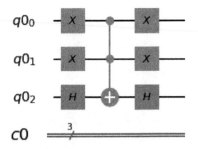

Figure 9.22 – A CCX-driven oracle for $|\mathbf{100}\rangle$

We will be using the same sample functions as in *The Grover search algorithm* recipe.

# How to do it...

To create a three qubit Grover circuit, let's follow these steps:

1. In your Python environment, run `ch9_r3_grover_main.py`.

2. When prompted, enter the oracle answer you want to find in the form of a three-digit string consisting of only 1 and 0, for example, `100`.

3. The program now steps through the building process for your three qubit Grover, just like for the two qubit one we built in the previous recipe. We will highlight the important steps, but not go into any real details. The output should speak for itself.

4. Create the Grover circuit.

   With three qubits, we have a total of N = 8 ($2^3$) possible outcomes, as we discussed in *Building Grover's search algorithm* recipe.

   For a database of size N=$2^q$, the optimal number of searches or repetitions is set by the following formula: $n = \pi \frac{\sqrt{N}}{4}$. For 3 qubits, we thus get n = 2.22. This we round to 2, for 2 repetitions of the oracle and amplifier circuits.

   The final circuit will look something like this:

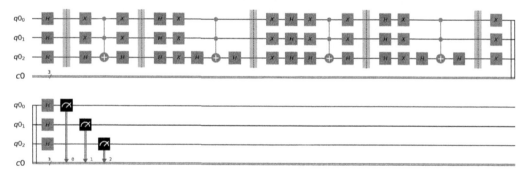

Figure 9.23 – Three-qubit Grover circuit with two repetitions for oracle $|\mathbf{100}\rangle$

As you can see, the first step of the Grover circuit is to set all the qubits in an even superposition by using the H gate. Then we add two repetitions of the oracle and the amplifier circuits. Finally, we finish by adding measurement components for all the qubits so we can read out the end result.

If you have the Boolean `showsteps` parameter set to **True**, you will see the individual steps and temporary results for the Grover circuit, with the final step looking like this:

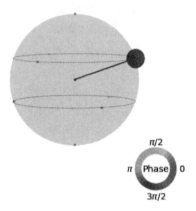

```
Statevector:
  -0.088 |000⟩  -0.088 |001⟩  -0.088 |010⟩  -0.088 |011⟩  0.972 |100⟩  -0.088 |101⟩  -0.088 |110⟩  -0.088 |111⟩
```

Figure 9.24 – Three-qubit Grover with the oracle coded for |**100**⟩

In this final step, you can see that the correct answer, |100⟩, has been amplified and now has ~94% probability (0.9722) whereas all other results have in the order of 0.8% (-0.0882) probability.

5.  Now, let's run the circuit and see what result we get:

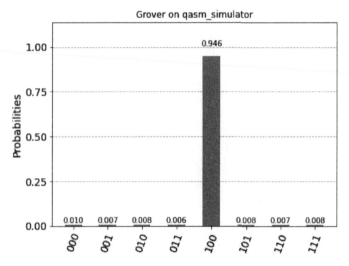

Figure 9.25 – Three-qubit Grover search outcome for a |**100**⟩ oracle on a simulator

Notice how the results nicely match what we predicted from the final statevector.

6.  Enter Y to run the Grover circuit on the least busy five qubit IBM Quantum® backend:

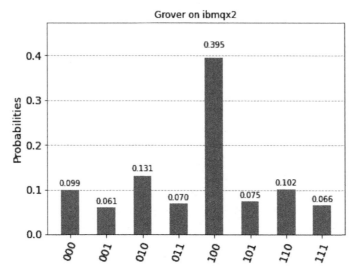

Figure 9.26 – Three-qubit Grover search outcome for a $|100\rangle$ oracle on an IBM Quantum® backend

So, what is going on here? How come we are not getting the super-precise outcome that the oracle and amplifier circuits promised? With the simulator, we had about a 94% chance of getting the correct result. Here, we are apparently down to ~40%. Can we use error mitigation to do better?

7.  See the final, mitigated results:

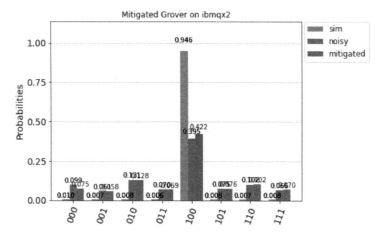

Figure 9.27 – Error-mitigated results of a 3-qubit Grover search outcome for a $|100\rangle$ oracle on an IBM Quantum® backend

Nope, that didn't do it. Even though the results are slightly better, error mitigation didn't fix it. Why? Remember that basic error mitigation mainly concerns measurement errors and doesn't take into account issues that might crop up with the gates that make up the circuit.

The explanation is in the size of our final Grover circuit. Let's run the final step of the program, which transpiles the final circuit and provides us with the size, depth, and width of the circuit that is actually run on the backend.

8.   Press *Enter* to see the final, transpiled circuit:

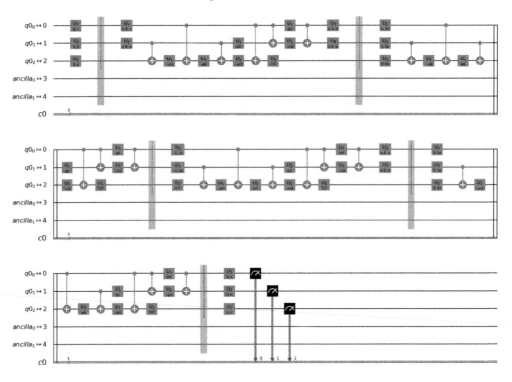

Figure 9.28 – Final backend executable quantum circuit for the 3-qubit Grover circuit

9.  And finally, we have the answer, the circuit size:

```
Circuit data
Depth:  49
Size:   76
```

Our Grover circuit has a total depth, from left to right, of 49 gate manipulations; there are a total of 76 individual gates. If you take a quick look at *Chapter 8, Cleaning Up Our Act with Ignis* again, you'll remember that we pulled out the gate error rates for the basis gates for each qubit. Although these errors are pretty small, in the order of tenths of a percent and less, when you run in the order of 100 or so gates as in the preceding circuit, chances are that there will be errors.

So, in the final analysis, the slightly higher probabilities of getting results other than the expected $|100\rangle$ are mainly due to gate errors, and not measurement errors.

# Adding more qubits to the Grover search

So far, we have done reasonably well in our Grover coding. We built our two and three qubit circuits using unique Qiskit® gates for the number of qubits that our circuits contained: CX and CCX. For a four qubit and more Grover, we will use a multi-control NOT gate, MCX, to dynamically create the right number of control inputs.

## Getting ready

We will use the same sample functions as in the *Building the Grover's search algorithm* recipe.

For two and three qubit Grovers, we could use the prefabricated CX and CCX gates to create our oracle and amplifier circuits. As we are using the same model to build a four and more qubit Grover, instead of using CCCX, CCCCX gates, and more, we use the MCX gate in our circuit, to let Qiskit® build the gate logic behind the scenes.

---

**Note**

To understand what we are doing here, take a look back at *Chapter 6, Understanding the Qiskit® Gate Library*, specifically at the CX and CCX gates.

---

Here's the unitary matrix for the CX gate, as seen in the *Building the Grover's search algorithm* recipe:

$$[CX] = \begin{bmatrix} 1 & 0 & 0 & 0 \\ 0 & 1 & 0 & 0 \\ 0 & 0 & 0 & 1 \\ 0 & 0 & 1 & 0 \end{bmatrix}$$

Here's the unitary matrix for the CCX gate (Toffoli), as seen in the *Searching with a 3-qubit Grover* recipe:

$$[CCX] = \begin{bmatrix} 1 & 0 & 0 & 0 & 0 & 0 & 0 & 0 \\ 0 & 1 & 0 & 0 & 0 & 0 & 0 & 0 \\ 0 & 0 & 1 & 0 & 0 & 0 & 0 & 0 \\ 0 & 0 & 0 & 1 & 0 & 0 & 0 & 0 \\ 0 & 0 & 0 & 0 & 1 & 0 & 0 & 0 \\ 0 & 0 & 0 & 0 & 0 & 1 & 0 & 0 \\ 0 & 0 & 0 & 0 & 0 & 0 & 0 & 1 \\ 0 & 0 & 0 & 0 & 0 & 0 & 1 & 0 \end{bmatrix}$$

The magic here is in the lower-right corner where the ones have left the diagonal and form a mini-diagonal the other way. The effect of this swap is to flip the value of the last qubit. Algebraically, this is an easy manipulation of the initial diagonal identity matrix; all we have to do is swap the two last rows.

**A controlled-controlled-controlled NOT (CCCX)** gate unitary matrix will then look like this:

$$[CCCX] = \begin{bmatrix}
1 & 0 & 0 & 0 & 0 & 0 & 0 & 0 & 0 & 0 & 0 & 0 & 0 & 0 & 0 & 0 \\
0 & 1 & 0 & 0 & 0 & 0 & 0 & 0 & 0 & 0 & 0 & 0 & 0 & 0 & 0 & 0 \\
0 & 0 & 1 & 0 & 0 & 0 & 0 & 0 & 0 & 0 & 0 & 0 & 0 & 0 & 0 & 0 \\
0 & 0 & 0 & 1 & 0 & 0 & 0 & 0 & 0 & 0 & 0 & 0 & 0 & 0 & 0 & 0 \\
0 & 0 & 0 & 0 & 1 & 0 & 0 & 0 & 0 & 0 & 0 & 0 & 0 & 0 & 0 & 0 \\
0 & 0 & 0 & 0 & 0 & 1 & 0 & 0 & 0 & 0 & 0 & 0 & 0 & 0 & 0 & 0 \\
0 & 0 & 0 & 0 & 0 & 0 & 1 & 0 & 0 & 0 & 0 & 0 & 0 & 0 & 0 & 0 \\
0 & 0 & 0 & 0 & 0 & 0 & 0 & 1 & 0 & 0 & 0 & 0 & 0 & 0 & 0 & 0 \\
0 & 0 & 0 & 0 & 0 & 0 & 0 & 0 & 1 & 0 & 0 & 0 & 0 & 0 & 0 & 0 \\
0 & 0 & 0 & 0 & 0 & 0 & 0 & 0 & 0 & 1 & 0 & 0 & 0 & 0 & 0 & 0 \\
0 & 0 & 0 & 0 & 0 & 0 & 0 & 0 & 0 & 0 & 1 & 0 & 0 & 0 & 0 & 0 \\
0 & 0 & 0 & 0 & 0 & 0 & 0 & 0 & 0 & 0 & 0 & 1 & 0 & 0 & 0 & 0 \\
0 & 0 & 0 & 0 & 0 & 0 & 0 & 0 & 0 & 0 & 0 & 0 & 1 & 0 & 0 & 0 \\
0 & 0 & 0 & 0 & 0 & 0 & 0 & 0 & 0 & 0 & 0 & 0 & 0 & 1 & 0 & 0 \\
0 & 0 & 0 & 0 & 0 & 0 & 0 & 0 & 0 & 0 & 0 & 0 & 0 & 0 & 0 & 1 \\
0 & 0 & 0 & 0 & 0 & 0 & 0 & 0 & 0 & 0 & 0 & 0 & 0 & 0 & 1 & 0
\end{bmatrix}$$

It turns out that building a unitary matrix that represents CCCX is not that hard for just a few qubits, but the matrix grows in size as $2^n$ so the next one, CCCCX, will be quite large.

This is all great, but what do we now do with this glorious matrix? The answer is to let Qiskit® code it into gates for us by using the MCX gate. This gate takes a set of control qubits and a target qubit as input. You can also specify to use **ancilla** qubits for handling the phase kickback, but for our circuit, we will not do that. Look back at the ancilla sample in the *There's more* section of the *Building Grover's search algorithm* recipe.

Here's what using that gate looks like in Python:

```
quantum_circuit.mcx([control qubits], target qubit)
```

For more help on the MCX gate, use Python `help`:

```
>> help(QuantumCircuit.mcx)
```

With the nitty-gritty behind the CCCX gate taken care of, building the 4+ Grover circuit is done exactly like the two and three qubit Grovers.

## How to do it...

We will be a little less stringent in covering and displaying all the steps here as the four qubit Grover takes up a lot more space than the others we have worked with. Feel free to revisit the previous recipes for details, and just apply them to the Grover we are building here.

To create a 4-qubit Grover, follow these steps:

1.  In your Python environment, run `ch9_r3_grover_main.py`.

2.  When prompted, enter the Oracle answer you want to find in the form of a 3-digit string consisting of only 1 and 0, for example, `1000`.

3.  Let's build the Grover circuit.

    The program now steps through the building process for your three qubit Grover, just like for the two qubit one we built in the previous recipe. We will highlight the important steps, but not go into any real details. The output should speak for itself.

    With three qubits, we have a total of N = 16 ($2^4$) possible outcomes, and as we discussed in the *Building the Grover's search algorithm* recipe, the ideal number of repetitions of the circuit is $n = \pi \frac{\sqrt{2^q N}}{4}$. For 3 qubits, we thus get n = 3.14. This we round to 3, for 3 repetitions of the oracle and amplifier circuits.

The final circuit will look something like this:

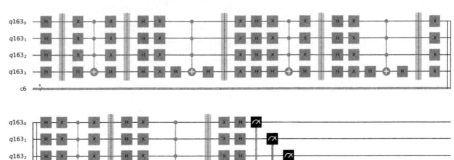

Figure 9.29 – Four-qubit Grover circuit with three repetitions for oracle |**1000**⟩

If you have the Boolean `showsteps` parameter set to **True**, you will see the individual steps and temporary results for the Grover circuit, with the final step looking like this:

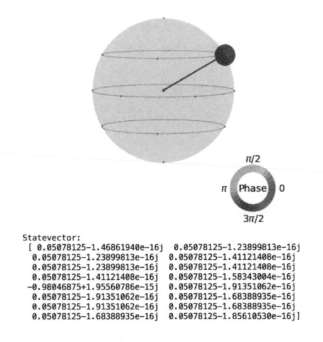

```
Statevector:
[ 0.05078125-1.46861940e-16j   0.05078125-1.23899813e-16j
  0.05078125-1.23899813e-16j   0.05078125-1.41121408e-16j
  0.05078125-1.23899813e-16j   0.05078125-1.41121408e-16j
  0.05078125-1.41121408e-16j   0.05078125-1.58343004e-16j
 -0.98046875+1.95560786e-15j   0.05078125-1.91351062e-16j
  0.05078125-1.91351062e-16j   0.05078125-1.68388935e-16j
  0.05078125-1.91351062e-16j   0.05078125-1.68388935e-16j
  0.05078125-1.68388935e-16j   0.05078125-1.85610530e-16j]
```

Figure 9.30 – Four-qubit Grover with the oracle coded for |**1000**⟩

In this final step, you can see (after some digging) that the correct answer, |1000⟩ has been amplified (-0.98046875) and now has ~96% probability whereas all other results have in the order of 0.02% probability.

4.  Now, let's run the circuit and see what result we get:

```
Sending job to: qasm_simulator
Job Status: job has successfully run
Grover search outcome for |1000) oracle
```

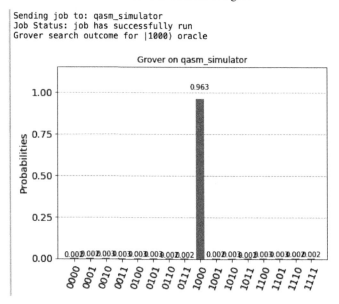

Figure 9.31 – Four-qubit Grover search outcome for a |**1000**⟩ oracle on a simulator

5.  Enter Y to run the Grover circuit on the least busy five qubit IBM Quantum® backend:

```
Loading IBMQ account...
Getting least busy backend...
Sending job to: ibmqx2
Job Status: job has successfully run
Grover search outcome for |1000) oracle
```

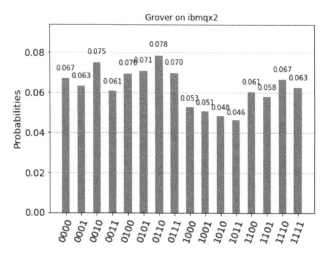

Figure 9.32 – Four-qubit Grover search outcome for a |**1000**⟩ oracle on an IBM Quantum® backend

This time, we seem to be getting nothing but noise. Surely there is no clear answer in that randomness. The correct answer is nowhere near the top of this list. Let's see the results after error mitigation.

The explanation is again in the size of our final Grover circuit. The final step of the program will give us the transpiled circuit.

6.  Press *Enter* to see the final, transpiled circuit. The result this time is pretty overwhelming:

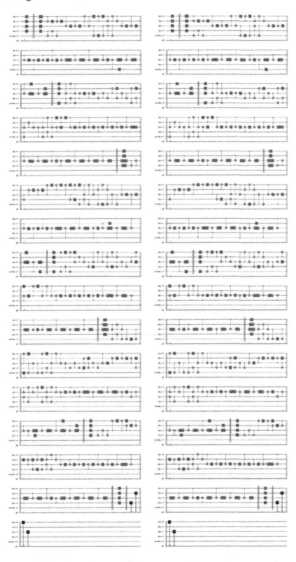

Figure 9.33 – Final backend executable quantum circuit for the 4-qubit Grover circuit

Again, we have the answer, the circuit size:

```
Circuit data
Depth:   311
Size:   409
```

Our Grover circuit has a total depth, from left to right, of 311 gate manipulations; there are a total of 409 individual gates. Again, just like in the *Searching with a three qubit Grover* recipe, the fact that we just get noise is due to gate errors and not measurement errors. The circuit has grown too big for efficient execution on a NISQ machine. There is nothing wrong with our Grover circuit, it is just too large!

## There's more...

Now go ahead and create a five qubit Grover and see where it takes you. The simulator should be able to handle it gallantly and give you the expected results, say for a $|10000\rangle$ oracle. But running it on a real quantum computer will just give you noise:

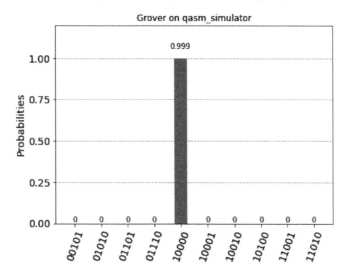

Figure 9.34 – Five-qubit Grover search outcome for a $|\mathbf{10000}\rangle$ oracle on a simulator

The final results of a five qubit Grover circuit when run on a real quantum computer are displayed:

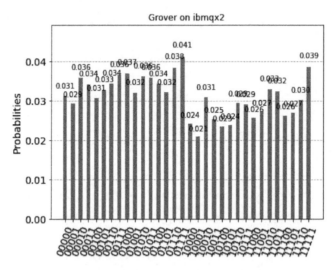

Figure 9.35 – Five-qubit Grover search outcome for a $|\mathbf{10000}\rangle$ oracle on an IBM Quantum® backend

Take a look at the final, transpiled circuit. Depending on which IBM Quantum® machine that you run your circuit on, you might get a different size and depth depending on the machine topology. Creating a CCCCX gate (using the MCX gate) on a machine with just five qubits will require a *lot* of swapping, not to mention repeating the oracle and amplifier four times.

Here's a circuit size example from running on the ibmqx2 five qubit backend:

```
Circuit data
Depth:   830
Size:   1024
```

A circuit this size will have to wait for a universal quantum computer; it is too big to successfully run on a NISQ machine.

# Using the Grover circuit in your own code

There's quite a bit of code going into the combined ch9_r3_grover_main.py and ch9_grover_functions.py scripts. The interactive main program is not needed to just run Grover if, for example, you want to utilize it in another Python program.

# Getting ready

The sample Grover functions code that you need is included here: `https://github.com/PacktPublishing/Quantum-Computing-in-Practice-with-Qiskit-and-IBM-Quantum-Experience/blob/master/Chapter09/ch9_grover_functions.py`.

# How to do it...

1.  Technically, all you need to do is to include the following short code snippet in your own code:

```
from ch9_grover_functions import *
oracle=create_oracle("01",2)
amplifier=create_amplifier(2)
grover=create_grover(oracle,amplifier,False)
print(grover)
```

2.  The preceding code should give the following result:

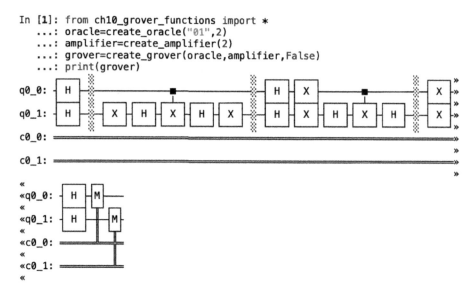

Figure 9.36 – Using the Grover functions in a minimal script to create a $|01\rangle$ Grover circuit

From a Qiskit Terra circuit point of view, we are now done, and you can include your `grover` circuit with your own hybrid classical/quantum code to get the Grover search results.

## There's more...

But we can do even better! Qiskit Aqua actually includes a `Grover()` function that you can use directly without having to write any code. More on this in the *Running Grover as an Aqua function* recipe in *Chapter 10, Getting to Know Algorithms with Aqua*.

# 10
# Getting to Know Algorithms with Aqua

So, we have finally come to the part where we will slow down a bit on coding our own circuits and instead take a look at what is arguably the most interesting part of Qiskit®—Qiskit Aqua.

As we were building the various Grover implementations in the last chapter, we saw how that seemingly simple algorithm turned into an unwieldy beast of coding when you implemented it in Qiskit Terra. If you are building a hybrid classical/quantum program (where you just want to use the Grover search function), it would be vastly simpler if you could just import and run a Qiskit® implementation of it, or other quantum algorithms, and not have to code from scratch.

So, with a fanfare and a drum roll, we now take an initial look at a couple of Qiskit Aqua algorithms (Grover and Shor) that you can use out of the box.

In this chapter, we will cover the following recipes:

- Running Grover's algorithm as an Aqua function
- Running Shor's algorithm as an Aqua function
- Exploring more Aqua algorithms

When we are done here, you will have looked at how to incorporate Qiskit Aqua algorithms into your own code and will know where to find more algorithms to test with, and how to start exploring how the algorithms are actually built using Python inside Qiskit® code.

# Technical requirements

The quantum programs that we discuss in this chapter can be found here: `https://github.com/PacktPublishing/Quantum-Computing-in-Practice-with-Qiskit-and-IBM-Quantum-Experience/tree/master/Chapter10`.

# Running Grover's algorithm as an Aqua function

At the end of *Chapter 9, Grover's Search Algorithm*, we promised that there was an easier way to include Grover's search algorithm in your quantum circuits. In this recipe, we will achieve the same results, but without having to build the circuit from scratch; Qiskit Aqua will set up the oracle, build the Grover circuit, and run it for us.

Just like importing and calling Python classes and methods for various things, such as `from math import pi` to get access to a numerical representation of π, you can do the same with Qiskit® components. Why reinvent the wheel and build your implementation of the Grover search algorithm when it is already included with Qiskit®?

## Getting ready

The sample code for this recipe can be found here: `https://github.com/PacktPublishing/Quantum-Computing-in-Practice-with-Qiskit-and-IBM-Quantum-Experience/blob/master/Chapter10/ch10_r1_grover_aqua.py`.

Before we jump in, let's take a look at the two forms of input that the Grover Aqua algorithm accepts to define the oracle:

- **Logical strings** using the `LogicalExpressionOracle` input type
- **Bit strings** using the `TruthTableOracle` input type

## Logical strings

Here's an example of a logical expression oracle for the $|\mathbf{10}\rangle$ oracle that we used in the *The two-bit Grover* recipe in *Chapter 9, Grover's Search Algorithm*, with the least significant bit (LSB) to the left in the logic:

```
'~A & B'
```

This literally translated into: NOT A and B, which then can be translated into our Dirac ket notation as first qubit (A) = 0 and second qubit (B) =1, or $|\mathbf{10}\rangle$.

## Bit strings

When you use truth-table oracle input, you create a bit-string that represents the expected output for the oracle. For the $|\mathbf{10}\rangle$ example, the bit string is as follows:

```
'0010'
```

We walked through this notation briefly for 1- and 2-qubit systems in the *A quick introduction to quantum gates* recipe in *Chapter 2, Quantum Computing and Qubits with Python*. Take a look at that if you need a refresher.

# How to do it...

To handle the creation and running of the Grover algorithm, we create four functions in the `ch10_r1_grover_aqua.py` script. Let's check out those first before we move on to test it:

## The sample code

1. First, we import the classes and methods that we need, and set some global variables:

```
from qiskit import Aer, IBMQ
from qiskit.aqua.algorithms import Grover
from qiskit.aqua.components.oracles import
LogicalExpressionOracle, TruthTableOracle
```

```
from qiskit.tools.visualization import plot_histogram
from IPython.core.display import display
global oracle_method, oracle_type
```

2. The `log_length(oracle_input,oracle_method)` function takes as input the oracle input (log or bin) and the oracle method (logical expression or bit string) and returns the ideal number of iterations the Grover circuit needs to include. If the oracle input is a logical string, we first calculate the number of qubits by counting the number of letters in the string, excluding tilde (~), ampersand (&), and space:

```
def log_length(oracle_input,oracle_method):
    from math import sqrt, pow, pi, log
    if oracle_method=="log":
        filtered = [c.lower() for c in oracle_input if
            c.isalpha()]
        result = len(filtered)
        num_iterations=int(pi/4*(sqrt(pow(2,result))))
    else:
        num_iterations = int(pi/4*(sqrt(pow(2,
            log(len(oracle_input),2)))))
    print("Iterations: ", num_iterations)
    return num_iterations
```

3. The `create_oracle(oracle_method)` function takes the oracle method as input and prompts for the oracle logical expression or bit string. From the input, it calls the `log_length(oracle_input,oracle_method)` function that calculates the required number of iterations based on the

$$\text{num\_iterations} = \pi \frac{\sqrt{N}}{4} \quad \text{formula.}$$

This is how it looks in Python:

```
def create_oracle(oracle_method):
    oracle_text={"log":"~A & ~B & C","bit":"00001000"}
    # set the input
    global num_iterations
    print("Enter the oracle input string, such
        as:"+oracle_text[oracle_method]+"\nor enter 'def'
        for a default string.")
    oracle_input=input('\nOracle input:\n ')
    if oracle_input=="def":
        oracle_type=oracle_text[oracle_method]
    else:
```

```
        oracle_type = oracle_input
    num_iterations=log_length(oracle_type, oracle_method)
    return(oracle_type)
```

4. The `create_grover(oracle_type)` function takes the `oracle_type` string, for example, `~A&B` as input, and uses the `Grover(LogicalExpressionOracle(oracle_type),num_iterations=num_iterations)` function to create the algorithm with the appropriate number of iterations.

In Python, it will look as follows:

```
def create_grover(oracle_type, oracle_method):
    # Build the circuit
    if oracle_method=="log":
        algorithm = Grover(LogicalExpressionOracle(
            oracle_type),num_iterations=num_iterations)
        oracle_circuit = Grover(LogicalExpressionOracle(
            oracle_type)).construct_circuit()
    else:
        algorithm = Grover(TruthTableOracle(
            oracle_type),num_iterations=num_iterations)
        oracle_circuit = Grover(TruthTableOracle(
            oracle_type)).construct_circuit()

    display(oracle_circuit.draw(output="mpl"))
    display(algorithm)
    return(algorithm)
```

5. The `run_grover(algorithm,oracle_type)` function takes the algorithm that we just created as input and runs it first on a local Aer simulator, and then on the least busy IBM Quantum® backend with five qubits.

This is how we build that in Python:

```
def run_grover(algorithm,oracle_type,oracle_method):
    # Run the algorithm on a simulator, printing the most
    # frequently occurring result
    backend = Aer.get_backend('qasm_simulator')
    result = algorithm.run(backend)
    print("Oracle method:",oracle_method)
    print("Oracle for:", oracle_type)
    print("Aer Result:",result['top_measurement'])
    display(plot_histogram(result['measurement']))
    # Run the algorithm on an IBM Q backend, printing the
    # most frequently occurring result
```

```
print("Getting provider...")
if not IBMQ.active_account():
    IBMQ.load_account()
provider = IBMQ.get_provider()
from qiskit.providers.ibmq import least_busy
filtered_backend = least_busy(provider.backends(
    n_qubits=5,, operational=True, simulator=False))
result = algorithm.run(filtered_backend)
print("Oracle method:",oracle_method)
print("Oracle for:", oracle_type)
print("IBMQ "+filtered_backend.name()+
    " Result:",,result['top_measurement'])
display(plot_histogram(result['measurement']))
print(result)
```

6.  The `main()` function prompts for the oracle method, then creates the oracle and runs the Grover algorithm:

```
def main():
    oracle_method="log"
    while oracle_method!=0:
        print("Ch 11: Grover search with Aqua")
        print("-----------------------------")
        # set the oracle method: "Log" for logical
        # expression or "Bit" for bit string.
        oracle_method = input("Select oracle method (log
            or bit):\n")
        type=create_oracle(oracle_method)
        algorithm=create_grover(type, oracle_method)
        run_grover(algorithm,type, oracle_method)
```

## Running the code

To create and run an Aqua-generated Grover circuit using a logical expression as input, do the following:

1.  In your Python environment, run `ch10_r1_grover_aqua.py`.

2.  When prompted, select the logical expression oracle method by entering `log`.

    Feel free to test the same oracle with the bit string input by entering `bit`.

3.  Now enter a logical expression like in the previous example:

```
~A & B
```

If you read out the logical expression, you get NOT A AND B, which corresponds to $|10\rangle$. Remember, A is the least significant bit, and in Qiskit® corresponds to the rightmost digit in the key notation.

For a bit string oracle, the input would be 0010.

4.  The oracle input and optimal number of iterations are displayed, together with the Aqua-created oracle circuit:

Figure 10.1 – The Aqua-created oracle circuit for $|10\rangle$

5.  The oracle is now run on a local Aer simulator, and the results are displayed as follows:

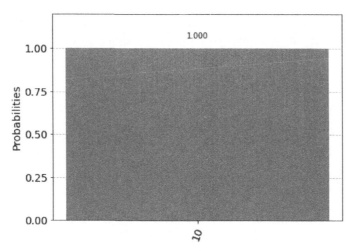

Figure 10.2 – Results of running the $|10\rangle$ oracle on your local Aer simulator

6. The oracle is now run on the least busy IBM Quantum® backend and the results are displayed as follows:

```
Oracle method: log
Oracle for: ~A & B
IBMQ ibmqx2 Result: 10
```

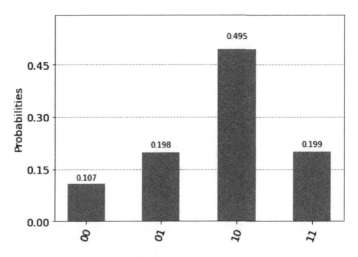

Figure 10.3 – Results of running the |**10**⟩ oracle on an IBM Quantum® backend

## How it works...

If you look over the ch10_r1_grover_aqua.py program, then you will find in the order of 100 lines of code. Most of this is not needed to run the Grover algorithm. Assuming that you get the logical expression or bit string oracle input from somewhere, you can run this in just four lines of code:

```
In [1]: from qiskit import Aer
In [2]: from qiskit.aqua.algorithms import Grover
In [3]: from qiskit.aqua.components.oracles import
LogicalExpressionOracle
In [4]: Grover(LogicalExpressionOracle("~A&B")).run(backend)
["top_measurement"]
Out[5]: '10'
```

The first three lines of code import the required classes. This fourth line of code creates and runs the Grover circuit with a logical expression oracle as input – in this case, ~A&B, to code for |10⟩, and pulls out the top measurement, the winner coded by the oracle.

# There's more...

Again, just like with your Terra-built circuits, things happen when you go from two qubits to three qubits. Let's take a look. To see what the final transpiled circuit (run on the IBM Quantum® backend) looks like, you can log in to IBM Quantum Experience® to see the fully detailed results of your run:

1.  Go to the following URL, and then log in with your IBM Quantum Experience® account: `https://quantum-computing.ibm.com/`.

2.  In the **Welcome** panel, scroll down to **Latest results**.

3.  Locate the job that you just ran and click it:

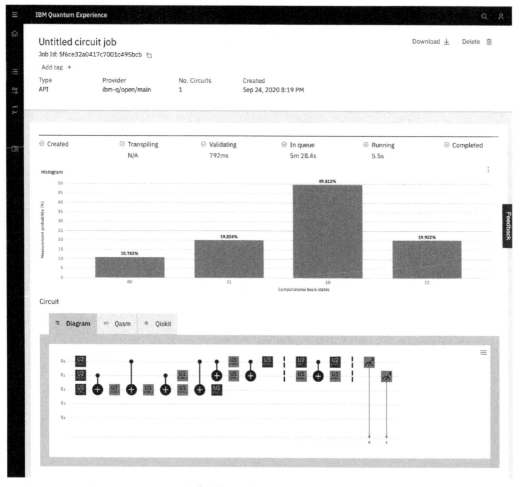

Figure 10.4 – The job results for the $|10\rangle$ oracle on an IBM Quantum® backend in IBM Quantum Experience®

4.    Compare the circuits.

By taking a look at your jobs here, you can compare the size of the circuits that you ran as a part of *Building Grover's search algorithm* recipe in *Chapter 9, Grover's Search Algorithm*, and your new Aqua-created circuit:

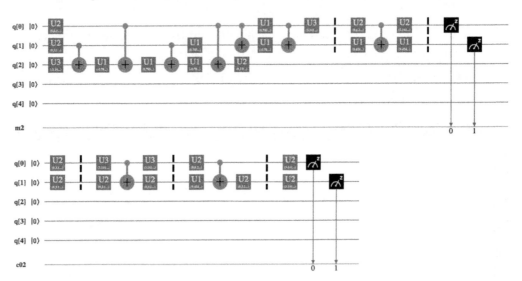

Figure 10.5 – 2-qubit Aqua Grover for $|\mathbf{10}\rangle$ versus your Terra-built 2-qubit $|\mathbf{10}\rangle$ Grover

For the 2-qubit circuit, the size is corresponding to what you saw with your Terra-built circuit. What you can see from the difference is that the Aqua-built circuit uses an **ancillary** qubit to handle the phase-shifting mechanism. This makes the circuit a little bit larger, with a depth of 15 for the Qiskit Aqua Grover versus 9 for the Qiskit Terra Grover. The size also grows to 24 from 15.

5.    Now, run a 3-qubit Qiskit Aqua-created Grover and take a look at the results.

Run the ch10_r1_grover_aqua.py program again, select the log oracle type, and use the following logical string to code for $|100\rangle$ : ~A & ~B & C.

The results of the Qiskit Aer-run Grover should look like the following:

```
Oracle method: log
Oracle for: ~A & ~B & C
Aer Result: 100
```

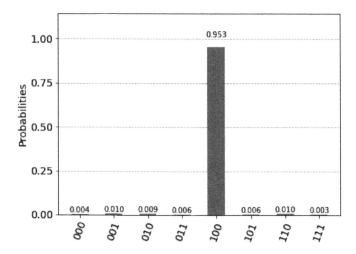

Figure 10.6 – Aer result for the Aqua-created $|\mathbf{100}\rangle$ Grover

And the result of the Grover run on an IBM Quantum® backend should look something like this:

```
Oracle method: log
Oracle for: ~A & ~B & C
IBMQ ibmqx2 Result: 001
```

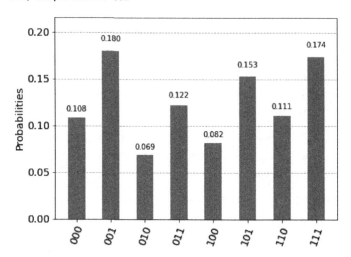

Figure 10.7 – IBM Quantum® result for the Aqua-created $|\mathbf{100}\rangle$ Grover

Look at these results. They do not look like the 3-qubit results we got in *The three-qubit Grover* recipe in *Chapter 9, Grover's Search Algorithm*, but more like the messy 4+ qubit results we saw in the *Adding more qubits to the Grover search* recipe. As we discussed in that recipe, we have clearly exceeded the circuit depth for a NISQ machine, getting more noise than the signal from our experiment.

So, how was that for some fun? We have seen how Qiskit Aqua codes the same algorithm that we spent so much time putting together in *Chapter 9, Grover's Search Algorithm*. But Qiskit Aqua contains so much more.

We have barely scratched the surface. If you have spent some time looking over quantum information history, you might have a few favorite algorithms picked out; one of these is likely Grover's algorithm, but the most famous one is probably Shor's algorithm, and that's what's next. Read on!

# Running Shor's algorithm as an Aqua function

Another one of the real luminaries of quantum computing algorithms is Peter Shor's algorithm dating back to 1984, in which he proved that with a sufficiently powerful quantum computer, you can prime factorize really large integers. This is important not only from an academic point of view but also because, for example, factorizing really large (thousands of digits) numbers into constituent prime numbers is the core behind today's RSA encryption that is used to secure online transactions, from banking and social media to the computers built into your car.

At the point when these sufficiently large quantum computers enter the stage, crypto keys that would take weeks, months, years, and longer to break can theoretically be broken in a matter of minutes.

To level-set our expectations here, running Shor's algorithm on today's NISQ machines is more of an academic interest. As you will notice, the Shor circuits tend to grow pretty large even for relatively small factorization exercises, and as you have seen in the previous chapters, as circuits grow, so do the errors.

Through IBM Quantum Experience®, you have access to quantum computers up to 15 qubits in size and simulators up to 32. As you will see, the qubit count limits us regarding the size of the number to factorize.

And a final issue to take into account is the sheer size of the simulation. The great theoretical advantage of using quantum computers is that they have the potential for exponential speedup for certain problems. On the flip side of this is the fact that simulating quantum computers gets exponentially harder for each added qubit.

When we run Shor's algorithm for bigger numbers, and by bigger, here I mean once we pass 63 going upward, your local simulator will start complaining and it is time to switch to the IBM Quantum® simulator provided.

Take a look at this table for some suggested numbers to test with:

| Number | Prime Factorization |
| --- | --- |
| 1 | Not composite |
| 3, 5, 7 | Prime |
| 9 | 3 x 3 |
| 11, 13 | Prime |
| 15 | 3 x 5 |
| 17, 19 | Prime |
| 21 | 3 x 7 |
| 23 | Prime |
| 25 | 5 x 5 |
| 27 | 3 x 3 x 3 |
| 29, 31 | Prime |
| 33 | 3 x 11 |
| 35 | 5 x 7 |
| 37 | Prime |
| 39 | 3 x 13 |

Table 10.1 – Prime factorization of numbers smaller than 40

Tip

For more factorization fun, see `https://www.mymathtables.com/numbers/one-hundred-factor-and-prime-factor-table.html` and `https://www.mathsisfun.com/prime-factorization.html`.

The Qiskit Aqua Shor algorithm accepts odd numbers larger than 1 as input, so the table only lists those. The numbers listed as primes themselves cannot be factorized, but the rest are fair game. Test a few of these.

## Getting ready

The sample code for this recipe can be found here: `https://github.com/PacktPublishing/Quantum-Computing-in-Practice-with-Qiskit-and-IBM-Quantum-Experience/blob/master/Chapter10/ch10_r2_shor_aqua.py`.

## How to do it...

To handle the creation and running of the Grover algorithm, we will build three functions in the `ch10_r2_shor_aqua.py` script. First, let's check the code and then run it.

### The sample code

1.  First, we import the classes and methods that we need:

    ```
    from qiskit import Aer, IBMQ
    from qiskit.aqua.algorithms import Shor
    import time
    ```

2.  The `display_shor(N)` function takes an integer as input and uses the `Shor()` method to construct and display the short circuit and the circuit data:

    ```
    def display_shor(N):
        print("Building Shor circuit...")
        shor_circuit = Shor(N=N).construct_circuit()
        print(shor_circuit)
        print("Circuit data\n\nDepth: ",shor_circuit.
            depth(),"\nWidth: ",shor_circuit.width(),"\nSize:
            ",shor_circuit.size())
    ```

3.  The `run_shor(N)` function takes an integer as input, creates the Shor circuit, and runs it on a local simulator. The function then displays the results of the run:

    ```
    def run_shor(N):
        if N<=64: #Arbitrarily set upper limit for local
                  #simulator
            print("Getting local simulator backend...")
            backend = Aer.get_backend('qasm_simulator')
        else:
            print("Getting provider...")
            if not IBMQ.active_account():
                IBMQ.load_account()
            provider = IBMQ.get_provider()
    ```

```
        print("Getting IBM Q simulator backend...")
        backend = provider.get_backend(
            'ibmq_qasm_simulator')
    print("Running Shor's algorithm for",str(N),"on",
        backend,"...")
    results=Shor(N=N).run(backend)
    print("\nResults:")
    if results['factors']==[]:
        print("No prime factors: ",str(N),"=",str(N))
    elif isinstance(results['factors'][0],int):
        print("Prime factors: ",str(N),"=",
            results['factors'][0],"^ 2")
    else:
        print("Prime factors: ",str(N),"=",
            results['factors'][0][0],"*",
            results['factors'][0][1])
```

4.  The `main()` function process prompts and verifies an odd input larger than 1, and
    then runs the preceding functions. Start and stop times are used to measure the
    time it takes to construct the circuit and to run it:

```
def main():
    number=1
    print("\nCh 11: Shor's algorithm with Aqua")
    print("----------------------------------")
    while number!=0:
        number=int(input("\nEnter an odd number N >1 (0
            to exit):\n"))
        if number>1 and number % 2>0:
            type=input("Enter R to run the Shor
                algorithm, D to display the circuit.\n")
            start_time=time.time()
            if type.upper()=="D":
                display_shor(number)
            elif type.upper()=="R":
                run_shor(number)
            elif type.upper() in ["RD","DR"]:
                display_shor(number)
                run_shor(number)
            end_time=time.time()
            print("Elapsed time: ","%.2f" % (
                end_time-start_time), "s")
        else:
```

```
                        print("The number must be odd
                        and larger than 1.")
```

## Running the code

1.  In your environment, run `ch10_r2_shor_aqua.py`.

2.  When prompted, enter N, an odd number larger than 1.

    This is the number that we want to prime factorize. For starters, try the three following numbers: **5, 9, 15**

3.  The algorithm returns one of three results:

    **No prime factors**: If the number that you entered is a prime number that cannot be factorized, for example:

```
Enter an odd number N >1 (0 to exit):
5

Enter R to run the Shor algorithm, D to display the circuit.
r
Getting local simulator backend...
Running Shor's algorithm for 5 on qasm_simulator ...

Results:
No prime factors:  5 = 5
Elapsed time:  0.66 s
```

Figure 10.8 – The result of Shor's algorithm with an input of 5

**Factorized square**: If the number can be expressed as a factorization of a prime multiplied by itself:

```
Enter an odd number N >1 (0 to exit):
9

Enter R to run the Shor algorithm, D to display the circuit.
r
Getting local simulator backend...
Running Shor's algorithm for 9 on qasm_simulator ...

Results:
Prime factors:  9 = 3 ^ 2
Elapsed time:  0.00 s
```

Figure 10.9 – The result of Shor's algorithm with an input of 9

**Two prime factorization**: If the number can be expressed as a factorization of two different prime numbers. This is the result that we are after:

```
Enter an odd number N >1 (0 to exit):
15

Enter R to run the Shor algorithm, D to display the circuit.
r
Getting local simulator backend...
Running Shor's algorithm for 15 on qasm_simulator ...

Results:
Prime factors:  15 = 3 * 5
Elapsed time:   1.43 s
```

Figure 10.10 – The result of Shor's algorithm with an input of 15

4. Now try the algorithm with bigger numbers and watch how the elapsed time to build and execute the circuit increases.

You will notice that your local simulator finds it harder and harder to keep up as the numbers get bigger. On my workstation (Apple iMac, 16 GB RAM), I run out of memory to build the circuits beyond the number 63. The run_shor(N) function code has a built-in breakpoint where it switches over to the IBM Quantum® simulator backend at 64.

Feel free to move the local/IBM Quantum® breakpoint if you feel like testing the performance of your local machine. Remember that the IBM Quantum® simulator backend runs on an IBM POWER9™ server, with quite a bit of horsepower!

## There's more...

Just like for the Grover algorithm that we discussed in the *Running Grover's algorithm as an Aqua function* recipe, you can run the Shor function with just a few lines of code:

```
In [1]: from qiskit import Aer
In [2]: from qiskit.aqua.algorithms import Shor
In [3]: backend = Aer.get_backend('qasm_simulator')
In [4]: results=Shor(N=15).run(backend)
In [5]: results['factors']
```

In this example, we run the Shor algorithm for the number 15. Running this code sample should result in the following output:

```
Out [5]  [[3, 5]]
```

What we have done so far is just run the Shor algorithm with one input parameter, N – the integer that you want to factorize. By default, if your run `Shor()`, with no input, it will default to 15, the smallest non-trivial integer that can be factorized. Verify this from the preceding table.

The Shor function optionally takes another input parameter, a, a co-prime smaller than N and with a greatest common divisor of 1:

```
In [4]: results=Shor(N=15, a=2).run(backend)
```

By default, a is set to 2, and for the smallish size integers that we are playing with here, it will likely make no difference, but feel free to experiment.

## See also

- Scott Aaronson has a delightful blog entry on Shor's algorithm: *Shor. I'll do it*, at `https://www.scottaaronson.com/blog/?p=208`.

- For a nice, detailed overview of Shor's algorithm on Python and Qiskit®, see *Chapter 12, Shor's Algorithm* in *Mastering Quantum Computing with IBM QX*, by Dr Christine Corbett Moran, Packt Publishing.

- And directly from the Qiskit® textbook, here is Shor's aglorithm broken down in Python and Qiskit®: `https://qiskit.org/textbook/ch-algorithms/shor.html`.

# Exploring more Aqua algorithms

We have now reached the end of our book, and with that, the end of our trip through Qiskit® together. On our trip, we have looked at some basic quantum programming and explored the IBM Quantum® backends – the actual quantum computers! We have run our programs on these and gotten quantum results back.

We started poking at the real meat of quantum computing, the algorithms. This book, however, is not about algorithms; we have just scratched the surface with some very basic ideas of how quantum algorithms differ from their classical counterparts and how it might feel to write them.

And after touching on how to write algorithms and the sometimes-counterintuitive approach to getting the answer compared to classical algorithms, we also looked into prefabricated algorithms that are included with Qiskit Aqua: Grover's algorithm and Shor's algorithm. I like to think of this part of Qiskit® as an appstore of quantum computing.

This is where you go when you have a problem that might require a quantum computing solution, but you do not necessarily want to sit down and code the algorithm yourself. Just like most people do not write their own programs just to get a weather forecast; they just use a readily available weather app.

## Getting ready

Qiskit Aqua has more algorithms than just Grover's and Shor's. The IBM Quantum® team, and collaborators all around the world, are filling it out with implementations and pure algorithms that target promising fields for near future as well as preparing for slightly further off implementations as quantum computers grow in strength and capabilities.

Firstly, the Qiskit Aqua components include a set of **pure algorithms** in the `qiskit.aqua.algorithms` package.

Among these are the Grover and Shor algorithms that we have tested, but also other specific algorithms such as QSVM (Quantum Support Vector Machine), VQE (the Variational Quantum Eigensolver algorithm), and more. Explore this library to learn how to explore various algorithms on the backends that are available today, and to understand how to expand them for use on the universal quantum computers of the future:

- **Chemistry**: Qiskit Aqua also includes specialized algorithms for chemistry, one of the promising fields of future quantum computing. The Qiskit® chemistry module (`qiskit.chemistry`) lets you experiment with energy calculations on molecules using your favorite modeling tool.

- **Finance**: If you are interested in finance, and have this nagging feeling that the stock market behaves quantum mechanically, you can start investigating using the Qiskit® finance module (`qiskit.finance`), which includes a set of functions that are structured in the form of Ising Hamiltonians applied to financial models.

- **Machine learning**: To start exploring quantum machine learning, take a look at the Qiskit® machine learning module (`qiskit.ml`), which contains sample sets. You can use these Aqua classifiers and SVM algorithms.

- **Optimization**: This is a much-hyped field for quantum computing, which you can now easily explore with the help of the Qiskit® optimization module (`qiskit.optimization`). This module contains several submodules with specific algorithms, applications, problems, and more.

## How to do it...

We won't go any deeper into these specific Qiskit Aqua modules, but to start exploring the algorithms, you can follow this path example:

1.  Import the package that you are interested in, for example, if you want to explore chemistry, this one:

    ```
    import qiskit
    from qiskit.chemistry import *
    ```

2.  Then take a look at the built-in docs.

    Qiskit® provides excellent Python help where you can start your exploration; for example:

    ```
    help(qiskit.chemistry)
    ```

3.  Explore the general Qiskit® resources to further explore the field that you are interested in.

    For example, the Qiskit® tutorials here: `https://qiskit.org/documentation/tutorials/chemistry/index.html`.

    And in the *Learn Quantum Computation Using Qiskit* textbook, for example: `https://qiskit.org/textbook/ch-applications/vqe-molecules.html`.

4.  And finally, experiment!

    Pick up on the various algorithms and integrate them into your own hybrid classical/quantum Python code to suit your purposes, much like we have done throughout the various recipes in this book.

There are many Qiskit® features that we have not touched yet, such as mixing in Boolean logic with your circuits, programming qubits directly with **OpenPulse**, more advanced error simulation, and much more. All of these features, and many more, are available for your exploration. If you do not want to go it alone, take a look around and see whether you can find some quantum computing meetups or workshops in your neighborhood.

The Qiskit Slack channel at `qiskit.slack.com` is an excellent starting point for your quantum social exploration. Sign up from the Support page on IBM Quantum Experience®: `https://quantum-computing.ibm.com/support`.

# There's more

The Qiskit Aqua algorithms didn't spring out of thin air; someone wrote them and added them to the collection. Qiskit® is open source and is built by an ever-growing collection of open source contributors. How about you?

Even if you are not planning to become a Qiskit® contributor, do go ahead and explore the source code. If you installed Qiskit® locally, you have the source right at your fingertips. If you installed it with the suggested Anaconda, your Qiskit® source might be in a location similar to this (example from macOS):

```
/Users/<your_user_name>/opt/anaconda3/envs/<your_environment>/
lib/python3.7/site-packages/qiskit/
```

Look around in the functions and classes that build the features and functions that we have used throughout the book. Who knows, perhaps you can come up with a better way to present qubit states, or come up with a brand-new algorithm, and then contribute that method back to Qiskit®.

Information about how to contribute to Qiskit® is available here: https://qiskit. org/documentation/contributing_to_qiskit.html.

# See also

Today's algorithm development is largely theoretical as we can successfully run them on the available but currently limited NISQ machines and on quantum simulators, but we do not have access to backends with hundreds or thousands of qubits. Remember that simulators size up exponentially with the number of qubits; running simulators at those circuit sizes proves immensely challenging.

This might change in the not unforeseeable future, at least if IBM Quantum® gets its way. In early September 2020, IBM Quantum's Jay Gambetta presented IBM's roadmap at the yearly IBM Quantum Summit. It is a bold plan, reaching 1,121 physical qubits by late 2023. With this amount of physical qubits, it will be possible to start exploring in earnest error-corrected qubits as per the *Exploring your qubits to understand T1, T2, errors, and gates* recipe in *Chapter 8, Cleaning Up Your Quantum Act with Ignis*. So watch this space.

Here's the roadmap document: *IBM's Roadmap For Scaling Quantum Technology*, September 15, 2020, Jay Gambetta: https://www.ibm.com/blogs/ research/2020/09/ibm-quantum-roadmap/.

# Thank you!

So, dear reader, you have followed me this far, or at least you have flipped to the last page of the last chapter to see how the story ends... Spoiler alert: It's a cliffhanger!

Quantum computing is still very much in its infancy, and the recipe building that you have taken part in in this book, while putting you on track for further exploration, are not enough to confidently establish your career as a quantum computing programmer; this takes time and effort.

Just like a basic course in C programming might lead you onto the path of making your fortune building the next social media phenomenon, this basic dipping-your-toes-in-the-water that you have now been exposed to might do the same. With what you now have, go ahead, take the plunge, become a Qiskit Advocate, check with your college or university for courses and programs to chart out your career path as a quantum computing developer or researcher, or why not just start the next big quantum start-up in your garage?

Have fun!

# Other Books You May Enjoy

If you enjoyed this book, you may be interested in these other books by Packt:

**Learn Quantum Computing with Python and IBM Quantum Experience**

Robert Loredo

ISBN: 978-1-83898-100-6

- Explore quantum computational principles such as superposition and quantum entanglement

- Become familiar with the contents and layout of the IBM Quantum Experience

- Understand quantum gates and how they operate on qubits

- Discover the quantum information science kit and its elements such as Terra and Aer

- Get to grips with quantum algorithms such as Bell State, Deutsch-Jozsa, Grover's algorithm, and Shor's algorithm

- How to create and visualize a quantum circuit

**Quantum Computing and Blockchain in Business**

Arunkumar Krishnakumar

ISBN: 978-1-83864-776-6

- Understand the fundamentals of quantum computing and Blockchain
- Gain insights from the experts who are using quantum computing and Blockchain
- Discover the implications of these technologies for governance and healthcare
- Learn how Blockchain and quantum computing may influence logistics and finance
- Understand how these technologies are impacting research in areas such as chemistry
- Find out how these technologies may help the environment and influence smart city development
- Understand the implications for cybersecurity as these technologies evolve

# Leave a review - let other readers know what you think

Please share your thoughts on this book with others by leaving a review on the site that you bought it from. If you purchased the book from Amazon, please leave us an honest review on this book's Amazon page. This is vital so that other potential readers can see and use your unbiased opinion to make purchasing decisions, we can understand what our customers think about our products, and our authors can see your feedback on the title that they have worked with Packt to create. It will only take a few minutes of your time, but is valuable to other potential customers, our authors, and Packt. Thank you!

# Index

# Z

Printed in Great Britain
by Amazon

87693347R00235